T0305214

# The International Monetary System and the Theory of Monetary Systems

NEW THINKING IN POLITICAL ECONOMY

**Series Editor:** Peter J. Boettke, *George Mason University, USA*

New Thinking in Political Economy aims to encourage scholarship in the intersection of the disciplines of politics, philosophy and economics. It has the ambitious purpose of reinvigorating political economy as a progressive force for understanding social and economic change.

The series is an important forum for the publication of new work analysing the social world from a multidisciplinary perspective. With increased specialization (and professionalization) within universities, interdisciplinary work has become increasingly uncommon. Indeed, during the 20th century, the process of disciplinary specialization reduced the intersection between economics, philosophy and politics and impoverished our understanding of society. Modern economics in particular has become increasingly mathematical and largely ignores the role of institutions and the contribution of moral philosophy and politics.

New Thinking in Political Economy will stimulate new work that combines technical knowledge provided by the 'dismal science' and the wisdom gleaned from the serious study of the 'worldly philosophy'. The series will reinvigorate our understanding of the social world by encouraging a multidisciplinary approach to the challenges confronting society in the new century.

Titles in the series include:

The Rediscovery of Classical Economics
Adaption, Complexity and Growth
*David Simpson*

Economic Futures of the West
*Jan Winiecki*

Entrepreneurial Action, Public Policy, and Economic Outcomes
*Edited by Robert F. Salvino Jr., Micheal T. Tasto and Gregory M. Randolph*

Sweden and the Revival of the Capitalist Welfare State
*Andreas Bergh*

Competition, Coordination and Diversity
From the Firm to Economic Integration
*Pascal Salin*

Culture and Economic Action
*Edited by Laura E. Grube and Virgil Henry Storr*

Politics as a Peculiar Business
Insights from a Theory of Entangled Political Economy
*Richard E. Wagner*

Liberty and Equality in Political Economy
From Locke versus Rousseau to the Present
*Nicholas Capaldi and Gordon Lloyd*

The International Monetary System and the Theory of Monetary Systems
*Pascal Salin*

# The International Monetary System and the Theory of Monetary Systems

Pascal Salin

*Honorary Professor, University Paris-Dauphine, France*

NEW THINKING IN POLITICAL ECONOMY

 Edward Elgar
PUBLISHING

Cheltenham, UK • Northampton, MA, USA

Published by
Edward Elgar Publishing Limited
The Lypiatts
15 Lansdown Road
Cheltenham
Glos GL50 2JA
UK

Edward Elgar Publishing, Inc.
William Pratt House
9 Dewey Court
Northampton
Massachusetts 01060
USA


A catalogue record for this book
is available from the British Library


Library of Congress Control Number: 2016942191


This book is available electronically in the **Elgar**online
Economics subject collection
DOI 10.4337/9781786430304

ISBN 978 1 78643 029 8 (cased)
ISBN 978 1 78643 030 4 (eBook)

Typeset by Servis Filmsetting Ltd, Stockport, Cheshire

*For Cassandre
my granddaughter*

# Contents

## PART IV   MONETARY PROBLEMS

# Introduction

The explicit aim of this book is to help readers to get a good understanding of the working of what is called the 'international monetary system'. In fact, it would be perhaps more correct to speak of 'the international set of monetary systems' insofar as there is not a single system, so the 'international monetary system' can only be the juxtaposition of different monetary systems. This is why an analysis of the international monetary system cannot be carried out without referring more generally to the working of monetary systems. Moreover, one cannot really understand any economic problem without using the general principles of economic theory. Contrary to what is too often believed, there is not a specific analysis of international monetary economics, of industrial economics, of the economy of health, development economics or any other economics: regardless of the specific purpose of an analysis, general economic theory should be applied, because there is necessarily and logically a single approach to economic problems (and even, more generally, to all social phenomena).

This is why a study of monetary systems cannot be made independently of the general economic theory, and the analysis of the international monetary system cannot be done independently of monetary theory (itself, therefore, constituting a particular application of general economic theory). That is also why, beyond specific issues studied in this book, it aims to show how the general economic theory allows one to understand the concerned phenomena. Thus, this book pursues a methodological target, since it has been written with the hope that the approach which is used here can help to develop parallel approaches when studying all kinds of different problems. The analysis proposed in this book is therefore a practical example of a method of reasoning which can be used in any field of knowledge, about any phenomenon.

I do not intend, therefore, to provide the reader with a lot of information concerning, for example, specific facts of history or current events; all of these can be found in documents which are easily accessible. It is useless, indeed, to possess and accumulate information if one does not have a method of analysis to understand the meaning and scope of this information. Moreover, employing an analytical method helps in selecting the significant facts. This is why I give only a limited amount of factual information in this book, just in cases where it seems able to illustrate an analysis. The reader will also find only a limited number of references to economic literature, since I mainly want to focus on the logical consistency of reasoning, and not give an extensive review of ideas or of the history of ideas. I only hope that mastering the intellectual instruments proposed in this book will not only help readers to better understand the specific facts that are of interest for them, but also provide them with a framework of critical analysis for the readings they may be inclined to undertake later on in the specific field of the present work, or in any other field.

A last statement is undoubtedly necessary. I have stressed above that it is impossible to analyse any phenomenon without referring to the general economic theory. But the objection may be raised that there is actually not one theory, but several, and even that economists are often in deep disagreement over them. This is certainly true. But I have tried hard to make my analysis compatible with the principles of economic theory which can be considered as indisputable, so that my statements are perfectly consistent between them and correctly correspond to the way individuals act in a human society.

# PART I

# Basic statements and analyses

In the Introduction to this book, I made its aims clear, and particularly stressed that a good understanding of the international monetary system could not be achieved without referring to the general economic theory. This is why I feel it necessary to first clarify certain concepts and analyses, the knowledge of which allows a rigorous approach. Therefore, I first clarify concepts such as those of 'nation' or 'equilibrium' and explain, for example, the analysis of exchange, of the demand for money, and of money creation.

# 1. The concept of nation

Whether one is considering international trade or the international monetary system, one cannot develop a rigorous analysis unless making clear the meaning of the terms used, in this case the word 'international'. But speaking of an international phenomenon necessarily leads to questioning the notion of 'nation' (since international means 'between nations'), as international exchanges are exchanges between traders located in different nations, and the international monetary system is a system which involves several nations. Thus, a meaning cannot be given to the word 'international' without having first defined a nation.

Looking for an economic definition of the nation is an old problem, which first concerned trade. In fact, for a theory of international trade to be developed, there must be differences between international trade and intra-national trade. Of course, in both cases, the same general theory is used, that is the general theory of exchange (which is covered in Chapter 2). But the theory of international trade has to add a specification, so that it can be a particular application of the general theory of exchange.

One of the criteria that has long been used and which is still used most frequently in the theory of international trade is the criterion of the mobility of goods and factors of production. Most generally, economic theory assumes that goods and factors of production are perfectly mobile, which means that they can move without costs. One may study the consequences of a restriction on mobility (for example, arising from transport costs or information costs). Traditionally the trade theory assumes – as hypothesized by David Ricardo – that commodities are internationally mobile, whereas factors of production are mobile within a nation, but immobile internationally. In other words, a nation in the economic-commercial sense can be defined as the space within which factors of production are perfectly mobile, although they are totally immobile between nations. There is no need at this stage to investigate the specific causes of this immobility (natural or linguistic barriers, state controls and bans on trade, and so on).

This traditional definition therefore contrasted 'perfect' mobility for commodities and factors of production within the nation, to the 'total' immobility of factors of production between nations. But one can give a less extreme version of this theory by defining a nation according to the assumption that the mobility of factors of production is relatively greater within a nation than between nations. Thus, the mobility of factors is not necessarily 'perfect'[1] – without cost – inside the nation, and not necessarily non-existent between nations. Moreover the theory of protection is precisely designed to analyse what is happening when the international mobility of commodities is not 'perfect' (tariffs, quotas or state authorizations constituting barriers to exchange).

Thus, traditionally, international economics retains a definition of the nation which could be called a commercial definition, since it is concerned with trade in commodities. But there can obviously be all sorts of other definitions of the nation using other criteria. Thus, we could define a nation in the linguistic sense as the space in which a language is mobile in absolute or relative terms; that is, the language in question is the most commonly used communication tool between residents of this space, while it is relatively less used in their dealings with residents of other linguistic areas. One could even, of course, define a nation in the gastronomic sense (circulation in a gastronomic space) or the artistic sense. But most often it is the legal and institutional meaning which is considered in defining a nation. From this point of view, a nation is the place in which a given system of law is used (or is 'mobile', while it is not between different nations). However, nowadays we usually consider that the creation of law is made by a state monopoly, contrary to what exists in jurisprudential systems in which the law is revealed by the judges, on the basis of the general principles of law (which can be considered as universal and not strictly 'national'). Thus, in present systems, there is a coincidence between the legal space and the political space (in which the state exercises its power). But, from a more general point of view, there is not necessarily such a coincidence between the political and the legal space.

This coincidence, so common in our time, does not correspond to any 'natural' need. It is the consequence of the working of the political power, which gets a monopoly of legal coercion on a space called the 'nation' and which uses its power of coercion to impose its monopoly in the development and the implementation of legal rules (laws and regulations).

What will mainly be used in this book, however, is the monetary

---

[1]    The use of the term 'perfect' is traditional, but it can lead to some ambiguity. When it is said that mobility is 'perfect', it is not to state a normative proposal representing an ideal which should be moved towards. Indeed, the reality is necessarily 'imperfect' in the sense that there are necessarily obstacles to trade, in particular the fact that information can never be 'perfect'. But the assumption of perfection must be considered as an instrument to facilitate a first step in reasoning.

definition of the nation. Using criteria similar to those given above, a nation can be defined in the monetary sense as a space within which the currency is perfectly 'mobile', while it is immobile between nations. Of course, a relative definition can also be provided of the 'monetary nation', described as a space within which the currency is relatively more mobile than it is between 'monetary nations'.

But what does the mobility of a currency mean?[2] It is simply the fact that it is accepted as a medium of exchange in transactions. But, as we shall see, the acceptability of a currency may result from a selection process voluntarily implemented by those concerned, or the result of a legal obligation to use a given currency, in which case one speaks of 'legal tender'. Thus the use and circulation of currencies can be the result of the freely expressed choice of individuals or the result of an obligation imposed by states using their legal right to coerce. This is obviously a fundamental distinction, but it is unfortunately all too often neglected in analyses of monetary systems. The fact remains that with currencies the same problem arises as with the law: there is no reason a priori for the monetary space – namely, the space of circulation of a currency – to coincide with the political space. But nowadays the political power uses its power of coercion to impose a monopoly on the production and circulation of money, which in particular implies the existence of a 'legal tender', that is, a prohibition on currencies other than the 'national' currency.

When speaking of the present-day international monetary system, one makes the implicit assumption – which in fact is coherent with the modern reality – that all currencies have a 'national' character in the political sense, that is, that there is coincidence between the nation in the monetary sense and the nation in a political sense. The study of the international monetary system, then, consists in finding out the role of different national currencies in transactions which take place between people using different national currencies. But to understand the operation of an 'international monetary system' it seems important to adopt a broader perspective by first analysing relations between currencies belonging to different monetary areas in cases in which there is no coincidence between the monetary area and the political area. This being done, it is then possible to add the assumption that this coincidence exists – as is generally the case

---

2   What is meant by 'a currency' should also be defined. Indeed, a currency is composed of a set of more or less heterogeneous monetary instruments (for instance, banknotes and deposits, possibly produced by different organizations). What makes it possible to say that these instruments constitute a single currency? I will not give an answer to this question here, but will do so in detail later on. But this issue is at the heart of any analysis of monetary systems.

nowadays – and to look for its implications. The analysis of the international monetary system is therefore only a particular application of a more general analysis, namely the theory of monetary systems. One will thus better understand the functioning of the international monetary system if one has first explored the broader operating processes which concern all monetary systems. But to avoid confusion, this general analysis of the monetary systems will not use the term 'nation' (although, as we have seen, a nation in the monetary sense can be defined), but will instead use the term 'monetary area' or 'monetary zone'. And use of the term 'nation' will be reserved for when there is coincidence between the monetary and political areas, which means that 'nation' refers to a reality of political order.

In other words, the theory of monetary systems is concerned with both the study of the internal structure of a monetary system and the study of relations between different monetary systems. Insofar as there is a plurality of currencies, and therefore a plurality of systems of production and circulation of currency, there are necessarily problems of relations between these different systems. But there are some specific characteristics in the functioning of these systems and of their interrelationships, depending on whether currencies are 'national' or not.

# 2.   The theory of exchange

Chapter 1 explained that the theory of international trade – that is the theory of international trade in commodities – was often based on the assumption that commodities were internationally mobile, but not the factors of production. As is well known, this theory – also called the theory of international specialization or theory of comparative advantage – revealed that each country specializes in commodities for which it has a relative advantage, either because it has relatively more productive techniques for these commodities, or because there is a relative abundance of factors of production needed for the production of these products. As a result, trade in commodities is a substitute for the mobility of factors of production.

Regardless of the specific assumptions that one makes, these statements are rigorously logical and therefore it is essential that they are made. In general terms it can be said that a country specializes in the productions for which it has a comparative advantage, whether due to the techniques used and/or to its holdings of factors of production.[1]

Let me stress, however, that it may be somewhat dangerous to speak about the specialization of a country or a nation. Indeed, a country does not produce and does not trade. Only individuals produce and trade, and they are possibly organized under the form of a firm and located in a given national territory.[2] In reality, the theory of international trade is only a particular application of a more general theory that I will just call the 'general theory of exchange'. I summarize its main proposals by using a simple example.

---

[1]   The theory of international trade can attain great technical sophistication because one can indefinitely add specific hypotheses concerning the production functions for different goods. But there is always the risk that this excess of sophistication will eventually hide the general principles of explanation. These principles only are relevant for us here, especially the idea that trade is not explained by the existence of an absolute advantage, but by a relative advantage: if the residents of a country are more productive than those of other countries in all productions, it is no less true that they have an interest in specializing in the productions for which they have a comparative advantage (that is, in which productivity is relatively higher).

[2]   A useful linguistic precaution would, for example, be to avoid saying 'France exports such a commodity', but instead say 'French people – or French residents – export such a commodity'.

Assume a world inhabited by two people, A and B, who produce two goods, wheat and tomatoes. There is no money, so it is a barter economy (exchanging one of the commodities against the other). There is a single factor of production, work (measured in working days); or, rather, it is assumed that only work is rare, while other factors – land, for example – are in surplus, which means that one can use as much land as needed without additional cost, regardless of the scale of production.

Now suppose that A can produce in a day's work 1 pound of wheat or 1 pound of tomatoes, while B can produce 4 pounds of wheat or 2 pounds of tomatoes. B is, therefore, more productive than A, for example because he has better techniques of production or land more suitable for agriculture. This hypothesis can be summed up in the table below:

|          | A        | B        |
|----------|----------|----------|
| Wheat    | 1 pound  | 4 pounds |
| Tomatoes | 1 pound  | 2 pounds |

The productive characteristics of the two individuals, A and B, can be represented in Figure 2.1 which represents the quantities produced

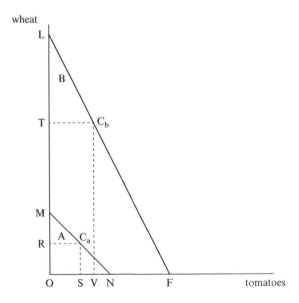

*Figure 2.1    Production and consumption in isolation*

of wheat and tomatoes by A and B within a day when there is no trade between these two individuals. Thus, individual A can produce a maximum quantity of 1 pound of wheat (*OM*) or 1 pound of tomatoes (*ON*). But he can also move on its production constraint *MN* and produce any combination of wheat and tomatoes on this line. He knows, for example, that by sacrificing 0.1 pound of wheat he can get 0.1 pound of tomatoes. The rate of substitution between wheat and tomatoes is the amount of one commodity which can be obtained by renouncing the production of a certain amount of the other commodity. In the present case, the rate of substitution between the two commodities for A is equal to 1/1. It is represented by the slope of the *MN* line. Similarly, the rate of substitution for B in isolation is equal to 2/4, that is, 1/2 (B may substitute the production of one unit of tomatoes for the production of two units of wheat). This rate corresponds to the slope of the *LF* line.

In isolation, A is obliged to consume only what he produces himself and he will adjust the structure of his production to his needs. Thus, he chooses, for example, for reasons which we do not know, point $C_a$ which represents both the distribution of production among wheat and tomatoes and the distribution of consumption (which is obviously identical): he will produce and consume a quantity *OR* of wheat and *OS* of tomatoes. Likewise B will choose, for example, point $C_b$ where he distributes his production and consumption between a quantity *OT* of wheat and a quantity *OV* of tomatoes. For each individual, the consumption is limited to what is compatible with the budget constraint, that is, the lines *MN* and *LF*.

But let us imagine now that trade becomes possible between A and B, either because natural or administrative obstacles to trade disappear, or because they discover each other's existence, which means that their information has improved. Trade is possible because the rates of substitution in production are not the same for A and B. Each will therefore agree to trade if they can get a larger amount of a commodity by selling a certain amount of the other commodity than if they themselves produced the first commodity. Thus, knowing that in isolation he can override one unit of wheat against one unit of tomatoes, A will agree to sell tomatoes to B if he can get more than one unit of wheat against one unit of tomatoes. Likewise, B will agree to sell wheat to A if he can get more than one-half unit of tomatoes against one unit of wheat (because he knows that in isolation, by sacrificing the production of one unit of wheat, he can get only half a unit of tomatoes). Trade will take place if the two individuals can reach an agreement about the rate of exchange – that is, a relative price – located between their two rates of substitution in isolation, that is, between 1/1 and 1/2 (or 0.5/1). The price they will agree will be such that the amount of wheat that B wants to sell will be equal to the amount that A wants to buy (and therefore the quantity of tomatoes which is exchanged will also be desired by the two partners in exchange). This exchange will take place if one assumes, as it is normal to do, that the two individuals are rational, that is, they are able to determine what is in their interest. Now, exchange is beneficial for the two individuals, otherwise it would obviously not have taken place.

Thus, it is in the interest of B to specialize in the production of wheat, in which he is relatively more productive than in the production of tomatoes in comparison with the capabilities of A. Likewise, A has a relative advantage over B in tomato production (he must sacrifice less production of wheat to produce more tomatoes). The general theory of exchange therefore leads to this basic statement: even if an individual is more productive than another in all productions, he gains by specializing in the productions for which he has a relative advantage. And if he is rational – as we must assume – he will recognize his interest in doing so, and he will do so.

This situation can be represented in Figure 2.2. Individual A totally specializes in the production of tomatoes, which means that he is placed at the point of production *N*, while B specializes in the production of wheat and is placed at the point of production *L*. But by delivering a certain amount

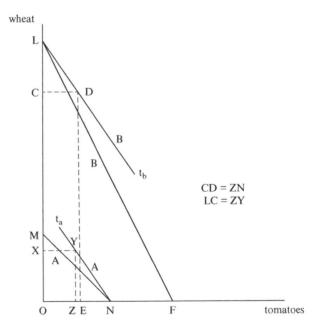

*Figure 2.2    Exchange*

of tomatoes to B, individual A gets a quantity of wheat more important than if he was in isolation. If, for example, both individuals have agreed on a price of 1/1.5 (1 pound of tomatoes exchanged against 1.5 pounds of wheat), A produces $ON$ of tomatoes (and no wheat), he sells $NZ$ to B and gets in return $ZY$ of wheat (the slope of the line $t_a$ represents the price of tomatoes in terms of wheat). He keeps for his own consumption a quantity $OZ$. The point of consumption $Y$ – which indicates the distribution of consumption between the two commodities – is then different from the point of production $N$. Likewise, B produces a quantity $OL$ of wheat, he sells $LC$ to A and gets $CD$ of tomatoes. He keeps for his consumption the amount of wheat $OC$. Obviously $LC = ZY$ and $CD = ZN$: what is sold by one of the partners is equal to what is bought by the other.

Or course, A and B could decide another relative price and they would thus move along other lines than the lines $t_a$ and $t_b$. But in any case it is possible for both, thanks to exchange, to stand at points of consumption placed higher than what was possible in isolation. The specialization of each in the production for which he is relatively better fitted allows them both to obtain a greater quantity of goods or, more specifically, to increase their satisfaction. If the exchange takes place on a voluntary basis (although it could have not taken place), that is logically because it brings a higher level of welfare to each of the two partners. To be sure, it is not necessary to undertake opinion polls or any statistical research about the gains from trade to be persuaded of the existence of these gains. It is important to note that the idea that exchange is productive – in the sense that it increases the satisfaction of traders – is an idea that is necessarily true because it is the result of a logical reasoning from the single assumption that individuals are rational.[3]

Thus, we have assumed that two traders agreed to an exchange of 1 (pound of tomatoes) against 1.5 (pounds of wheat). This exchange ratio is called the market price, which is directly observable and measurable by the traders concerned and by possible external observers. This price is the relative price of one commodity relative to another. It cannot be expressed in monetary terms since, for the time being, we have assumed that money does not exist and therefore this relative price may be called a real price (a price in terms of a commodity). To mention this price one should obviously choose a standard of value. We could choose either of the two commodities that exist in the studied economy. Choosing wheat arbitrarily as a standard of value leads wheat to be distinguished as an object of production, consumption and exchange. By definition, 1 pound of wheat

---

[3]   I will later consider the definition of rationality.

traded has a value of 1 pound of wheat in terms of the standard of value. As regards tomatoes, given the price assumed above, 1 pound of tomatoes has a market value of 1.5 pounds of wheat in terms of the wheat standard. There is equivalence on the market[4] between 1 pound of tomatoes and 1.5 pounds of wheat.

Now let us assume that, given this price, A sells 2 pounds of tomatoes – with a market value of 3 pounds of wheat – and buys in return 3 pounds of wheat, which obviously have a market value equal to 3 pounds of wheat in terms of the wheat standard (which corresponds to a relative price of 1/1.5). We have here an illustration of the well-known fact that, in any transaction, the market value of what is sold is equal to the market value of what is purchased. It can be represented in the following table:

Transaction by A

| Purchases | Sales |
| --- | --- |
| 3 pounds of wheat worth 3 pounds of wheat | 2 pounds of tomatoes worth 3 pounds of wheat |

This statement is the basis for double-entry accounting. It corresponds to the fact that, in the account of a transaction, the value of sales is equal to the value of purchases, and there is always a net balance equal to zero.[5]

But it is essential to stress that this equivalence between exchanged values does not hold if one gives another definition to 'value', namely if one is interested in the 'subjective value'. Indeed, we have seen that, if the exchange takes place, it is because what A buys (3 pounds of wheat) has more subjective value for him than what he sells (the 2 pounds of tomatoes); otherwise he would have not made the exchange. And, likewise, what B purchases (2 pounds of tomatoes) has more (subjective) value for him than what he gives (3 pounds of wheat). Thus, exchange is the creator of value (subjective). The equivalence of market values – or objective values – in exchange does not prevent each trader from obtaining a gain. It is not achieved by the despoilment of one by the other, but by a process of simultaneous creation of value for both traders. However, what is relevant

---

4    The market can be defined as an abstract place where the exchange of goods takes place between the traders. The market may be more or less materialized in various forms (such as the market in a village, or on the internet).

5    I will later introduce a third good, money. It is possible – but not necessarily desirable – to use money as a numéraire, that is, as a market standard of value. This will obviously change nothing in the statements developed in the present chapter.

for each of them is precisely the subjective value, which is not measurable. An outside observer cannot know to what extent there is such a creation of value and this creation cannot be measured. But he must know that it exists necessarily. Thus it is a great mistake to focus on what is visible and measurable: market prices are nothing but an instrument to create what is truly desired, namely subjective values. Yet there are many economists who wrongly believe that they only need to care about the phenomena which are measurable. And there is also a conceptual error when it is claimed, for example, that an exchange is unequal between two parties. Indeed, if an exchange is done freely and not under coercion, it is necessarily beneficial to all traders. As it is impossible to measure the gain in value – or gain in satisfaction – by each trader, since it is of a subjective nature, every trader can only say that they made a gain thanks to exchange, but without being able to measure this gain. It is therefore impossible to compare the gain in satisfaction obtained by each of them, so that it is meaningless to speak of an unequal exchange.

Let me therefore take this opportunity to point out that there are statements which are necessarily true in economics. Such is the case with the statement that each trader gains from an exchange, at least if it is done freely and not under coercion. It is universally and eternally true. On the other hand, if a transaction between two traders is made through coercion, we can be sure that there is a gain for one of them, namely the one who uses the coercion (otherwise, as a rational agent, he would not use it, since any action necessarily has a cost). But there is necessarily a loss for the one who is coerced: since one must exercise coercion to force him to act, it means that he had no interest in doing the action which is required of him. We thus see that the distinction between a free and a forced act is fundamental in any economic reasoning, but it is unfortunately too often forgotten, especially by those who believe that only what is measurable must be considered in a scientific approach. In reality, a statement has a scientific foundation if it corresponds to the actual characteristics of the object of study. Thus, studying exchange without mentioning the duo 'free act – forced act' must be considered as a non-scientific approach, whatever its degree of sophistication or its use of mathematics.

But take the case of free exchange. According to the basic proposition of the theory of exchange, each party gets a gain in an exchange. But still, it should be noted that this gain is a foreseen gain. However, it may be the case that the goods purchased by A do not give him the satisfaction that he was expecting. Thus, he will be tempted to say: 'Ah! If I had known, I would not have made this exchange.' But that does not invalidate the fact that, when he made the transaction, he believed that he was gaining. This simply means that one can never have perfect information and that, in this situation of natural uncertainty, one may well be wrong. But the general theory of exchange is obviously not affected so far.

The central statement of the theory of exchange depends itself on an assumption which has not yet been specified: the assumption of individual rationality. Saying that an individual is rational is saying that he is capable of determining targets which are specific to him, and determining how to best achieve his purposes. This assumption is justified, on the one hand, because it corresponds to what we can observe about human nature, maybe just by introspection; but also because there is only one other conceivable assumption, the assumption of fundamental irrationality of individuals. But in the latter case, we would have to admit that human actions are only the result of chance, which is not consistent with what we know of human nature and which would prevent the existence of any social science, such as economics. It is necessary, however, to specify what entails this assumption of rationality. It does not mean that individuals are fully informed, in particular about the means for achieving their targets, but only that they are able to decide and to act according to their own goals and their own knowledge of the means. More specifically, the acquisition of information is one of the objectives of the action, among other objectives. But nobody chooses to have perfect information, because it would require an infinite cost and therefore make it impossible to reach any other goal (without, moreover, being able to achieve the goal of perfect information). Everyone must therefore compare the costs – for example the costs of looking for information – and all the potential gains of other activities, and arbitrate between them. Looking for information stops when the net marginal gain (expected gain minus cost) falls below what it is in other activities (specifying that this net marginal gain is itself uncertain, since one never knows in advance, by definition, what will be the value for oneself of the information which is sought).

The theory of international trade, already mentioned, is only a particular application of the general theory of exchange. It results simply from the additional assumption according to which both traders (or groups of traders) are located in different national territories, which leads to clarification of the definition of the nation, as I have done previously. But it is not because the traders are in different national territories, instead of being in the same national territory, that the principle of exchange should be amended. The general principle remains true, namely that two traders earn by exchanging, if they exchange freely. The principle of exchange being universally and eternally true, it obviously remains true when applied in the particular case of two traders located in different nations. It is expressed in the theory of international exchange – or theory of international specialization – when one says that the two 'nations' will gain through exchange (but it would obviously be better to say that both traders or groups of traders, located in different countries, earn through exchange). This is of course a definitive argument against any form of protectionism, that is, any policy consisting of preventing individuals from exchanging between different national territories, or of limiting their trade. This is the most rigorous logic and one cannot afford to take liberties with the requirements of logic. However, this does not prevent a number of authors from saying, for example, that the exchange between nations may be uneven, or claiming that the principles of the theory of international trade could have been valid at the time of Ricardo, but that they are no longer. Indeed, an universal principle cannot become obsolete.

# 3.  Equilibrium and disequilibrium

The notion of equilibrium is an absolutely central concept of any economic analysis. Often mentioned, for instance, are a market equilibrium (or disequilibrium), a balance of payments equilibrium (studied in detail in Part II of this book), a monetary equilibrium, and so on. But this term is unfortunately used too often without sufficient attention to the precise definition which is implicitly given to it, or which should be given to it. When speaking of 'equilibrium' one may think of an accounting equilibrium (equality between the two sides of double-entry accounting) and this definition will be considered in this book when studying the balance of payments. But this definition is not of main interest in this book, which does not aim at developing accounting principles, but rather aims at an economic analysis. Therefore, what can be said about the meaning of the term 'equilibrium' from the point of view of economic science?

## 3.1  THE CONCEPT OF EQUILIBRIUM

It may be necessary first to avoid the confusion that can exist with a frequent use of the term, for instance in physics. A system is said to be in equilibrium – or stable equilibrium – when the parameters which define it take values which will no longer change, except if an exogenous shock was to occur (that is, a shock which does not come from the inner working of the system, and therefore from the interdependence which exists between the variables which characterize it). We can take the example of Foucault's pendulum: if it receives an exogenous shock, it starts to oscillate, but it follows increasingly smaller paths until it reaches a position of immobility, that is, of equilibrium.

In the field of economics, it may be useful to refer to a similar concept, for instance by making the assumption – generally unrealistic – that a system is in a situation of stable equilibrium, which would mean that all the variables which characterize it have immutable values; then one may assume that a shock modifies this steady state of the system and causes a 'disequilibrium' before any return to an equilibrium, which can be identical to the previous one or different. Making such an assumption is useful because it makes it possible to isolate the influence of a given variable in a complex system in which interdependencies are numerous.[1] However, it would not be correct to argue that it constitutes the bulk of a scientific approach in economics. Indeed in economics we are not dealing with an inert reality, but with human beings who are all different and whose activities are developing over time so that they are never in a 'stable equilibrium'. What characterizes it is human action,[2] that is, the ability of individuals to choose their own targets – in fact continually changing – and the best ways to reach them. This also makes clearer that the confusion about the precise meaning of the term 'equilibrium' often comes from the fact it is used in relation to macroeconomic concepts which are designed arbitrarily, without caring about what constitutes the basis of any economic system or any social system, namely the behaviour of individuals who constitute a society. Such is the case of the expression 'main macroeconomic equilibria' defined, for instance, in an arbitrary and questionable way by the absence of inflation, the absence of unemployment and the so-called 'external equilibrium'. However, because it is impossible to understand the working of a society without first understanding the behaviour of individuals who compose it, one should recognize that it is impossible to define a macroeconomic equilibrium regardless of 'individual equilibrium'.

But what exactly is an individual equilibrium? What do we mean when we say that an individual is in equilibrium? For the reasons we have seen – the continually changing nature of human behaviour – there cannot be a stable equilibrium, that is, a sort of situation of nirvana from which an individual will not move once he has reached it. The only interpretation that seems acceptable consists in defining an individual equilibrium as a situation in which an individual is satisfied. Indeed, what determines human behaviour is looking for satisfaction, whatever it is: for instance physical, intellectual, spiritual or emotional. It is in fact a very useful and rewarding exercise to systematically replace the term 'equilibrium' by the word 'satisfaction'. In so doing, we can understand reality.[3]

---

[1]  This is why I will use this type of assumption.

[2]  This is also the beautiful title of the fundamental work by Ludwig von Mises (1949): *Human Action*.

[3]  Unfortunately, it is often assumed that one is doing a scientific analysis by using terms which seem to be learned, such as the term 'economic equilibrium'. But a scientific approach requires that one knows precisely what one is talking about, and it is therefore preferable to use unambiguous terms, as is the case for the word 'satisfaction', in contrast to the word 'equilibrium'. And insofar as colloquial terms are being used, one has more chance of giving a correct description of the reality than by using arbitrary abstractions. But this requires abandoning an attitude of intellectual arrogance which consists in differentiating oneself from the general public by using a sophisticated language reserved for insiders. Unlike a common bias, it is not necessary to be incomprehensible to develop a scientific work.

This thus reveals the basic assumption which is the basis for any economic analysis (or which should be), namely that the aim of an individual is to maximize satisfaction. Of course, this effort towards maximization meets limits, in particular because there are resource constraints and information constraints. Resource constraints are well known and they are, for example, made explicit in any textbook of microeconomics, usually in a chapter on what is called 'consumer behaviour'. However, this formulation is questionable because it may let people believe that there are two types of behaviour – the behaviour of the consumer and the behaviour of the producer – each obeying different operating modes. In fact, it is not correct to 'split' an individual in this way into two parts whose behaviours would be different and independent one from the other. Any individual is producing to consume, and he consumes only on the basis of what he is producing. This means, by the way, that the 'income constraint' is not exogenously imposed on the 'consumer'. An individual chooses simultaneously his productive effort and his consumption. He compares the (subjective) marginal cost of his production effort and the marginal gain of satisfaction (of a subjective nature) which he gets by consuming the product of his efforts (after having possibly practised acts of exchange, for example between the outcome of his work – his wage – and the commodities obtained by spending this wage). But productive efforts being the subject of choices, the income constraint (also known as the budget constraint) is not an exogenous and immutable datum. It is the consequence of the active behaviour of any individual. However, insofar as any human action takes place over time, it is not possible to change this income constraint instantaneously. Therefore, if it is reasonable to assume that the resource constraint is given at a given point of time, there is a maximum amount of resources that the individual can use to maximize his satisfaction. These resources are the result of the choices made in the past to maximize satisfaction.

One may say something similar about the information constraint. Information is not exogenously given, but it is the result of choices made by the individual. Indeed, information is never free, especially because, to get it, one has to use material resources, but also and mainly the rarest of resources, namely time.[4] Being fully informed would imply spending infinite resources and infinite time to this purpose, which obviously no one can do. We are therefore all obliged to choose a degree of information which is optimal for us, or to desire a certain level of ignorance (which is also optimal). But, as in the case of the income constraint, if this takes

---

[4]    This resource would not be scarce if men were immortal.

place at a given moment of time, it is possible to consider that information is a given datum.

If, at a given time, an individual has made his choices freely, in the absence of coercion, arguably he is in equilibrium, which means that he gets the maximum satisfaction, taking into account the constraints of resources and information, constraints which he has chosen. Therefore, there is a strict equivalence between maximizing one's satisfaction and acting freely. Indeed, if an individual is free to choose his own acts, why would he decide something that would not allow him to maximize his satisfaction? This would assume that he is not rational, since rationality can be defined as being able to determine one's own targets and to seek the best ways to reach them. Thus, insofar as he is acting, a free and necessarily rational human being maximizes his satisfaction. We do not need anything else than logic in order to be convinced, without needing to carry out opinion polls about the behaviour and the satisfaction of people

Therefore, although we can be sure that an individual who decides freely is in equilibrium, this does not mean that his wishes will necessarily come true. It may be the case, in fact, that the decisions he has taken do not bring him any of the benefits he hoped, in particular because his information was not perfectly correct. The individual may then say: 'If I had known, I would not have decided this'. But, precisely, he had rationally decided not to know. The fact that he is not satisfied with the result of his action does not prevent us from asserting that he had maximized his satisfaction at the precise time he made his decision. And it may also be the case that suffering some disappointment reveals better information which will improve his future decisions. In such a case, it is possible that an outside observer may be tempted to say that the individual in question is not rational, since he took bad decisions, and that he did not look for the right information. But such a statement is wrong. Saying that someone is rational does not mean that he is fully informed and that he cannot make a mistake. On the contrary – as we have seen – it is rational to choose an optimum level of ignorance.

All these considerations may seem far removed from what are the topics of this book, namely the working of monetary systems. In fact, they allow a better understanding of the exact scope of common concepts of economic analysis that are used frequently, in particular the concepts of supply and demand.

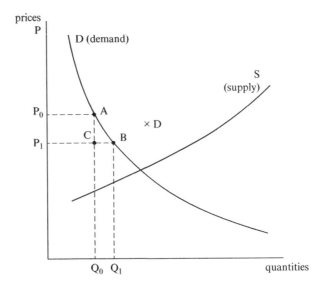

*Figure 3.1    Equilibrium, supply and demand*

## 3.2    EQUILIBRIUM, SUPPLY AND DEMAND

Supply and demand curves are the basic tools of any economist, but it is still necessary to define the exact scope of this instrument to avoid any error in reasoning. A simple supply curve and a demand curve are represented in Figure 3.1, and we will begin by analysing the meaning of the demand curve *D*.

We will first consider the microeconomic level, representing the behaviour of an individual demanding a good which will be called good *i*. The demand curve is a representation of the fact – well known by both theoreticians and practitioners – that the quantity demanded of the good *i* increases when its price decreases, hence the negative slope of the curve. The general shape of this curve is directly derived from the assumptions concerning the evaluation of the utility of a good by an individual, as it is explained by the theory of marginal utility in microeconomics. But it is worth remembering that the latter is itself a logical consequence of the rationality assumption of individuals, that is, of the assumption that they make choices and that their behaviour is not random.[5]

---

[5]    It is important to recall these sequences of logic insofar as I will subsequently continue my arguments by using some more logical sequences; ultimately that all the proposals put

All along the demand curve the representative individual is in equi-librium, which means that he is satisfied. The demand curve can thus be defined as the locus of the points in the space 'price-quantity' for which the individual is satisfied (in equilibrium). But all the points on the curve are not identical and they do not have the same subjective value for the indi-vidual. Thus, if the price at which the individual can get good $i$ equals $P_0$, he will be satisfied by purchasing the quantity $Q_0$ (point $A$). But if the price drops and becomes $P_1$, the individual will be even more satisfied. He could simply buy the same quantity $Q_0$ (which corresponds to point $C$, giving him rationally a greater satisfaction than point $A$ did) and this is what can happen in a limit case. But most likely, he will take the opportunity from the decline in price to buy a larger quantity, for instance $Q_1$ (correspond-ing to point $B$). One can be certain, according to the logic of individual behaviour, that the point $B$ is preferred to the point $A$ (or, more specifi-cally, that $B$ is preferred to $C$ which is preferred to $A$). Thus, the individual is the happier the more he is going down his demand curve and we will later see that this proposal – which is irrefutable since it corresponds to the logic of human behaviour – has important implications for the evalu-ation of monetary systems. Of course, saying that the individual increases his satisfaction does not imply that we can measure this satisfaction. This satisfaction is purely subjective and the classification made between differ-ent points is ordinal and not cardinal.

The demand curve has previously been defined as the set of equilibrium points of the individual. But it would in fact be more accurate to define it as the boundary between the space which is acceptable for the individual and the space which is not acceptable: thus point $C$, even though it is not actually selected, would be acceptable for the individual, since he could get $Q_0$ at a price lower than $P_0$. On the other hand, a point above the demand curve, such as $D$, would be unacceptable. The set of points on the curve or below the curve are therefore acceptable for the individual; they are satis-factory for him, but to varying degrees. On the contrary, all points above this curve are not acceptable.

Of course, the demand curve represents the equilibrium of an individual at a given time and under specified conditions, in particular because his behaviour depends on the resources available to him at the moment, on other choices available to him, on the information he possesses (for example about the price of good $i$, but also on the prices of other goods). His choices – and therefore his level of satisfaction – change if his resources

---

forward in this book about monetary systems and the international monetary system are logical consequences of the rationality assumption, which is the very foundation of any economic theory.

change, if he gets new information, or if his tastes vary. Anyway, the concerns of this book do not involve any precise and measurable knowledge of demand curves and of the factors which determine them. As we shall see, it is sufficient to have information of purely qualitative nature – in particular, the fact that a demand curve is decreasing and that the satisfaction of an individual increases when he moves down his demand curve – in order to have the instruments of reasoning that allow us to understand and evaluate monetary systems.

But, to be sufficiently accurate, it is still necessary to add an important remark about the demand curve. According to the usual presentation of all economics textbooks, I have previously said that the individual demands a certain amount of good *i* for a certain price of this good. But the demand curve is in fact supposed to describe the behaviour of an individual who is undertaking an exchange. Now, as we saw earlier, it is not possible to separate the demand for a good from the corresponding supply of another good: an individual wishes simultaneously to get a certain good and to pay for it with another good (or service, for instance his work). This is why a price is always a relative concept: it is the price of a good in terms of another good. In an economy in which money is used, the habit is to consider that the purchase of a good is always made against a supply of money, and one names the 'price' of a commodity in terms of money. But let us for now assume that we are in a barter economy, for example an economy where there are only two goods, wheat and tomatoes. The demander for wheat is at the same time a supplier of tomatoes, as we have seen when studying the theory of exchange. Thus, the price of wheat is expressed in terms of tomatoes (or, conversely, the price of tomatoes is expressed in terms of wheat). As a result, the demand curve of 'wheat against tomatoes' represents at the same time the supply of 'tomatoes against wheat'. This simple remark calls into question the traditional presentation of microeconomics in which one explains the demand function by the so-called theory of the consumer, and the supply function by the so-called theory of the producer (for which one uses a great number of analytical devices to determine the 'costs of production'). Actually, there are not two different kinds of behaviours, that of the consumer and that of the producer. There is only the behaviour of the individual who is acting. He creates wealth to gain satisfaction, either by consumption (current or future), or through exchange.

As we know, nowadays there is usually no recourse to barter, but money is used as an intermediary in trade. The individual who wants to purchase wheat supplies money as a counterpart in exchange (this currency having been previously bought against the supply of another good), and the price of the good *i* is expressed in terms of the quantity of currency units. But, as will be seen later on, even to analyse the workings of a monetarized economy – as in this book – it may be useful, in order to understand the phenomena, to express the price of a good in terms of a real commodity (or a 'basket of commodities') and not in terms of money. Thus, I will not use money as a standard of value in exchange, but this will not remove its other functions (which I will summarize later on). It is especially useful to express the price of money in terms of real goods (what will later on be called its 'purchasing power').

It is now possible to shift from the micro level to the macroeconomic level, keeping in mind that, in so doing, the nature of the problem does not change: there is no macroeconomic reality separable from the microeconomic reality. The shift from one to the other is simply done by a process of aggregation. If we could know and measure the quantities demanded or supplied by all individuals in a society for all possible prices, we could draw an aggregate demand curve and an aggregate supply curve. This is obviously an illusion. But, as said previously, it is quite sufficient for the purpose of this book to have a qualitative understanding of the phenomena. Thus, we know that, for any individual, the demand curve is decreasing and that an individual always has an interest in moving down his demand curve. Likewise, we know that the supply curve is increasing and that an individual always has an interest in moving up his supply curve (this statement is logically deduced from the previous one concerning the demand curve). Thus, the demand and supply curves drawn in Figure 3.1 can be assumed to represent the behaviour of a set of individuals. What is true for an individual is true for any number of individuals, in particular the decreasing slope of the demand curve and the increasing slope of the supply curve. Therefore, the representations made in this figure correctly express a 'collective demand' (or 'macroeconomic demand') and a 'collective supply' (or 'macroeconomic supply').

## 3.3  THE CONCEPT OF DISEQUILIBRIUM

In the light of the above, saying that an individual is in disequilibrium – or not in equilibrium – is saying that he is not satisfied. But we have also seen that satisfaction is always relative in the sense that it takes into account the resource and information constraints. This implies that an individual can never be in a situation of disequilibrium if he acts freely and not through coercion. At the time when an act is decided, a free and rational individual chooses what he prefers, given the constraints which apply to him or which he has freely chosen: thus, he is satisfied with what he is doing, given the degree of information that he decided to obtain. He may regret his decision later on or regret not having invested more time and resources in the search for better information, but nevertheless, the decision is rational – at the point of time where he takes it – and it brings him a maximum of satisfaction. Thus, it may be that an individual, looking at the results of his action, considers that his satisfaction is less great than he had hoped, or less than what he could have obtained by taking another decision. But at the time of the decision he was necessarily in 'equilibrium', which means that he took the decision that gave him the highest possible satisfaction.

On the other hand, an individual is in disequilibrium if, at a given time, he would like to take a certain decision, given the resources and information available to him, but he is obliged through coercion to take another decision. This coercion may be exercised by an individual – for example, a thief who forced him to hand over his wallet – or by a public authority enjoying the privilege of exercising legal coercion. But it is also true that the borders between a free act and a compulsory act are not always easy to determine. Thus, if a thief says to someone: 'Your wallet or your life', he leaves to them a certain degree of freedom in the decision. And the individual will probably be 'satisfied' – in a very relative sense – to give up his wallet rather than his life. Even if a citizen considers that he is a victim of an excessive fiscal despoilment he will be satisfied by choosing exile rather than plunder, but he would obviously have preferred not to undergo this coercion and be able to remain in his country while paying less tax. But it is no less true that the distinction between a free and a forced act is a fundamental distinction, too often overlooked in most approaches of economic theory which do not sufficiently consider the motivations of behaviours and the systems of incentives.

What has been said at the individual level can obviously be transposed at the level of a society. A macroeconomic equilibrium prevails when all individuals are satisfied, which means that they can freely choose the position they prefer, given their resources, their information and the consequences of interactions between them (which determine, in particular, the different prices). Thus, the collective demand and supply curves mentioned earlier correspond to situations of macroeconomic equilibrium insofar as they do not result from acts of coercion.

Let us apply these concepts, for example, to the market for loanable funds, that is, the market of saved resources that are lent and borrowed. In Figure 3.2, supply and demand for loanable funds determine an equilibrium interest rate $r_e$. If a public authority imposes a lower interest rate, $r_1$, there is a disequilibrium: those who demand loanable funds would borrow an amount $OB$ of loanable funds for the interest rate prevailing, but supply is reduced due to the decline in the interest rate, so that they can get only $OA$. Some of them are therefore not satisfied (but those who can

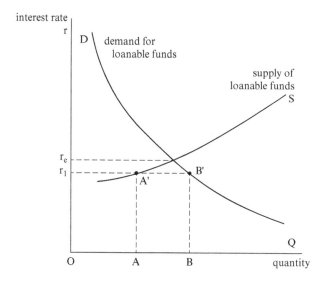

*Figure 3.2   Disequilibrium created by a state intervention*

borrow are satisfied because they benefit from a lower rate than $r_e$). Thus, there is a macroeconomic disequilibrium.

Saying that an economic system is in equilibrium means that the concerned individuals are satisfied, but it absolutely does not imply that their situation remains the same over time, that is that the equilibrium is stationary. It may be convenient to simplify economic reasoning by assuming a given situation and considering the consequences of a change of one variable, all other things being constant. This is a comparative static analysis, but the human reality is rather dynamic. Because human beings are free beings, they constantly modify information and resources, as well as their personal goals. As a consequence there are continuous changes in economic variables, for example in prices. This is why the supply and demand curves should be considered more as instruments to facilitate reasoning rather than as faithful representations of reality.

# 4.  The demand for money

This book aims at understanding and assessing the working of monetary systems. But to this end, it is necessary to clearly specify the criteria of the good working of a system. Now, analysing a monetary system is analysing how a currency is created, how it is circulating, which services it may supply. In very simple terms a good monetary system is a system which allows individuals to have 'sound money'. But what is a 'sound currency'? This is obviously a currency that fulfils its role (or roles). Analysing the roles of a currency and the reasons for which it is desired is therefore a necessary step in the analysis of monetary systems. The latter follows logically from the study of the functions of a currency.

## 4.1  THE ROLES OF MONEY

Money plays two key roles and it is precisely because it plays both these roles that, probably, it was invented, although its appearance cannot be dated: money makes indirect exchange possible, and it facilitates exchanges over time.

### 4.1.1  Indirect Exchange

In the absence of a currency – that is in a barter economy – each potential trader is obliged to find another trader who wishes to achieve an exchange which is exactly symmetrical to the one which he desires to do: thus, if someone wishes to sell wheat and to buy tomatoes in exchange, he must first find people who want to buy wheat and to sell tomatoes; but he must also find, among all the people who would be willing to do this sort of barter, those who would be ready to do it at an exchange rate between wheat and tomatoes which is acceptable for him. It is obvious that such searches are costly, at least in terms of time. Information on the relative prices in markets is difficult to obtain and to keep in mind, since in a universe with $n$ goods, one needs to know the relative prices between a commodity and each of the $n - 1$ other ones. Thus, there is a very large number of prices.

Information costs are considerably reduced if there is a good with monetary characteristics. It can be one of the $n$ existing goods – which is then desired both for its own characteristics and for its monetary nature – or any other good which has only a monetary role. Historically it seems that a spontaneous selection process has occurred by which members of a society have chosen to give a monetary value to a specific good. Most likely, this selection has not been the result of a deliberate choice or an obligation imposed by a public authority, but rather the result of habits that have gradually developed and extended. Thus, a large number of goods have been able to play a monetary role through history, for example silver, bronze, gold, pieces of fabric, salt, seashells (cowry shells), cattle, and so on. It is also striking that many currencies got their name from a unit of measure for the good that originally played a monetary role, for example the pound (weight unit) or the dollar.

Whatever it is, when a currency exists, it is no longer necessary to know the relative prices of each good with each of the other goods, but only the relative price of each good against one of them: that which plays the role of a currency. And it is also no longer necessary to find a potential trader who wishes to make an exchange which is perfectly symmetrical to the exchange which one wishes to do. Let us assume, for example, that a silver ounce is selected as the monetary unit. The individual who wishes to exchange wheat against tomatoes will sell his wheat against a certain amount of money (silver). He does not have any direct need for the money in question because he does not wish, for instance, to hold a silver jewel, but he is assuming that the money will be exchangeable against tomatoes. The seller of these tomatoes will likely undertake the same type of reasoning: he does not need silver directly, but he believes that it will easily be accepted against the commodity which he wishes to buy. Thus, it is no longer necessary that there is a coincidence of wants between the seller of wheat and the seller of tomatoes, but each will eventually get the goods they want against the goods which they wish to sell and these exchanges will take place at a lower cost through indirect exchange: instead of an exchange of wheat against tomatoes, there is first an exchange of wheat for money and then of money against tomatoes. Of course, from the price in terms of money of wheat and tomatoes, one can easily deduce the relative price of wheat against tomatoes. Thus, if one exchanges 1 pound of wheat against 1 ounce of money and 1 ounce of money against 2 pounds of tomatoes, the relative price between wheat and tomatoes is 1/2 (1 pound of wheat against 2 pounds of tomatoes).

### 4.1.2   Exchange Over Time

Holding money enables an individual to distribute expenses and incomes over time in the most satisfactory way for him. Figure 4.1 illustrates this idea. It represents the evolution of expenditures and incomes of an individual during a period, for example a year. Let us assume that he evaluates the total value of his production during the year as being equal to 100 units. These units of measure may consist of monetary units (for example, 100 ounces of silver) or units of physical goods (for example, 100 pounds of wheat). Let us choose, for example, the latter: it implies that the individual gets an income each year the value of which, in terms of wheat, is equal to 100 pounds of wheat. He may be a producer of wheat and he may

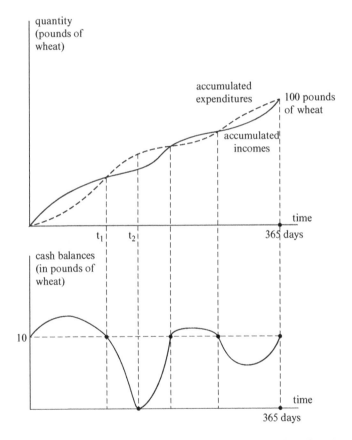

*Figure 4.1    Accumulated incomes and expenditures (panel a, above), and variations of money cash balances within a year (panel b, below)*

produce 100 pounds of wheat each year, but one may also assume that he produces another commodity the value of which, expressed in wheat-units, is equal to 100 pounds of wheat. Thus, if he produces 200 pounds of tomatoes and if 1 pound of tomatoes is traded against half a pound of wheat, the value of his 200 pounds of tomatoes in terms of wheat is equal to 100 pounds of wheat. This example therefore takes a pound of wheat as a numéraire, that is, as a unit of measurement.

The individual cannot spend more than his total income during the period, but he does not know exactly how his income and his expenditure will be phased over the period. Thus, Figure 4.1a represents the curve of the accumulated income from the first day of the year until the last day. This curve is constantly increasing, but it evolves in an irregular manner, and it leads to a point corresponding to 100 pounds of wheat. Similarly the curve of cumulative expenditure from the first to the last day of the year is represented. In the absence of money, the curve of cumulative expenditure can never exceed the curve of cumulative income. But imagine that the individual has begun the year with a monetary cash balance worth 10 pounds of wheat (for example, 10 ounces of silver, the value of which in wheat is equal to 10 pounds of wheat). He can then deal with a situation where his desired cumulative expenditure exceeds cumulative income by an amount equal to a maximum of 10 pounds of wheat. This is what happens, for example, at time $t_2$.

Figure 4.1b represents the evolution in time of the corresponding money cash balance of the individual. This is equal to 10 pounds of wheat on the first day of the year, and then fluctuates depending on gaps between cumulative expenditure and cumulative income, without ever being able to become less than zero. The money cash balance of the individual has a value of 10 pounds of wheat at the beginning, goes back to 10 pounds of wheat in $t_1$ and then becomes zero in $t_2$, before being reconstituted, and so on.

This figure can be used to specify what is meant by 'the demand for money'. Indeed, the money holding changes continuously during the period, but it can be considered that the individual wishes, on average, to hold a money cash balance worth 10 pounds of wheat, that is, a cash balance which allows him to bear a situation in which he has at the most an excess of expenses over income of 10 pounds of wheat. He began the period with a cash balance position of this value and he finishes it with this same cash balance.

Thus, we see that a currency derives its usefulness, *inter alia*, from the freedom it gives to its holder in his efforts to better coordinate expenditure and income over time, which is especially desirable in a (normal) situation of uncertainty. Its usefulness comes from the fact it is held, and it constitutes a 'pending' purchasing power. It is similar in some respects to an insurance policy: in a world of uncertainty it gives the guarantee that one can temporarily finance expenditure in excess of income (for example because at any given time there are exceptional needs or a non-forecasted decrease in the pace of income). Money supplies services – which can be called liquidity services – corresponding, on the one hand, to the possibility of indirect exchange, and on the other, to the possibility to distribute expenditure and income over time in the way one prefers, given the uncertainties of life.

In the example above it was assumed that the individual began the year holding cash balances worth 10 pounds of wheat. But he necessarily had to obtain this cash previously, and to that end he had to accept a sacrifice of consumption; that is, to renounce spending all of his income. Thus, if all his cash was accumulated in the previous year and the annual income of the individual was equal to 100 pounds of wheat that year, he will have consumed only a value of 90 pounds of wheat and saved 10 pounds of wheat to buy his money cash balances. Let me note in passing, because this is very important, that money cash balances are not savings, but they are purchased in exchange for savings. This can be compared to a good investment: by saving, one can buy a production good which will supply services in the future, or money cash balances which will supply liquidity services at any time in the future. Normally an investment good depreciates in use (hence the need for depreciation allowances). This is not the case for money, which may give services for ever; except in the special case – unfortunately frequent – which will be addressed later on where there is what is called inflation.

### 4.1.3    Money as a Standard of Value (Numéraire)

It is often considered that a constitutive feature of a currency is its role as a numéraire, that is, a standard of value, and it is true that it is customary to express the prices of goods and services in terms of a currency. If we consider the emergence of money, as above, we can imagine two scenarios. It can first be assumed that people have found it convenient to express all prices in terms of one of the existing goods; that is, a good was first selected as a standard of value, before possibly taking on a monetary role subsequently, thus making possible indirect exchange and exchange over time. But maybe it is the opposite which occurred, namely that the role of a standard of value came after the other two roles. In fact, it is likely that these roles have emerged gradually and more or less simultaneously, so that it is not possible to consider that one clearly preceded the other.

But what is important from the point of view of economic analysis, and not of history – and therefore from the point of view which interests us in the present book – is that the role of a standard of value is not necessary for a good to be considered as a currency, unlike the other two roles. Moreover, it is assumed above that even the value of money cash balances could be expressed in terms of a commodity other than money (for instance, wheat) and it will be seen later on that, in order to understand the functioning of monetary systems, it is useful not to give the role of standard of value to a currency, but that one cannot, on the other hand, discard the two other roles. When using a currency as a numéraire, it is usual to say that prices and values are expressed in nominal terms. When using a real good (or a basket of goods, as is the case when using a price index), it is usual to say that prices and values are expressed in real terms. However, from the point of view of economic analysis, it is useful to express the value of a currency not in terms of a monetary standard, but in real terms. Indeed, one essential feature of a currency consists in its ability to be a potential purchasing power; thus, expressing the value of cash balances in real terms yields a direct assessment of this purchasing power (at least in terms of the commodity serving as numéraire). In the simplified example of the monetary behaviour of an individual over time seen above, what interests the holder of money is the purchasing power he has at his disposal – how many pounds of wheat in money – in order to finance an excess of expenditure over income. Knowing that he has 10 euros or 10 dollars is less useful for him than knowing what is the real value of these cash balances. This is why I will very often use the distinction between nominal cash balances (expressed in terms of money) and real cash balances (expressed in terms of a real purchasing power, by using a real numéraire).

But let us assume that, as is generally the case nowadays, a currency is used both as the numéraire and as an intermediary in trade, and let us assume that this currency is called the Ecu and that it is defined as equal to 1 pound of wheat (1 Ecu = 1 pound of wheat). Then, let us take the example used in Chapter 2 in which, in a barter economy, an individual exchanges 2 pounds of tomatoes against 3 pounds of wheat. There is now a double transaction which can be represented thus in the transaction account of the individual:[1]

Transaction account of individual A

| Sales | Purchases |
|---|---|
| 2 pounds of tomatoes worth 3 Ecus | 3 Ecus of money |
| 3 Ecus of money | 3 pounds of wheat worth 3 Ecus |

---

[1]  It is possible to stress already that the balance of payments – which will be studied in Part II of this book – is nothing but a transaction account concerning not an individual, but all those who are inhabitants of a country, and their transactions with the inhabitants of the rest of the world.

Instead of exchanging 2 pounds of tomatoes against 3 pounds of wheat – as in the case of a barter economy – our individual begins by selling 2 pounds of tomatoes and buys as a counterpart 3 Ecus in money. Later on, he resells these 3 Ecus against 3 pounds of wheat. Thus, he will have sold, indirectly, 2 pounds of tomatoes against 3 pounds of wheat. The nominal price of 1 pound of tomatoes equals 1.5 Ecus, the nominal price of 1 pound of wheat is equal to 1 Ecu. But the relative price between tomatoes and wheat remains what it was in the barter economy, that is, 1 pound of tomatoes = 1.5 pounds of wheat (which constitutes a real price expressed in the numéraire 'pound of wheat'). This means that the general principle of exchange is not changed by the fact that one uses money as numéraire and/ or as an intermediary in trade.

But let us assume now that the individual wishes to accumulate a certain amount of currency during this period. His transaction account will be for instance the following:

Transaction account of individual A

| Sales | Purchases |
| --- | --- |
| 4 pounds of tomatoes worth 6 Ecus | 6 Ecus of money |
| 3 Ecus of money | 3 pounds of wheat worth 3 Ecus |

Using the conventional terms of accounting, we can say that the balance of his transactions on commodities will be 'positive' for an amount of 3 Ecus (monetary value of the excess of sales over purchases) and that its monetary account balance is 'negative'[2] for an amount of 3 Ecus (excess of purchases of currency over the sales of currency). The double-entry accounting which necessarily exists in any transaction obviously implies that the absolute value of a balance is equal to the absolute value of the other balance (or other balances if there are several items in the account).

---

[2]  Using such terminology is dangerous since it suggests that a positive balance is desirable, while a negative balance would be regrettable. This is obviously not the case since the individual wishes to make the transactions in question: he wants to obtain 'positive' balance for the item 'commodities' and a 'negative' balance for the item 'currency'. These two balances are interdependent and desired at the same time. Part II of this book will show that it is very important to avoid giving a normative meaning to the terms thus used.

## 4.2   THE DEFINITION OF MONEY

From what we have seen about the roles of money, a definition of money can be proposed. The definition which I propose and use thereafter is the following: money is a generalized purchasing power, that is, money can be redeemed against anything, at any time, and with anyone. It is a pending purchasing power and it supplies services as long as it is held. Of course, no currency can perfectly match this definition; for example, because a dollar or a pound is not necessarily accepted by everyone in the world. That is why, instead of talking about money, it may be more correct to speak of the (more or less) 'monetary quality' or 'moneyness' of goods. All goods, in fact, to a more or less significant degree, have this character-istic of exchangeability. But a field, for example, is less 'monetary' than a pound or a dollar because it is less easily redeemable against anything, at any time, with anyone. The goods which are commonly called 'currencies' are goods which have relatively higher levels of tradability. But it is neces-sary to distinguish this 'natural' definition of a currency from the 'formal' definition which is usual nowadays: for instance, the name 'currency' will be given to banknotes, the purchasing power of which deteriorates over time. But these so-called currencies – which enjoy state privileges for their use – have a very low 'monetary quality'. It is in any case essential to always bear in mind that the very nature of a currency is to constitute available purchasing power. As such, it opens up freedoms to its holders because they know that holding money balances allows them to meet their future needs in a world of uncertainty.

Two features appear to be essential in specifying the factors which allow a good to have a monetary nature:

- First of all – and this is obvious – a good is closer to being 'money' insofar as it better keeps its purchasing power over time. Of course, the definition and the measurement of the purchasing power of the currency are subject to debate, and this is a problem that I will discuss later on.
- Secondly, a currency is more 'money' insofar as its area of circula-tion is greater, namely that it is more exchangeable with anyone and against anything else. But I will also consider this issue more specifi-cally later on.

There will be frequent opportunities to discuss these two features as they make it possible to assess the extent to which a currency is 'good money'. They also make it possible to evaluate and to compare different monetary systems, since a monetary system is obviously better if it provides a better currency. We thus have very relevant criteria with which to evaluate monetary systems.

## 4.3    THE MONEY DEMAND FUNCTION

The explanatory factors of the money demand function can now be specified. Let us assume first that the currency is not used as a numéraire, so that the variables are measured in terms of a real commodity, for example pounds of wheat. The amount of money cash balances owned by an individual (or a group of individuals) will then be measured in terms of this real standard of value, which implies that we are concerned with the demand for real cash balances, which is logical since a currency is desired as a purchasing power. What is desired – and therefore in demand – by individuals is purchasing power in a monetary form, rather than a number of nominal monetary units regardless of the purchasing power they represent.

According to convention, lowercase letters will be used to denote variables expressed in real terms and uppercase letters to denote variables expressed in nominal terms (that is, with a monetary numéraire). As a first approximation we will assume that there are only two goods, wheat and currency.[3] We can write:

$$m^d = ky \text{ (with } dm^d/dy > 0) \qquad (4.1)$$

where $m^d$ represents the demand for real cash balances of an individual during a period, and $y$ his real income during the same period. It is logical to make this assumption of a positive relationship between the demand for real cash balances and the real income of an individual, simply because the currency has a specific characteristic, which means that it has no close substitutes. This implies that it is not what is called an 'inferior good', that is, a good the demand for which declines with increasing income (because this increase would allow substitution of a much more desirable – but more expensive – good for the so-called 'inferior good'[4]). The positive relationship between income and real cash balances can also be justified by

---

[3]    This is obviously an extreme assumption in which the currency cannot fully play its role since there is only one commodity – wheat – so that one therefore cannot exchange one product against another one via the currency. It plays a role only as a means to cover the gaps in time – possibly unpredictable – between production and consumption.

[4]    Thus, with an increasing income an individual abandons a portion of his consumption of bread to buy cakes or cheese. Bread is then considered to be an 'inferior good'.

the fact that the increase in income will normally increase the number and/ or the amount of transactions, which increases the need for the currency in its role of intermediary in exchange. We will not try to give a quantitative estimate of the parameter $k$ in equation (4.1). It is sufficient, in order to complete the reasoning developed in this book, to possess the qualitative information that there is a positive relationship between the demand for real cash balances and real income. Of course, a lot of econometric work has attempted to calculate the parameters of money demand functions (in a more elaborate form than has been presented here on a provisional basis). It all confirms this positive relationship.

### 4.3.1 Substitution between Money and Financial Assets

If the currency has no close substitute in the sense that it is the best fitted to fulfil the function of 'generalized purchasing power' (at least, if it is a 'good' currency the real value of which is not deteriorating, or only slightly, over time), there is, however, a certain degree of substitutability between money and other assets. Thus, we now add to our model a third good: financial claims. They represent property rights on future goods (of future wheat in this case). As is the case for money, a financial claim is a potential purchasing power. But it is less liquid than a currency because it is not generally accepted in exchange, in contrast to what occurs with a currency. If I hold a claim which is exchangeable one year later against 1 pound of wheat, and I need to finance expenditure before the maturity of this claim, I have to bear transaction and risk costs: I have to exchange it against money, and its market value is necessarily less than its value at maturity. From this point of view, a claim is less useful than money cash balances. But, on the other hand, it supplies an interest rate usually higher than the interest rate which may be available for holders of a currency. Nowadays, moreover, legislation often prohibits paying interest on money cash balances (demand deposits and banknotes). In the absence of this legislation, money would probably bring interest (as can be seen when this ban does not exist), but the rate of interest on cash balances would necessarily be lower than that on claims. Given his desire to own a pending purchasing power, an individual must therefore arbitrate between money and claims, money offering greater liquidity and claims a higher real interest rate. We can therefore write:

$$m^d = k(r) \, y \text{ (with } dk/dr < 0) \tag{4.2}$$

This reflects the fact that the demand for money decreases when the rate of interest on claims increases. Allowing money cash balances to collect an interest rate, $r_m$, the function (4.2) becomes:

$$m^d = k\,(r_m,\, r)\, y \text{ (with } dk/dr_m > 0 \text{ and } dk/dr < 0) \qquad (4.3)$$

### 4.3.2   Substitution between Money and Commodities

Leaving aside for the time being the existence of claims, let us assume that a currency is constituted by a real commodity – for instance, gold – and let us assume (still temporarily), that it does not play the role of a numéraire. There is a relative price between gold and wheat, $P_{g/x}$, which represents the quantity of gold ($G$) which can be obtained in exchange for a unit of wheat ($X$). One will be more induced to hold the currency insofar as one anticipates an increase in its purchasing power in terms of wheat (that is, one anticipates a decline in the price of wheat in terms of gold). We can therefore write:

$$m^d = k\,(P^a{}_{g/x}) \text{ (with } dm^d/dP^a{}_{g/x} > 0) \text{ (where } P^a \text{ means anticipated price)} \qquad (4.4)$$

The evolution of the relative price between gold and wheat obviously depends on the relative change of the supply and demand of the two goods. Thus, if the growth of the stock of monetary gold is lower than the growth of the production of commodities (wheat) – that is, the growth of incomes – there is a growing relative scarcity of gold compared to wheat and therefore an increase in the price of gold in terms of wheat; that is, a drop in the price of wheat in terms of gold.

But suppose now that money is used as a numéraire, so that we express the price of commodities (wheat) in terms of money (gold). $P_{w/g}$ is the price of wheat in terms of gold, but, for the sake of simplification, we will agree to use the variable $P$ to refer to the price of a good in terms of the currency (for example, the price of wheat in terms of gold). To shift from the numéraire 'wheat' to the numéraire 'money' we just have to multiply a value expressed in numéraire 'wheat' by $P$. Thus, we can express the demand for money as a demand for nominal cash balances, and no longer as a demand for real cash balances: equation (4.1) then becomes:

$$Pm^d = k()\, Py \qquad (4.5)$$

which one can also write, taking into account the notation conventions:

$$M^d = k()\, Y \qquad (4.6)$$

where $M^d$ is the demand for nominal cash balances, and $Y$ is nominal income (expressed in terms of money).

But it must always be remembered that, with money being desired as purchasing power, the equations of the demand for real cash balances reflect the actual behaviour of individuals. What is called a demand for nominal cash balances is nothing else than an expression 'derived' from the demand for money, obtained by a mathematical manipulation in order to change the standard of value.

For the time being we have assumed that there is a single commodity, wheat, so that $P$ is the money price of wheat. But in order to get gradually closer to the reality, which is obviously more complex, let us assume now that there are several products and that $P$ represents the price in money of a 'basket' composed of a certain amount of each of the existing products.[5] An increase of $P$ represents a decrease in the purchasing power of the currency: a currency unit allows the purchase of increasingly smaller fractions of the 'basket' as long as $P$ increases. This is called inflation. On the other hand, there is deflation when $P$ decreases, meaning that the price of products decreases in terms of money, which means an increase in the purchasing power of money.

Thus, let us assume that there is a continuous variation of $P$ over time, for example an increase at a constant rate. We assume for the moment that the prices of all goods are increasing at the same rate (an assumption which will be abandoned later on). Let us use the symbol $\pi$ to express the rate of increase of $P$ during a period. We can specify the shape of the demand for real cash balances function (assuming provisionally that claims do not exist) in the following forms:

$$m^d = k\,(\pi^a)\,y \;\text{(with } dk/d\pi^a < 0) \tag{4.7}$$

or

$$M^d = k\,(\pi^a)\,Py \;\text{(with } dk/d\pi^a < 0) \tag{4.8}$$

in which $\pi^a$ represents the anticipated rate of change of $P$ by period.

This equation expresses the fact that people demand less money cash balances insofar as they anticipate a higher inflation rate (the $k$ coefficient varies in the opposite direction of the rate of change of $P$). This statement follows logically from the assumption of rationality: since an individual wants to hold money insofar as it plays its role as a store of value, he holds less currency the less well it plays its role. But it is important from this

---

[5] The relevance of what is called a price index, intended to measure the price of a basket of goods, will be examined later on.

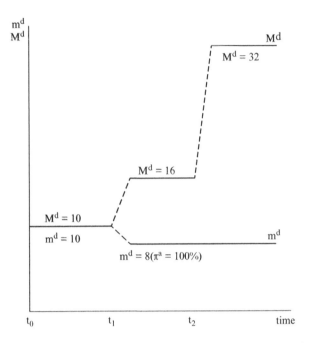

*Figure 4.2    Nominal cash balances ( $M^d$ ), real cash balances ($m^d$) and inflation*

point of view to distinguish between the demand for real cash balances and the demand for nominal cash balances. Their evolution over time are represented in Figure 4.2.

Let us take the case of an individual who is at $t_0$ at the beginning of a period (of one year, for example); and let us assume that the individual whose monetary behaviour we represent is anticipating a zero inflation rate for this period (and for subsequent periods), that is, $\pi^a = 0$. For this anticipated inflation rate the individual wishes to hold a real cash balance worth 10 pounds of wheat. And if we assume for the sake of simplicity that one can exchange 1 pound of wheat against 1 Ecu at $t_0$, the desired nominal cash balance at the beginning of this period – for this price level $P$ and for this anticipated inflation rate $\pi^a$ – is equal to 10 Ecus. Finally, suppose that the real income anticipated for the coming period, $y$, is equal to 100 so that, in accordance with equation (4.1), the parameter $k$ is equal to 0.1 (the real cash balance desired at the beginning of the period is equal to one-tenth of the real income for the period). Thus, throughout the period from $t_0$ to $t_1$, the desired real cash balance will be equal to 10 (in terms of pounds of wheat), which obviously does not mean that the individual will hold this same amount of money at any time during the period since, as we have seen, this amount is necessarily changing during the period. To simplify, we will also assume that the individual is doing what is necessary in order to hold the desired amount of real cash balances at the beginning of each period, taking into account his expectations regarding the inflation rate and the level of income. Let us also assume for the time being that his expectations are correct, so that he does not need to amend his behaviour during the period to take account of the actual values of the rate of inflation and of his real income.

Let us assume now that the individual anticipates in $t_1$ a doubling of prices during the coming period. This doubling necessarily comes from an increase in the quantity of money (which will be specified later on). Because money loses a part of its purchasing power, the individual will want to hold less real balances, for example a cash balance worth 8 pounds of wheat (instead of 10 pounds of wheat). According to equation (4.8), $Pm^d = M^d = k\,(\pi^a = 100\%)\,Py$. Using the data of our example, it yields: $2 \times 8 = k \times 2 \times 100$, so that $k = 0.08$. This means that the real cash balance required per unit of income has decreased (the $k$ coefficient decreased from 0.1 to 0.08). This is what is represented in Figure 4.2. Of course, the adjustment to the new level of real cash balances is not necessarily immediate and this is why it is included in the form of a dotted curve. Furthermore, the nominal cash balances have increased: to be consistent with the anticipated increase in prices and the new level of desired real balances, the amount of nominal cash balances must become 16 Ecus, which is represented in Figure 4.2 by the curve at the top.

If in $t_2$ the individual still forecasts the same increase in prices (100 per cent for the period), the desired level of real balances remains equal to 8 (pounds of wheat), but the nominal cash balance increases (it shifts from 16 to 32 Ecus). The desired real cash balance will remain constant as long as the individual anticipates a constant inflation rate; it will increase if this rate decreases, and it will decrease again if this rate increases.

Thus, it can be seen that, due to the increase in monetary prices, there is a double movement: the desired real cash balance decreases, while the desired nominal cash balance increases. This is what might be called the paradox of money: individuals hold less money (in real terms) insofar as there is more money (in nominal terms). Indeed, money creation implies an increase in monetary prices, and therefore a deterioration in the purchasing power of money and a flight away from money. The best way to create money (in real terms; that is, the kind of money which is actually desired) is by not creating money (in nominal terms). Indeed, if one creates no money, while the quantity of goods increases, the prices of goods fall, meaning that the purchasing power of the currency increases. In this case, there is deflation and the coefficient $k$ (in the equation of the demand for money) increases. It can be considered quite rightly that this is the most satisfactory assumption for money-holders, since the purchasing power of the cash balances they hold increases so that money is therefore particularly suited to supply the services one may expect from it.

Conversely, inflation imposes upon money-holders a number of costs (which we will encounter in this book). For the time being, there is one which is particularly obvious: since, in the case of inflation, the real value of money cash balances decreases, a person who holds such a currency is obliged to reconstitute the value of his cash balance. But, of course, as we have seen, his demand for real cash balances decreases with inflation, which means that he does not reconstitute the full real value of his cash balance. In the previous example, his desired real cash balance changes from 10 to 8 (pounds of wheat) when the rate of inflation which he anticipates changes from 0 to 100 per cent. But, while he held a monetary cash balance worth 10 Ecus, he is nevertheless obliged, in order to achieve this new level of real cash balance, to bring his nominal cash balance from 10 to 16 Ecus. Now, to obtain this additional nominal cash balance he must sell goods and services, for a value in this case of 6 Ecus (3 pounds of wheat with the new value of $P$). And this cost must be borne at each period for as long as he anticipates the continuation of inflation.[6] In fact, for the time being it has not been made clear what relationship could exist between the forecast inflation rate and the actual rate of inflation. Let us then assume, as a simplification, that expectations are correct and that the two rates therefore coincide.

There is, from this point of view, a situation very similar to the one which exists, for instance, in industrial activities: the deterioration of a capital good in a firm obliges it to implement a depreciation allowance, that is, to devote resources to the renewal of this equipment. In the monetary field, we can say that inflation deteriorates the 'monetary capital' and therefore requires that the money-holders reconstruct its value, that is, implement a depreciation allowance. But while it is impossible to avoid the wear and tear on a material equipment good, the 'wear of monetary capital' could very easily be avoided, since it would just be sufficient not to create nominal cash balances. Inflation therefore imposes a levy on the

---

6   In fact, from $t_1$ to $t_2$, the individual must sacrifice 4 pounds of wheat, rather than 3, since the desired nominal cash balance shifts from 16 to 32, and $P$ doubles again and becomes equal to 4. But it is impossible to say that the (subjective) sacrifice to perform in $t_2$ is higher than in $t_1$: indeed, in $t_1$ the individual sacrificed resources worth 3 pounds of wheat, but he also had to accept a sacrifice to accept to hold real cash balances with a purchasing power of 8 pounds of wheat instead of 10.

resources of currency-holders. There is a real transfer (with a value of 3 or 4 pounds of wheat, in each period, in our example) from money-holders to the producers of money. Therefore, it is legitimate to speak of an inflation tax, at least in the monetary systems which are managed by a public authority.

From this analysis – based on absolutely indisputable proposals, since they are consistent with the logic of human behaviour – two very important (and too much ignored) statements must be drawn:

- First of all, and contrary to widely held ideas, deflation is preferable to inflation.
- Secondly, it is absolutely not necessary, and it is even harmful, to create money.

Indeed, creating money means creating nominal cash balances; but we have seen that there are certainly less real cash balances whenever there are more nominal cash balances. If one refrains from creating nominal cash balances and there is an increase in the demand for real cash balances because of the growth of production and trade, individuals become demanders of cash balances and suppliers of commodities in return, so that the price of the currency in terms of goods and services increases: that is, the monetary price of goods and services decreases (deflation). This is what is called the 'real cash balance effect'. It is this effect which makes it possible to adjust the level of real balances to the needs of people.

So far we have analysed the demand for money of an individual. But one can express the demand for money of a set of individuals (for example, the residents of a country) by a process of aggregation. As I have said, it is sufficient for the upcoming demonstrations to have qualitative information on the relationships between different variables, and it is not necessary to quantify precisely the parameters of the demand for money functions. Thus, if the demand for money function is positively related with income for one person, it has the same characteristic for any set of individuals. Similarly, this function is negatively related with the real interest rate.

Moreover, we have assumed above that individuals correctly anticipated price changes so that the actual inflation rate is equal to the forecast one. One could certainly make very different assumptions, and there is in fact a considerable literature on the formation of inflationary expectations and on the relations between anticipated inflation and actual inflation. But the goal in this book is to seek the logic of the working of monetary systems and, from this point of view, it is concerned with a long-term perspective. That is why the assumption of a coincidence between anticipated inflation and actual inflation (or forecast deflation and actual deflation), although it does not strictly correspond to the reality, is acceptable to achieve this objective.

### 4.3.3  Money, Financial Assets and Commodities

We have studied successively and separately the substitution between money and financial assets and the substitution between money and commodities. We can now make the synthesis of these two analyses and write a demand for money function which takes into account both the substitution between money and financial assets, on the one hand, and money and commodities, on another hand, since individuals have to arbitrate between these three goods. This function can be written:

$$m^d = k(r, \pi^a) \, y \text{ (with } dk/dr < 0 \text{ and } dk/d\pi^a < 0)\text{)} \qquad (4.9)$$

We know that the interest rate is determined by the supply and demand for loanable funds. But so far we have considered only a real interest rate, that is, a rate of interest expressed in terms of commodities (written $r$ by convention). But if one is using a monetary numéraire on the market for loanable funds, the interest rate will be determined in nominal terms and not in real terms and is represented by $i$. Suppose that a certain nominal interest rate, $i_0$, is determined on the market. Suppose also that the individual whose behaviour we are studying anticipates a certain inflation rate $\pi^a_0$. The real return which he may hope to get is equal to $r_0 = i_0 - \pi^a_0$. In other words, if he lends, for example, 1 Ecu worth 1 pound of wheat at time $t_0$, if he gets a 10 per cent nominal interest rate, but if he anticipates an annual inflation rate of 5 per cent, he will get at the end of a year 1.1 Ecus, which will allow him to obtain about 1.05 pounds of wheat. His anticipated real rate of return is therefore roughly 5 per cent.

Of course, the nominal interest rate desired by lenders and borrowers depends on the rate of inflation expected by each of them, and there is no reason for them all to have the same expectations. The nominal interest rate which prevails on the market is in any case determined by these expectations of inflation rates as well as by the intertemporal preferences of everyone. This nominal interest rate being thus determined, each person evaluates the real interest rate which he anticipates, taking into account his own inflationary expectations.

It may be convenient, from the point of view of the analysis, to make simplifying assumptions, for example to assume that all people have the same expectations about the rate of inflation (or deflation) and that their expectations are correct, which means that the expected inflation rate is equal to the actual inflation rate. If a person is in a regime with a constant inflation rate from period to period, we can then write that the nominal interest rate is equal to the sum of the equilibrium real rate of interest and of the rate of inflation:

$$i = r + \pi \qquad (4.10)$$

## 4.4  THE QUANTITY THEORY OF MONEY

We have just analysed the demand for money function and it can be written in the very general form of equations (4.5) and (4.6), or in the following form which is derived from them:

$$M^d = k() \, Py \qquad (4.11)$$

This equation can be regarded as an aggregate function of demand resulting from the addition of all individual money demand functions. As has already been said, to the extent that we do not seek to accurately measure a factor such as $k$, but simply to evaluate the consistency and to understand the working of monetary systems, we can be perfectly content with this very general form of the demand for money function for a set of individuals (for example, all those who use a given currency).

The money supply will be analysed in Chapter 5, but for the time being we will use a very simple form of this supply function, namely the following:

$$M^s = M^\circ \qquad (4.12)$$

in which $M^s$ represents the money supply and $M^\circ$ indicates an existing quantity of money (in nominal form). Therefore we assume here that the quantity of money existing at a given time is given exogenously and that it is not determined by the entire monetary model. We can assume for example that there is a certain amount of metal currency (gold) or that monetary authorities decide a priori to create a certain amount of money over a period. Chapter 5 will show to what extent such an assumption is justified.

The equilibrium between the supply and the demand for money is thus given by the following equation:

$$M^\circ = k()\, Py \qquad (4.13)$$

which can also be written according to the traditional formulation of the quantity theory of money in the following form:

$$M^\circ V = Py \text{ or } MV = Pt \qquad (4.14)$$

in which $t$ represents transactions (because there is a relationship between $y$ and $t$). The parameter $V$ is obviously equal to the inverse of $k$. It is traditionally called the 'velocity of money', which is a debatable term because there is no such thing (money is desired to be held as a store of value, and not to circulate). But it is worth remembering the true meaning of this equation: it expresses the equality between the supply and demand of nominal balances.

Assuming that we are in a steady state, namely that the forecast rate of inflation and the real interest rate do not change, it follows that $k()$ is constant. Then one can draw from equation (4.13), by computing derivatives, the following equation:

$$\mu = \pi + \rho \qquad (4.15)$$

in which $\mu$ represents the rate of change of $M$ per unit of time, $\pi$ is the rate of change of prices and $\rho$ is the real growth rate (rate of change of $y$). One can also write (always assuming a constant $k$) that:

$$\pi = \mu - \rho \qquad (4.16)$$

which states that the rate of change of the prices of commodities is equal to the difference between the rate of change in the money supply and the rate of change of the quantity of commodities. This result is quite logical: it implies that the monetary prices of commodities increase (decrease) if there is an increasing (decreasing) relative scarcity of commodities against money, that is, an increasing (decreasing) relative abundance of the currency against commodities. Of course these results are strictly valid only under the condition of 'all things being equal', that is, in this case, if the parameter $k$ is constant.

# 5.  Money creation

Throughout this book it will be necessary to study the creation of money, since it is a key concern of any analysis of monetary systems. For the moment, I will make a few very general remarks. Thus, this chapter will successively take the example of a real currency (for example, a metallic currency such as gold), and the example of a fiduciary currency, that is, a currency which has no intrinsic value, but the value of which is determined only by the greater or lesser confidence one can have in its ability to be exchanged against real goods.

## 5.1   THE CASE OF A REAL CURRENCY

Let us suppose, for instance, that gold has been chosen as a currency because of its specific qualities. It is held and it circulates in the form of coins. How does money creation take place? It results simply from the same principles as those governing the production of any good. Holders of factors of production – capital, labour, natural resources – decide to use them in any particular activity on the basis of the return they receive from each activity and, in turn, it depends on the demand for each type of product. Let us imagine that we are initially in a situation in which gold is not used as currency. The supply and demand for gold determine the price of gold on the market. It is normal to assume that the marginal cost of extraction of gold is growing because the most profitable gold mines are operated first, either because gold is particularly abundant in these places, or because the extraction does not require very complex technical means in these places. The factors of production will be used in the production of gold as long as the marginal cost is low enough to allow the gold producer to get at least the minimum marginal benefit he wants, taking into account the market price of gold. Of course, supply and demand change over time, and thus the price of gold also changes.

Imagine now that gold is desired not only for the needs of jewellery or industry, but also as a currency. The demand for gold will increase and hence its relative price relative to other goods. This will encourage gold producers to increase their production to meet this new demand, until an

*45*

equilibrium stock of gold is obtained, that is, one which makes it possible to meet both non-monetary and monetary needs.

During this period of transition between the barter economy and the monetary economy, there is a change in the structure of demands of individuals: instead of using their resources only to buy non-monetary goods – such as wheat – they devote a part of them to buy gold. This means that the working of a monetary economy in which money is a real commodity implies that individuals are willing to sacrifice a portion of their resources to acquire money, at least initially. It is clear, from this point of view, that a monetary economy of this type has a cost, but individuals freely accept to bear this cost because the benefit they get from the use of money is greater than the cost of buying the currency they desire. In the transition phase, in any case, there is indeed money creation in the sense that an additional quantity of gold is extracted to meet the new needs which emerge (assuming, for instance, that the conditions in gold production are such that it is better for all individuals to obtain a new quantity of gold rather than to melt down their gold jewellery).

What can happen after this transition phase? If there is real growth (a periodic increase of what we have called 'wheat', which is representative of all commodities), the need for real cash balances increases correspondingly, as we saw in Chapter 4. Let us assume for simplicity that the rate of growth of the demand for money is the same as the one of real goods and services (what would nowadays be called real gross domestic product). Therefore, there will be an increasing demand for gold. But there is no demand without a corresponding supply, as we know. In other words, individuals will demand gold, and supply goods and services. This implies an increase in the price of gold compared to goods and services, that is, a decrease in the price of goods and services in relation to gold. In these circumstances it is not at all certain that gold producers are required to increase their production. Indeed, the change in relative prices between gold and real goods is the least expensive way to achieve a constant growth of real cash balances: the value of an ounce of gold in terms of goods increases continuously, and to meet any need of money it is not necessary to use factors of production for the production of an additional quantity of gold.[1] These factors remain available for the production of other goods which are desired.

---

[1]    There is, however, a difficulty in this case because, for low-value transactions, it would be necessary to have extremely small coins, and their weight would constantly decrease if the price of gold increased relatively to commodities. Either alloys containing less gold would be used, or coins with a lower value (for example in bronze) would be introduced alongside gold coins.

We have here an illustration of the very important idea according to which the real cash balance effect is the most efficient way to create money (in real terms), that is, to meet all monetary needs. It is never necessary to create additional monetary units from the time when a certain amount of currency exists. In the transition phase resources had to be devoted to the production of additional gold stock to meet the new need for currency, insofar as there was no desire to sacrifice other uses of gold. But this is no longer necessary later.

Obviously, simplifying assumptions have been chosen, for example assuming that the demand for real cash balances increases at the same rate as production and as the demand for other goods, and assuming that the conditions of production do not change. But it is obvious that the conditions of supply and demand can change. Thus, if a new gold mine is discovered, the operating costs of which are very low, there will be an incentive to produce gold and the gold price will decrease compared with goods. Such a phenomenon was observed when Europeans plundered gold from South America after the discovery of the Americas. This was one of the rare periods of significant increase in monetary prices (inflation) in history until modern times, when phenomena of a much larger scale have occurred.

## 5.2   THE CASE OF A FIDUCIARY CURRENCY

Let us assume now that there has been a shift from real money to a regime of 'fiduciary money' (that is, a currency with no material content), setting aside for the time considerations of the reasons for this shift, and its voluntary or non-voluntary character. A monetary unit has no real content and it has the form either of a piece of paper (banknote), or even of a simple accounting entry (deposit), without anyone guaranteeing the exchangeability of this monetary unit against a certain amount of real commodities. This monetary unit therefore has a purely formal name. Let us call it, for example, the Ecu. At any one point of time there are therefore a certain amount of currency units, $M$, the value of which can be expressed in nominal terms and not in real terms. What is important in such a scheme is that the currency producers create nominal cash balances and not real cash balances. But from this characteristic comes a major problem which creates obstacles to the sound functioning of modern monetary systems: currency producers produce nominal cash balances, whereas individuals need real cash balances. But in addition, there is an important feature, namely that the production of nominal cash balances is done at a zero or close to zero cost. There is thus a considerable incentive for currency producers to produce money, because this creation is not expensive and it can bring a high return. However, we know that the more nominal cash balances are produced, the less real cash balances there are, and the less currency needs are satisfied. This is the extraordinary and dangerous feature of fiat money systems, which are dominant nowadays: there is a bias in the system which induces meeting the monetary needs of people in a less desirable way. We will see later how different monetary systems can possibly reduce this risk and how, in particular, monopoly positions are most likely to use this opportunity for the unlimited creation of money.

There is also in this field another paradox which illustrates the very specific nature of money. In the production of any good it is considered an improvement – which benefits consumers – to use fewer factors of production to produce one unit of a particular commodity. Yet, this is what happens when one moves from a system of real currency to a fiduciary currency system: it can be regarded as an improvement to no longer be compelled to spend resources, at least initially, to constitute the quantity of money. Moreover, shifting from one system to another, the stock of monetary gold can be got rid of and used for other purposes, which represents a gain. It could therefore be considered a considerable improvement to shift from one system to the other, since it is quite unnecessary to use any resources whatsoever to create money in a fiduciary money system. But this is to forget that there is still more considerable progress if, instead of creating money, the real cash balance effect is allowed to play its role. It can be considered that the real cash balance effect represents the most efficient method for the production of real cash balances (the only one that deserves to be taken into account), and that it will never be possible to invent anything better. Letting the real cash balance effect work is using the most advanced technology for producing money. And what is remarkable is that money-holders thus indirectly become producers of real cash balances by their free and rational behaviour.

## 5.3    THE BANKING FIRM

So far I have talked about 'producers of money' without using the term 'banks'. Yet there is a tendency nowadays to consider that money creation is specifically a banking activity. In fact, the real job of a bank is to be a financial intermediary, that is, holding equity capital and/or borrowing loanable funds and using the saving resources thus available either to invest in the equity capital of firms or to deliver loans to individuals, firms, and public and private organizations. But nowadays banks in general are engaged in three types of activities: financial intermediation, money creation, and the production of financial and monetary services.[2]

Certainly there is complementarity between these various functions, for example because the production of money in modern monetary systems has, as a counterpart, the distribution of loans. The experience of a banking firm in financial intermediation may therefore be useful in its role as a producer of money. But, however, it is very conceivable that these roles may be filled by different organizations, as was the case historically. It is probably because of the existence of regulations which define what a bank is that these activities are generally performed together.

Banks are therefore, nowadays, the producers of money. We can represent their behaviour as suppliers of money in the following simple way:

$$M^s = g(i - c_m) \tag{5.1}$$

where $M^s$ is the supply of money in nominal terms (by a bank or a set of banks), $i$ is the nominal rate of interest and $c_m$ the periodic marginal cost of production of a currency unit. This supply function is increasing, that is, the money supply is greater insofar as the gap between the nominal interest rate and the marginal cost of production of money is greater. Indeed, the nominal interest rate $i$ is the periodic return earned by the bank for the credit it delivers as a counterpart of the creation of a monetary unit, while $c_m$ represents the periodic cost of production of this unit. In the case of fiat money (non-material money) this cost is extremely low. For a banknote it is essentially the initial cost of manufacturing it, and the periodic cost depends on the greater or lesser durability of the banknote. For a deposit, the cost is essentially represented by the management costs of the deposit accounting and this cost can therefore be considered to be close to zero. This cost may also include the remuneration of deposit accounts. It is often zero nowadays, but this usually results from a regulation which prohibits paying interest on demand deposits. When this ban is lifted, it often occurs that the producers of a currency – at least if they compete – decide to pay interest to attract customers. But in all cases – whether banknotes or deposits – it is also necessary to take into account the cost of the risk

---

[2] People sometimes tend to conflate what is financial and what is monetary. In fact, it is necessary to carefully distinguish between both terms: financial activities involve the constitution, the circulation and the use of savings (in the form of equity capital or loanable funds); while monetary activities concern the production, the circulation and the holding of money. The confusion which often occurs between these expressions probably comes from the fact that nowadays the production of money is necessarily associated with a corresponding creation of credits, which establishes a relationship – incidentally very damaging, as we shall see – between these very different activities.

attached to the credit associated with the production of the currency unit. It is logical to consider that this cost is growing because the bank accepts increasingly more risky loans. From this point of view the marginal cost of production of money is therefore increasing, which can limit monetary production. It is no less true that the profit margin can be considerable, at least if there are a large number of low-risk credit activities, and it thus follows that there is a strong incentive to create money. The unit profit obtained from the difference between the nominal interest rate and the marginal cost of production of money is sometimes called 'seigniorage', which is a resurgence of an old term which referred to the benefit obtained by lords or kings when they had the privilege of minting coins.[3] But this term refers now simply to the profit obtained in the production of money.

Now, it can also be said that the marginal return of money production is decreasing, although this may be slow. Indeed, the higher the monetary growth, the more inflation there is, and the more people fly away from the currency. Because of inflation, individuals are forced to restore the value of their cash balances, which brings a gain to currency producers, but they restore their cash balances less when they anticipate higher inflation. In the limit, when there is hyperinflation, there is a complete flight away from money: people no longer use money, and thus there are no more profits from money creation. There is thus a positive relationship between the marginal return in the production of money and monetary growth, but the marginal return is decreasing. As the marginal cost in the production of money is increasing and the marginal revenue is decreasing, there is necessarily a point where the marginal profit becomes zero. Unlike most economic activities in which profit is the remuneration of the service supplied to others (in particular by innovation), in the field of monetary production it is instead the result of a production system where the profit increases with the deterioration of the quality of the production. It will be of interest to consider later on how this profit evolves in different monetary systems. However, it is a priori likely – and this is indeed what we will see – that a great part of the explanation of the situation in different systems will depend on whether the production of money is made by a monopolistic or a competitive system.

But it is now possible to make a clarification of terminology. We have just seen that the profit obtained in the production of money can be called 'seigniorage'. But one can also refer to the 'inflation tax', that is, the profit

---

3    In ancient times seigniorage existed not because there was a low cost of production of money, but because the lords and kings could impose a significant difference between the face value of a coin (in terms of the amount of metal) and the actual value of the metal used in its manufacture.

obtained by the producers of money because money-holders are forced to reconstitute their money cash balances in the case of inflation. But this inflation tax (a term which will be discussed later) is in fact only a particular category of this more general concept known as seigniorage.

The quick analysis of the production of money in this chapter leads to the following basic proposition: it is never necessary to produce nominal cash balances, and the production of real cash balances is achieved at best by allowing the real cash balance effect to play its role. In the field of international monetary economics, which will be discussed later, this statement will have the following consequence: contrary to what is often said, there is never a lack of international reserves. It thus follows that it is not necessary for an international organization to create international liquidity, as is done by the International Monetary Fund (IMF) with special drawing rights (SDRs).

# 6. The exchange rate

So far we have assumed for the sake of simplicity that there is a single currency, but it is now time to abandon this assumption. Let us consider a situation where there are several currencies, the characteristics of which are perceived[1] as different by currency users, so that they are not perfectly substitutable one with another and they constitute goods which are different. These currencies will be exchanged on the market and there are relative prices between them. The exchange rate is precisely the relative price of one currency relative to another. Of course, all currencies cannot simultaneously play the role of a numéraire, which proves also, as previously pointed out, that the function of numéraire is not necessary to enable a good to be considered as a currency. Thus, when considering the exchange rate between the Ecu and another currency called the 'pound', one may say, for instance, that a pound is worth 10 Ecus if the Ecu is chosen as the numéraire. The exchange rate would obviously be equal to 0.1 if the pound was chosen as numéraire.

As the exchange rate is a relative price, it is necessarily determined by the supply and demand for one currency against another. Thus, the decrease in the price of one currency relative to another means that there is a growing relative abundance of this currency as a result of the evolution of the demands and supplies concerning the two currencies in question. Of course, these developments are explained by the changes in some of the variables which determine supply and demand (among which are those we have met previously when studying the demand for money and money creation). It is not the purpose of this book to develop an exhaustive analysis of the determination of the exchange rate in the short, medium and long term; but to evaluate the working of different monetary systems and of different exchange rate regimes, the determinants of long-term exchange rates are obviously those which have the greatest importance and will be given attention.

On a foreign exchange market – that is, a market where currencies are traded one against another – which operates freely, the confrontation of supply and demand determines an exchange rate which can be called

---

[1] What is important is not the observable and measurable characteristics of currencies, but the perception that users of currencies may have.

the equilibrium exchange rate. But can it be that the observed exchange rate – the one which prevails on the market – at a given time is different from the equilibrium exchange rate? Thus, it may often be questioned whether in a floating exchange rate regime the observed exchange rate is an equilibrium rate. Given what has been said earlier regarding the notion of equilibrium, the observed rate is an equilibrium rate, to the extent that no coercion is exercised and contractual freedom prevails in the foreign exchange market. What is done is done freely, and corresponds to the satisfaction of individuals, which means that there is equilibrium. Likewise in fixed exchange regimes, in which consistent rules are used (rules which will be clarified later). Even the distinction between short-term and long-term equilibrium is questionable. There is always equilibrium and the concept of a long-term equilibrium is a construction of observers which does not match reality. The overnight rate is an equilibrium rate: everyone acts freely on the foreign exchange market, which results in an exchange rate which can only be an equilibrium rate. If there is, at any given time, a difference between the observed exchange rate and the alleged long-term equilibrium exchange rate, it is because, for example, the right information has not been obtained. Individuals decide a certain exchange rate for their exchange of currencies, taking into account their level of information, and this exchange rate is an equilibrium rate.

In Figure 6.1, point $B$ is the equilibrium point in flexible exchange rates. All individuals are satisfied (given their constraints in resources, time and

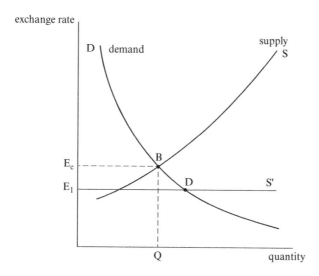

*Figure 6.1   Determination of the exchange rate*

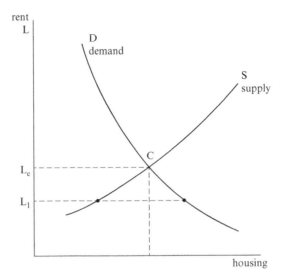

*Figure 6.2    Rent control*

information). The observed rate coincides with the equilibrium rate. This does not mean that point *B* is immutable, since the supply and demand curves move continuously.

Now suppose that an economic agent – for example, the central bank – 'imposes' an exchange rate $E_1$ different from the equilibrium exchange rate $E_e$. Are there reasons to say that the observed exchange rate is a disequilibrium rate because it does not coincide with $E_e$?

To answer this question, let us compare the working of the foreign exchange market with that of another market, for instance the housing market (Figure 6.2). $L_e$ is the equilibrium price of rentals, that is, the equilibrium rent. If the public authorities impose by decree or legislation a price $L_1$ smaller than the equilibrium price $L_e$, there is an excess of demand over supply. Among those who would be willing to pay $L_1$ to obtain housing, some cannot get it at this price and there is a disequilibrium. Suppliers, for their part, are less satisfied than they would be at point *C*, but they are still in equilibrium, taking into account the constraint which is imposed on them. Those who can find housing and are therefore on their demand curve are also in equilibrium and they are even more satisfied than they would be at point *C* (cheaper accommodation). But those who do not find accommodation are not in equilibrium. As a consequence the control of prices and rents – when the price is lower than the equilibrium price – increases the satisfaction of those, among

demanders, who are satisfied, but at the expense of the satisfaction of
other demanders and of suppliers.

But let us now go back to the foreign exchange market (Figure 6.1). If
monetary authorities were to implement the rate $E_1$ by imposing it by a law
or a decree – which is rare – it would result in a situation very similar to the
one just described in terms of the imposed price of housing: there would be
excess demand in cases of too-low prices and excess supply otherwise. But
in general, if there is a fixed rate $E_1$, it is because one or several economic
agents promise to exchange one currency for another at a fixed price
without limit. Participants in the foreign exchange market remain free to
conduct transactions at another price, but as some of them have no interest in doing it, it is the price $E_1$ which will prevail. We can interpret this
situation by saying that the promise of a convertibility between currencies
at a fixed rate leads to substituting the horizontal straight line *S'* for the
*S* curve. Therefore, there is not a situation of disequilibrium, since equilibrium can be achieved at point *D* which is located on both the demand
curve and the new supply curve. The observed exchange rate resulting
from this commitment of convertibility at a fixed rate coincides with the
equilibrium exchange rate (while the price imposed on the housing market
leads to a discrepancy between the observed price – equal to the imposed
price if there is no black market – and the equilibrium price). In the case
of a good such as housing, a compulsory fixed price results in a disequilibrium because it creates a scarcity of supply over demand. This cannot
happen in the special case of a currency because, the demand for money
cash balances being a demand for real cash balances, it can always be satisfied by the real cash balance effect,[2] which makes it possible to achieve
equality between demand and supply at a zero cost.

The problem is not, therefore, whether a fixed exchange rate regime
leads to a gap between the equilibrium price and the observed price, but
whether the action of the monetary authorities which transforms the curve
*S* into the curve *S'* is justified. This problem will be examined later on,
when discussing the possible justification for a regime of fixed exchange
rates.

To end, let me mention some problems of terminology. 'Parity' means
an exchange rate, the value of which is decided by monetary authorities.
It may be the case that the observed exchange rate is strictly equal to the
parity. But there are also exchange rate regimes in which the observed
exchange rate can fluctuate within certain limits around the parity. The

---

[2]   As discussed in Part III of this book, there are also transfers of cash balances between
countries under fixed exchange rate regimes which contribute to equilibrium.

parity is then a reference exchange rate, relative to which the exchange rate actually used by the traders can diverge.

Finally – and according to a questionable terminology – the 'effective exchange rate' is a variable which is in fact not an exchange rate, but rather an index which shows the evolution of the relative price of a currency compared with a 'basket of currencies', that is, a set of currencies among which each currency is assigned a certain relative weight in the 'basket'.

# 7. An overview of monetary systems and exchange rate regimes

Subsequent chapters will examine in rigorous detail the working of monetary systems and exchange rate regimes. The present chapter provides background to the coming analyses, emphazising the great potential diversity of monetary systems and exchange rate regimes. To this end I will represent these different systems and regimes on a line, where the system in which the fixity of the exchange rate is the greatest appears at the far left, and the flexibility of exchange rates increases along the line towards the right:

| 1. Single currency (one producer) | 2. Single currency (several producers) | 3. Multiple currencies (several monetary systems with fixed exchange rates) | 4. Flexible exchange rates | 5. Currency competition |
|---|---|---|---|---|

These different situations are examined below:

- Case 1. It is assumed that there is a single currency in the world, that all monetary units held and circulating are perceived by their holders as perfectly substitutable. If ever this currency is a commodity currency, for example coins, there is not too much concern about having a good knowledge of producers (except that it is important that a credible guarantee be given as regards the title and the weight of metal in a coin, as will be seen later on). If it is a fiduciary currency, that is, a currency made up of claims issued by a firm, it is thus assumed in this case that there is a single producer of monetary claims in the world, even though there may be subsidiaries of this firm spread across the planet. This situation may result from the spontaneous working of markets which has led people to select a single producer, or from a kind of international law giving the privilege of issuing money only to this firm, which is obviously a totally different hypothesis with totally different potential consequences.

- Case 2. Leaving aside the case of a commodity currency, let us assume that the currency is a fiduciary currency (banknote or deposit). If there are several producers of monetary claims, these are a priori different since they are claims against various debtors to whom is not necessarily attributed the same ability to honour their debts (it may be the case, for instance, that the bankruptcy of some of them can be considered as likely, so that the monetary quality of their claims is strongly affected). What can unify this system, however, given that there is a single currency, is for all monetary units to be perceived as perfectly substitutable. It means that there is a credible procedure guaranteeing the convertibility at a fixed price of all monetary units between one another. We will later look at the procedures which may be considered to obtain this result.

  The system involving different currency producers can be hierarchical (a producer supplies the convertibility guarantee and, optionally, can impose decisions on the members of the system) or non-hierarchical (each participant gives convertibility guarantees at a fixed rate). Each member of the system may have a monopoly on a certain area (for example, a national space) or not (in which case the activity areas of the various producers are overlapping). Producers can be private or public enterprises.

- Case 3. There are several currencies in the world, produced by different monetary systems. Each monetary system may include one or more producers of money who may be private or public; each system may be hierarchical or not, national or not. The fixity of the exchange rate between the different currencies is the result of guarantees of convertibility at a fixed price given by at least one member of each monetary system. These convertibility commitments or convertibility agreements make currencies perfectly substitutable between them, so long as the convertibility commitments or the convertibility guarantees are credible.

- Case 4. There are several monetary systems with different characteristics, producing different currencies, as in the previous case. But, as no producer of currency is giving a guarantee of convertibility at a fixed price, exchange rates vary depending on the developments in the respective supply and demand for these currencies. This is therefore a floating exchange rate regime. Each monetary system is managed by a monopolistic power in each national territory, and production decisions are taken by a public authority, which is the case at the present time.

- Case 5. There are several monetary systems producing different currencies, as in the previous case. But it is assumed now that there is no confusion between the monetary area of a monetary system and any national area. It is also assumed that there is no public decision about monetary affairs (particularly about money creation) and that anyone is free to produce a currency and free to use the currency (or currencies) of their choice. This is the assumption of monetary competition which will be studied later.

Thus it can be seen that there is, at least potentially, a considerable diversity of monetary systems, even considering only the few criteria retained (hierarchical nature or not, public or private nature, convertibility guarantees at fixed rate or not, coincidence between a monetary area and a national area or not). Each of these characteristics – possibly by combining them with others – determines the system of incentives for the producers of money and, therefore, the working of monetary systems. There will be the opportunity to study these effects later on. For the time being, simply note that the present monetary organization of the world is based on a particular combination of characteristics: the monetary systems are monopolistic, national, public and hierarchical. None of these characteristics is necessary for the proper functioning of a monetary system and we will see that they even have a harmful character. In the field of international monetary economics it is traditional to focus on the debate between advocates of fixed exchange rates and advocates of flexible exchange rates, but without calling into question the monopolistic, hierarchical, national and public nature of the systems involved. As we can see, there is a narrowing of the debate: thus, the working of a floating exchange rate regime or that of a fixed exchange rate regime is not the same if the monetary systems possess the above characteristics (monopolistic, public, hierarchical, national character) or if they have other characteristics. A proper assessment of the working of monetary systems implies taking account of all their characteristics. Therefore, one ought to be persuaded that the actual monetary organization of the world – with either fixed exchange rates or flexible exchange rates – represents a special case among the whole range of possibilities.

# PART II

# The balance of payments

The balance of payments situation of a country is often considered to be an important target of economic policy. Thus, policy-makers quite often mention the 'magic triangle' consisting of full employment, the absence of inflation and the balance of payments equilibrium, or lament a deficit in the trade balance, or try to achieve a trade surplus. Because of this importance given to the balance of payments in economic analysis and in the practice of economic policy – an excessive importance, in my opinion, as will be seen – it is necessary to understand what the balance of payments is, and that is what I aim to do in the chapters of Part II. I first distinguish the accounting and the economic approach of the balance of payments, and then present some practical implications of the analysis.

# 8. The accounting approach to the balance of payments

The balance of payments is an account which records all transactions carried out during a period – for example, a year – by the residents of a country (or group of countries) with the rest of the world. The rules and conventions for the recording of data are exactly those that are traditionally used in accounting, whether for individual transactions or for business transactions. The rules are those of double-entry accounting; they are the translation of the fact, already underlined, that any transaction consists of two inseparable components, a sale and a purchase. Furthermore the simple and convenient convention has been adopted according to which the sales in a transaction are given a plus sign (+) and the purchases a minus sign (−). This does not imply that any meaning should be assigned to these conventions: it could just as well have been decided to put a plus sign for purchases and a minus sign for sales, or to write purchases in blue and sales in red. Anyhow, the use of the plus and minus signs allows us to recall that the market value of the sales part is equal to the market value (or exchange value) of the purchases part. This implies that the value of purchases made over a period is equal to the value of sales over the same period, so that if one adds up the values with a minus sign and the values with a plus sign, there is necessarily a zero balance. There is therefore always equality between the two parts of an account, such as the balance of payments. In other words, there is always what is called – in a somewhat ambiguous way – a balance of payments equilibrium. Therefore, it should be noted that the traditional – and logical – accounting rules imply that the balance of payments is always in equilibrium from an accounting point of view. To illustrate these general remarks, some examples of accounting recording can be given.

## 8.1 FIRST EXAMPLE: A BARTER ECONOMY

Suppose first that there is no money and there is therefore a barter economy. Let us take the example of Chapter 2, in which wheat serves as a numéraire and where an individual sells 2 pounds of tomatoes (worth 3 pounds of wheat) against 3 pounds of wheat. Therefore, this individual may write in his transaction account:

| Purchases (imports) | | Sales (exports) | |
|---|---|---|---|
| wheat | −3 | tomatoes | +3 |
| balance | 0 | | 0 |

It is traditional to give the name of 'balance of payments' to this account if the transaction occurs between residents of different countries. Furthermore, instead of talking about purchases and sales, in this case one refers to imports and exports. But the difference in terminology should not be allowed to obscure the identical nature of an 'intra-national' transaction and an 'international' transaction. We will see that this implies major consequences.

## 8.2   SECOND EXAMPLE: A MONETARY ECONOMY

Suppose now that there is a currency, the Ecu, which plays the role of an intermediary in transactions. The exchange between tomatoes and wheat considered above will now be broken down into two phases. We have first the following account, if 1 pound of wheat is worth 1 Ecu:

| Purchases (imports) | | Sales (exports) | |
|---|---|---|---|
| | | tomatoes | +3 Ecus |
| money | −3 Ecus | | |

This account indicates that residents of the country exported tomatoes worth 3 Ecus and in return they have imported money to an amount of 3 Ecus.[1] In accordance with the usual terminology, we say that there is a surplus in the trade balance (balance of goods and services) amounting to 3 Ecus. But one can also say that there is a deficit of the monetary balance, of the same amount; the surplus and the deficit compensating each other, of course, so that the accounting balance of the balance of payments is equal to zero.

---

[1]   It is usual to say, for instance, 'the country exports . . . '. But I prefer to avoid this terminology since a country is an abstract concept which is not endowed with a will and an ability to act. Thus, international trade is not made by 'the countries', but by perfectly concrete human beings. This is why I prefer to use statements such as 'the residents of a country export' in order to underline that exchanges are the outcome of decisions taken by rational persons who act in conformity with their own aims and the environment in which they are living (which determine their incentives to act).

If, subsequently and during the same period, the currency which has thus been obtained is exported to buy wheat, there will be the following balance of payments for the whole period:

| Purchases (imports) | | Sales (exports) | |
|---|---|---|---|
| *trade balance* | | | |
| wheat | −3 Ecus | tomatoes | +3 Ecus |
| *monetary balance* | | | |
| money | −3 Ecus | money | +3 Ecus |

In this example there is an accounting equilibrium of the trade balance which means that the residents of the country are not net buyers or net sellers of money with the residents of the rest of the world. The currency was held temporarily and it served as an intermediary in exchange. But we will later on study cases in which there is a net purchase or a net sale of money. What is important is simply to note that one must apply exactly the same accounting rules regardless of the good concerned, whether commodities or money. Thus, what is called an import of money – according to a terminology which is unfortunately rarely used – corresponds to an accounting record with the minus sign. It may also be of interest to consider why one speaks of exports or imports of goods, but not of imports or exports of money. It seems to me that this can be explained by the fact that there is an underlying implicit analysis, which is to consider that currency flows result only from an accounting requirement, but that only the exchanges of commodities and services (or of financial assets) are actually desired or desirable. In other words, a purely passive monetary behaviour is thus assumed on the part of traders. But, given what has been confirmed about the demand for money, individuals exhibit active behaviour regarding their holdings of money: at any moment of time they wish to increase or decrease their stock of money, temporarily or more permanently. If an individual buys 1 pound of wheat and sells 1 Ecu, it cannot be said that only the 'purchase of wheat' part of the transaction is desired. Actually, the individual arbitrates between the satisfaction he will draw from the use of the wheat and the satisfaction which he might draw from liquidity services brought by the holding of money. He will make the transaction in question if the first is perceived by him as superior to the second.

## 8.3    THIRD EXAMPLE: TRANSACTIONS IN FINANCIAL ASSETS

Purchases or sales of commodities and services are not necessarily performed against monetary flows. Traders may agree to the payment being made in the form of a financial asset, for example because the seller of a commodity agrees to grant commercial credit. His transaction account (balance of payments) will then be as follows:

| Purchases (imports) | | Sales (exports) | |
|---|---|---|---|
| | | tomatoes | +3 Ecus |
| financial claim | −3 Ecus | | |

Thus, the seller of tomatoes buys, as a counterpart for his sale, a debt obligation issued by the purchaser. This financial claim represents a property right on future commodities: the individual who is both a buyer of tomatoes and the seller of a financial asset agrees to repurchase this debt obligation at a later date against a certain amount of money agreed in advance (or possibly a certain amount of real goods). As is well known, the future value of this debt is equal to its current value increased by the rate of interest agreed upon between the two parties. At maturity, the holder of the claim resells it to its issuer and he buys a certain amount of money in return. But it may also be the case that this debt has been sold by its original owner and therefore it will be the second (or $n$th) holder of the debt who will sell it back to the original issuer. In any case, the accounting rule is always the same: the sale of a financial claim is written with the plus sign, and a purchase with the minus sign. In the above example, using the traditional terminology, one says that there is a trade surplus and a deficit in the balance of financial assets. As it will be seen later, this balance of financial assets is sometimes called a 'capital balance', but this term is ambiguous, so that it seems preferable to use the expression 'balance of securities' or 'balance of financial assets'.

## 8.4    FOURTH EXAMPLE: A GIFT

The recording of a gift made by the resident of a country to a resident of another country may seem problematic, because it seems that there is a transaction without a counterpart and therefore it would be incompatible with the normal rules of double-entry accounting. In reality it is appropriate to interpret this situation in the following way: the recipient of the gift has an implicit claim on the donor. When the latter gives him either real goods, or money, the beneficiary of the gift gives back the claim he had on him. Therefore one has the following account of the beneficiary of the gift (in the case of a transfer in a monetary form):

| Purchases (imports) | | Sales (exports) | |
|---|---|---|---|
| | | gift | +3 Ecus |
| money | −3 Ecus | | |

The beneficiary of the gift exports his 'gift claim' (bearing the plus sign) and he imports money (bearing the minus sign).

Thus, even in the case of a gift, one uses the basic accounting rule according to which any transaction is subject to a double entry – purchases and sales[2] – so that there is always an accounting equilibrium in the balance of payments: the sum of the items with a plus sign must be equal to the sum of the items with a minus sign. But the mere record of accounting data is obviously of no interest by itself. What must be done now is to consider the economic meaning of these writings, that is, to develop an economic analysis of the balance of payments.

---

[2] Other terminologies are used – for instance 'credit' and 'debit' – but these terms can create ambiguities and it seems preferable to use easily understandable terms such as 'purchases' and 'sales'.

# 9. The economic approach to the balance of payments

The economic approach to the balance of payments consists, obviously, in applying to the specific question of the balance of payments the general economic theory, and particularly in this case, the analysis of exchange made earlier in this book. It is now necessary to go beyond the accounting record of transactions and to analyse the meaning and scope of accounting records. As already said, what is called 'the equilibrium of the balance of payments' is generally considered to be important. But exactly what does this equilibrium mean and to what extent is it really important? Given that any economic phenomenon is necessarily the result of human decisions, it is not possible to perform a proper analysis of the balance of payments from arbitrarily constructed macroeconomic concepts, and it is necessary to go back to the foundations of individual behaviour. This is why I will firstly present a few reminders about the intertemporal behaviour of an individual, before looking at its implications for the analysis of the balance of payments.

## 9.1 THE INTERTEMPORAL BEHAVIOUR OF AN INDIVIDUAL

Let us consider an individual who stands at the beginning of a period $t_1$ and who plans his activities for two periods, the current period and the next, $t_2$. He produces a certain amount of goods and services in each period and he uses the resources thus obtained. There are therefore production activities and 'absorption activities', that is, the uses of resources, which can be either consumption activities, or investment activities. Of course the structure of goods and services produced by this individual is probably not identical to the structure of the goods which he wishes to consume or invest. He will therefore proceed with exchanges to maximize the usefulness of his resources, as we have seen when studying the theory of exchange. But for the sake of simplicity, let us now put aside the question of the structure of production and the structure of absorption in order to focus on another problem: the intertemporal planning of production and of the use of resources. For this, we will take several successive steps.

### 9.1.1 First Step: A Lack of Money, Bonds and Savings

Let us take the simplest assumption, in which there are only commodities and services, but neither money nor bonds, in a barter economy in which loans and borrowings do not exist. In Figure 9.1, the $W_1$ axis represents the amount of resources produced or absorbed (used) during the period $t_1$ (or what the individual forecasts at the beginning of this period). Similarly, the $W_2$ axis represents the amount of resources produced or absorbed during the period $t_2$. If it is assumed that there are no durable goods, the individual is obliged to consume all of what he produces in each period and no investment is possible. Thus, if he produces $OM$ in period 1 and $ON$ in period 2, point $A$ represents both the distribution of production over time and the distribution of consumption over time. Of course, even in this extreme case, the individual retains some margin of freedom, since he can eventually produce more during a period if he wants to consume more during this period, by sacrificing part of his leisure time. But, for simplicity, we will not take account of this possibility of substitution in the following reasoning and we will therefore assume that the amount of production is a given datum for the individual in each period (we assume, for example, as illustrated in Figure 9.1, that the level of production is the same in each period).

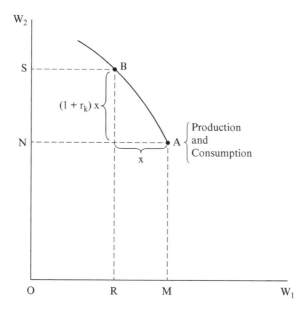

*Figure 9.1   Investment and savings in equity capital*

### 9.1.2    Second Step: Investing One's Own Resources

We now assume that the individual has the opportunity to save resources and invest them to obtain an increased level of production later. Thus, in Figure 9.1, the individual produces $OM$, but consumes only $OR$, so that he saves $RM$, that is, an amount of resources equal to $x$. He invests the saved resources, either individually or by pooling his savings resources with other investors, in which case he becomes the holder of property rights on future resources which we may call, for instance, securities. Whether he has individually held or pooled savings, we say that the amount $x$ is the equity capital of the individual (as opposed to the loanable funds which will be examined in the following cases).

In the previous case, point $A$ was the allocation of production and consumption over time. If savings and investment are possible, the individual can change the allocation of production and consumption. Thus, rather than remaining at point $A$, he can choose to stand at point $B$. If he actually makes this choice – although he could stay at $A$ – it is because he prefers point $B$ to point $A$; action reveals preferences. If he chooses to be at point $B$, he consumes $OR$ in period 1 and he saves and invests $RM$. As this amount of resources has a rate of return equal to $r_k$, the individual can obtain an income (a production) equal to $ON$ in period 2 – that is, a production equal to the one he received in period 1 – to which is added a supplement $NS$. The sacrifice of consumption $x$ decided in $t_1$ is thus more than compensated in the mind of our individual by the additional resources obtained in $t_2$, namely $(1 + r_k)x$. Of course, the individual may change his plans at will in period 2. Thus, he may decide to consume all or part of the additional resources obtained by the previous savings, but he can also decide to save and to invest again, in which case the time at which he will get a higher degree of satisfaction thanks to his initial sacrifice of consumption will be pushed forward. But man is not eternal and it is unlikely that he may choose indefinitely to create more and more resources from period to period without benefiting from at least a portion of what he will have been able to obtain thanks to his behaviour as a saver and an investor.

### 9.1.3    Third Step: Lending and Borrowing

Let us assume temporarily that the individual does not invest his savings himself, without caring about the possible reasons for this situation. Another way remains open however for him to carry a purchasing power over time; that is, to reschedule his structure of consumption: he can borrow or lend. Suppose that there is on the market a real interest rate $r$.

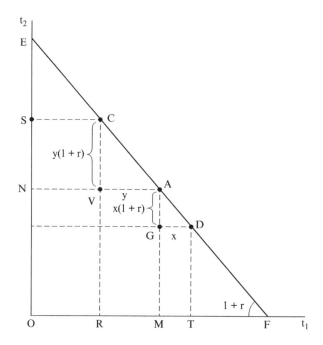

*Figure 9.2    Savings in loanable funds*

From point $A$ in Figure 9.2 (identical to point $A$ in Figure 9.1), the individual can move on the $EF$ line, the slope of which is equal to $(1 + r)$, which means that he can trade one unit of goods in the current period against $(1 + r)$ units in the next period, or get an additional unit today at the expense of $(1 + r)$ units of the next period. Thus, if the individual chooses to be at point $C$, this means that he produces $NA$ in period 1, but he consumes only $NV$. The difference between his income, $NA$, and his consumption, $NV$, represents his savings which are equal to $VA$. As the rate of interest is equal to $r$, he will be able to obtain in period 2, in addition to his income – equal to $RV (= MA)$ – the amount $VC$ so that his total consumption of the period 2 will be equal to $RC$: by sacrificing $y$ in period 1 he gets a surplus equal to $y(1 + r)$ in period 2. By standing at $C$, although he could have been at $A$, the individual proves that he prefers point $C$ to point $A$: this rescheduling in the structure of his consumption, made possible by saving and lending resources, increases his satisfaction.

On the other hand, if he moves to $D$, he consumes more than he has produced in period 1 ($OT$ instead of $OM$), which means that he is a borrower; but he will have to make a sacrifice of consumption in period 2, by taking

AG from his income to repay his borrowing from period 1. Of course, if he is doing so, it is because he prefers to consume more in period 1, even if it means that he will have to save in period 2.[1]

Generally speaking, we can say that the possibility to borrow or to lend allows an individual to enhance his well-being by distributing over time his production and the use of his resources in a way which he prefers. From this point of view, bonds provide a service similar to that provided by money, which we met previously. But, of course, so that an individual be able to borrow it is necessary that, in addition, there are one or more persons interested in lending; that is, that the 'time preference' (for the present in comparison with the future, or for the future in comparison for the present) is different for different individuals. We meet here a simple application of the 'principle of exchange' analysed previously. For an exchange to exist it is necessary that the capacities and needs of individuals be different. Exchange allows the increased satisfaction of each individual and it determines an 'equilibrium price' which allows the equalization of the supply and demand. In the present case, individuals trade time, and from their negotiations an equilibrium price of time appears; that is, an equilibrium interest rate, which equalizes the demand and supply of present goods against future ones. Because of their differences in capabilities or needs, some individuals specialize in the production of present goods and others in the production of future goods. Exchanges of bonds are therefore only a particular application of the general principle of specialization.

Thus, an individual can increase his consumption in period $t_2$ by reducing it in period $t_1$, either by investing his own resources or by lending his resources, as represented in Figures 9.1 and 9.2, respectively. The choice of the individual between own investment (equity capital) and lending (loanable funds) is represented in Figure 9.3, which incorporates elements of the two previous figures. Starting from point $A$, the individual can obtain a marginal return equal to $r$ (interest rate) by lending resources (which correspond to the slope of the line $EF$). If he uses his savings to make his own investments, he will first carry out the investment the performance of which is the highest, and then he will successively choose investments the marginal return of which is lower and lower. This is depicted in Figure 9.3 by the curve $AH$. The slope of the tangent to the curve at a point shows the

---

[1]    Of course, one can also assume that the individual borrows to invest, in which case his income in period $t_2$ will be higher and the surplus will allow him, more or less, to repay his loan and to pay the rate of interest instead of having to reduce consumption. But it has been assumed for the moment, for the sake of simplification, that the income was the same in both periods.

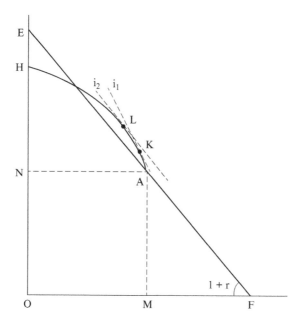

*Figure 9.3    Equity capital and loanable funds*

marginal return at this point. We see that the marginal return is decreasing. Thus, at point $K$, the marginal yield of capital, $r_k$, shown by the slope of the tangent to the curve $AH$ at point $K$, is higher than the interest rate which the individual would have received by lending resources (the slope of the tangent $i_1$ is greater than the slope of $EF$). He will therefore use his savings in his own investment (equity capital) and not in loanable funds. If he continues his own investments, he will go to point $L$, but not further. Indeed, in $L$ the slope of the tangent to the curve $AH$ is equal to the slope of the $EF$ line, which means that the rate of return on capital, $r_k$, becomes equal to the interest rate. Beyond this point, therefore, the individual has an interest in lending for a rate of interest $r$ rather than investing himself, because by investing he may get a marginal rate of return lower than the interest rate.

### 9.1.4    Fourth Step: Reintroduction of Money

During the three previous steps, it was assumed that people are able to allocate their resources over time thanks to their own savings (and therefore their own investment) or by exchanging bonds. But we know that facilitating the allocation of resources over time is also one of the roles of money. An individual will then compare these different possibilities and he will be in equilibrium at any given time – that is, he will get the maximum satisfaction, taking into account his information about the available opportunities – when in the following situation:

$$u_m(M) = u_m(T) = u_m(S_{own}) = u_m(X) \qquad (9.1)$$

which means that the individual equates the marginal utility of the future goods obtained via money ($M$) with the marginal utility of the future goods obtained via bonds ($T$), with the marginal utility of the future goods obtained by own savings and investments ($S_{own}$), and with the marginal utility of present goods ($X$). But it is still necessary to make clear that the marginal utility of money does not depend only on the future goods which it allows to buy, but also on the liquidity services it will supply in the future. To put it another way, from a certain amount of resources saved in the present, money enables obtaining a certain amount of goods in the future and a certain amount of liquidity services, bonds enable obtaining the same quantity of goods to which is added the interest earned in the period.

Thus, the savings of an individual can have as a counterpart his own investment, or the accumulation of money cash balances, or a purchase of bonds. In the two first cases savings are his own savings, meaning that the investor remains the owner of the saved capital, while in the latter case the property of saved resources is transferred to other people and the investor becomes the owner of future goods. In a barter economy the issuer of a claim will remit in the future a certain quantity of goods, increased by the amount of the interest; in a monetary economy he will, obviously, remit a certain amount of currency.

## 9.2    EXCHANGES OVER TIME BETWEEN RESIDENTS OF DIFFERENT NATIONS

The balance of payments records all transactions carried out during a period between the residents of a country[2] and residents from the rest of the world. From this point of view it is preferable to avoid speaking of the balance of payments of a country, because a country as such does not think, does not act and does not trade. Only individuals think, act and

---

[2]    Or, possibly, the residents of a group of countries, for example those of the European Union.

trade. Thus, in speaking of the balance of payments of a country, one may not forget that it is not the expression of a kind of global mechanics among countries, but the consequence of the decisions and behaviours of a very large number of individuals. This is why it is not possible to understand what it represents without referring to the intertemporal behaviour of individuals which has just been analysed. The balance of payments is arrived at simply by aggregating the exchanges made by all the residents of a country. When aggregating all the transaction accounts of individuals, the exchanges between residents of the same country vanish, since the sales of some are the purchases of others. The only remaining exchanges are those between residents and the rest of the world. This is called the balance of payments. The fact that different terms are used to refer to the transaction account of an individual and the transaction account of all the residents of a country should not create any illusions: it is exactly the same reality which is analysed. From this point of view it is unfortunate that different terms are used at the micro level and the macro level: misinterpretations would be avoided by speaking of the balance of payments of an individual (and not using this term only when referring to a set of individuals), or by avoiding using the term 'balance of payments' and using only the accounting terms which are usual at the microeconomic level, that is, for the accounting of an individual or of a firm. Because of this total similarity between both analyses, I shall proceed for the balance of payments exactly as I did for the intertemporal behaviour of the individual.

### 9.2.1   First Step: A Lack of Money and Bonds

The assumption is of a barter economy, that is, of an economy without money. Furthermore, it is assumed that it is not possible to transfer resources from one period to another, except by using one's own savings and own investment. In other words individuals save – which means that they decide not to consume part of their actual resources during the analysed period – but they use these savings themselves, possibly by putting them in common with the savings of some other people.[3] But there are no exchanges of future goods against present goods between residents of a country and therefore, necessarily, nor are there exchanges of future goods against present goods (exchange of bonds) between residents of the country and foreign residents. The only trade between residents and

---

[3]   In the analysis of the intertemporal behaviour of the individual, we introduced an additional reasoning step since we had first assumed that there were only exchanges of goods and services, then we introduced own savings and own investment in a second step.

non-residents – what is called usually 'international trade'[4] – relates to goods and services. This then concerns the usual assumption of what is called the theory of international specialization or the theory of comparative costs. Each individual or each group of individuals (firms) specializes in productions for which they have a comparative advantage. In this case, the balance of payments includes the account of trade in goods and services, usually called the trade balance. It is identical to the account contained in the first example of Chapter 8 (on the accounting approach of the balance of payments). It is reproduced below:

| Purchases (imports) | | Sales (exports) | |
|---|---|---|---|
| wheat | −3 | tomatoes | +3 |
| balance | 0 | | 0 |

This balance of payments – reduced only to the trade balance – reflects the fact that, on average, the residents of the analysed country specialize in the production of tomatoes, for which they are relatively more fitted, and they buy wheat in return for tomatoes. This does not mean that there are only tomato producers in the country and no producer of wheat, unlike what would happen in the rest of the world. It may well be that there are in the country some producers of wheat as 'competitive' as foreign producers, but when considering all the producers of the country, they are relatively more productive in tomato production than in wheat production, compared to foreign producers. As we know, the value of exports in terms of any numéraire (for example, wheat) is equal to the value of imports, but the exchange – which is, in this case, an 'international' exchange – is beneficial to all parties. Of course, this does not mean that all the residents of the country earn thanks to trade, since it may be that some do not wish to buy wheat and simply eat the tomatoes they produce. But it is absolutely certain that the 'international' trade is beneficial for some – otherwise it would not occur – without harming anyone. For this reason, globalization – that is, freedom of trade at the global level – is necessarily good, and all the arguments hostile to globalization are necessarily wrong.

---

[4]  I try to avoid the use of the term 'international trade', to emphasize that it is not the nations which exchange, but individuals (residents and non-residents). However, for brevity I later abandon this linguistic precaution. But the reader must keep in mind that those who exchange are the individuals and not the nations.

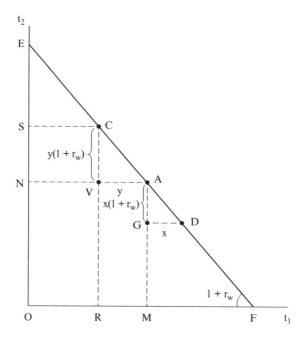

*Figure 9.4    Intertemporal choices and the balance of payments*

### 9.2.2    Second Step: Lending and Borrowing

In order to simplify the presentation, let us assume for the time being that there are no savings used for own investment, contrary to the assumption made in the first place in the study of the intertemporal behaviour of the individual to examine the transfer of resources over time. It is therefore by borrowing and lending that the residents of a country transfer purchasing power over time. This is represented in Figure 9.4, which is formally identical to Figure 9.2. There is a world-wide interest rate $r_w$, so that the price of time is equal to $1/(1 + r_w)$.[5] At point $A$ all the residents of the country consume exactly the entire amount of what they produce in the period. Moving on the $EF$ line, they can reallocate their resources over time. Let us assume, for instance, that they prefer to stand at point $C$ than at point $A$. Their total income (equal to the value of their production) is equal to $OM$, but they consume only $OR$ in the period $t_1$. The difference, that is, $RM\ (= VA = y)$, represents

---

⁵    I use $w$ to indicate the value of a variable in the world.

their overall savings, the amount of real resources not consumed in the period $t_1$. These resources are sold (exported) to the rest of the world and in return the 'country'[6] buys debt bonds issued by residents of the rest of the world, the actual value of which is obviously equal to $AV$ in period $t_1$. The world rate of interest being equal to $r_w$, the country will receive (import) a quantity of resources equal to $y(1 + r_w)$ during period 2. This is represented by the $VC (= SN)$ segment in Figure 9.4. In return for these purchases of real goods, the country will resell to the rest of the world the debt bonds it had bought from it in period $t_1$. These bonds, which were worth $y$ in $t_1$ are worth $y(1 + r_w)$ in $t_2$. Thus, the country was a net lender in $t_1$ and this corresponded to a trade surplus with a value of $y$ which was obviously equal to the real value of bonds purchased. In accordance with the usual accounting terminology one can therefore say that there was a trade surplus and a deficit in the capital balance. But this latter term is ambiguous, and it would be preferable to speak of a 'balance of bonds'.

It is very important to emphasize that the balance of the trade balance, and the balance of the balance of bonds, are determined simultaneously, which corresponds to the fact that there is no sale without purchase and no purchase without sale. One therefore cannot say that the trade balance determines the balance of bonds or vice versa: there is interdependence and not unidirectional causality. However, in practice, most people – whether they pretend to be economists or not – consider that the trade balance is determined independently and that it is the result of the so-called 'competitiveness' of a country. It should then be necessary to 'close' the balance of payments and, in a universe in which there is no money, the international flows of bonds would come to 'compensate' the balance of the trade balance. Implicitly, this assumes – incorrectly – that the balance of the trade balance would be desired, while the balance of the balance of bonds would have a passive, compensatory role. It is not a simple difference of language, but a fundamental difference in analysis which has important practical consequences, for example from the point of view of economic policies. Thus the usual – and mistaken – approach leads to the implementation of policies supposed to influence the trade balance. Based on false reasoning, they can only fail.

The balances of payments corresponding to Figure 9.4 can be illustrated in the following way:

---

[6]    As already mentioned, it is questionable to imagine that the country buys or sells. Those who act are the residents of the country. But in using this shortcut language, it is necessary to keep in mind that the term 'country' actually means 'residents of the country'.

Balance of payments of period $t_1$

| Purchases (imports) | | Sales (exports) | |
|---|---|---|---|
| | | y | trade balance |
| balance of bonds | $-y$ | | |
| balance | 0 | 0 | |

Balance of payments of period $t_2$

| Purchases (imports) | | Sales (exports) | |
|---|---|---|---|
| trade balance | $-y(1+r_w)$ | | |
| | | $y(1+r_w)$ | balance of bonds |
| balance | 0 | 0 | 0 |

Of course, the surplus of the trade balance in period $t_1$ does not mean that imports are non-existent. This is a net balance and it just means that exports of goods and services are greater than imports of goods and services for an amount equal to $y$. Also, the fact that the country is a lender (it sells real goods against bonds in period $t_1$) does not mean that all residents of the country saved during this period: there are very probably in the country people who save and others who borrow, but for the interest rate prevailing in the world the supply of savings by residents (the supply of loans) is higher than their demand for savings (the demand for borrowing). Here we see again that savings is a real concept (it is the amount of resources which is not destroyed by consumption during a period). It has here a financial counterpart (bonds), but it could have a monetary counterpart if money was being reintroduced in the analysis, as will be done later.

Alternatively, one may of course assume that the country, instead of lending in the period $t_1$, is a borrower. This is what is represented in Figure 9.4 by point $D$: the country borrows $GD$ ($= x$) in the period $t_1$ and therefore has a trade deficit and a surplus of the balance of bonds, which are both equal to $x$. In period $t_2$ it will export $x(1 + r_w)$, which will reduce its consumption relative to its production; and it will import bonds for the same value, that is, it will redeem – and thereby cancel– the debt bonds it had issued in $t_1$. It is therefore clear that exports represent a levy on available resources, which ought to lead to a revision of the usual view according to which it is desirable to have a trade surplus.

We assumed above that there was a world interest rate, $r_w$. But, of course, this interest rate is actually determined in the whole world by all the supplies and demands of loanable funds by individuals. To see how this world interest rate is determined one may proceed – in a way which is certainly somewhat artificial – as is commonly done in the field of the theory of international trade (or theory of international specialization): one first

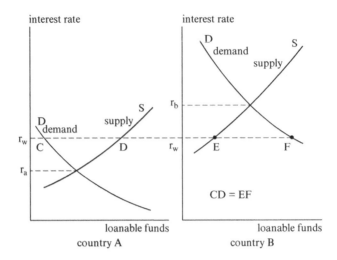

*Figure 9.5    International trade in loanable funds*

considers what is happening in isolation, that is, when exchanges between countries are not possible; then one examines the consequences of trade opening. In the 'two goods, two countries' model one gets the equilibrium relative price of one good relative to the other and each country specializes in the production of one of the two goods on the basis of its relative productive abilities and of the relative needs of its inhabitants. In the field that we are now studying – the market for loanable funds – we are interested in the relative price between two types of goods, present goods and future goods. As we do know, the relative price of these goods is $1/(1 + r_w)$.

Let us assume that there are two countries in the world, country A and country B. Figure 9.5 represents the supply and the demand for loanable funds in each of these countries in isolation, that is, when there is no exchange of loanable funds. The supply and demand curves for loanable funds are obviously obtained from the supplies and demands by the residents of the country concerned, via a process of aggregation. In the absence of an international trade of loanable funds, the equilibrium interest rate is equal to $r_a$ in country A and $r_b$ in country B. We see that these two interest rates in isolation are different, which means that there is a possibility of exchange. If exchanges of bonds become possible, the equilibrium will be achieved for the rate $r_w$. Indeed, at this rate country A exports loanable funds for an amount represented by $CD$[7] which represents the excess of

---

    [7]    It is very important to avoid confusion: if country A is a net supplier of savings (loanable funds), this does not mean that it exports debt bonds, quite the contrary. Saving

supply over demand and which is equal to *EF*, the amount of loanable funds imported by country B (excess of demand over supply). Country A exports present goods against future goods: it has a trade surplus and a deficit in the balance of bonds in the current period. In the future period, when its loan will be repaid, it will have a deficit in its trade balance (equal to the surplus of the current period, but increased by the amount of the interest) and therefore a surplus in its balance of bonds (it sells back to country B the bonds which it had purchased). Symmetrically, country B – which is a borrower – has a trade deficit in the current period and it will have a trade surplus in the future period (it must levy goods from its production of this period to repay the borrowings which it had carried out previously).

The trade deficit of country B in the current period (obviously equal to the trade surplus of country A) allows it to have a greater amount of goods than it produced itself during the period and therefore to invest more (at least to the extent that it is borrowing to invest and not to consume more, as it is most often the case). This obviously does not mean that country B imports capital goods, but the greater availability of goods, because of imports, helps to free factors of production which can be devoted to the realization of investment projects funded by the borrowings of the country.

### 9.2.3 Third Step: Loanable Funds and Equity Capital

Until now we have assumed, to simplify the analysis, that there are only loanable funds and not flows of equity capital. But let us now introduce equity capital in the analysis and consider the point of view of a country, for example country A. The behaviour of the residents of country A is exactly the same as the intertemporal behaviour of an individual, as shown in Figure 9.3: savers invest in equity capital up to the point where the expected return $r_k$ becomes equal to the world interest rate.[8] But own savings and own investment are not necessarily carried out inside the country, and individuals compare the returns of capital they can get in their country and in the rest of the world. If the rate of return expected for investments in the rest of the world is higher than the rate which can be achieved inside, there will be an outside investment in equity capital. This is the case, for example, if a resident of country A buys shares in

---

is a real concept and the export of savings is an export of real goods (against an import of bonds).

[8]  The rate of return on capital and the interest rate are here considered to be the only variables determining decisions. But investors obviously take account of other variables, such as the degree of risk of investments and loans, transaction and information costs, and so on. But to simplify the analysis, all of these variables are considered to be integrated in the rate of return and the rate of interest which are therefore partly subjective variables.

country B. The impact of such a transaction on the balance of payments is exactly the same as for the international exchange of loanable funds: if country A makes investments in country B, it buys shares (that is, property rights) from country B and it sells commodities as a counterpart, which means that it has a trade surplus. This surplus is the means by which actual resources are transferred from country A to country B, since it allows the increase of investments in country B. But if there is a similarity in the accounting records of the balance of payments between transfers of loanable funds and international flows of equity capital, the nature of the flows is different: in the case of loanable funds, country A – if it is a net lender – gives up the property of actual resources to residents of country B who will use them as they want. In return, country A gets property rights on future goods. In the case of a transaction concerning equity capital, the owners of resources in country A do not give up ownership of their present resources, but they transform the nature of this ownership. Thus, let us suppose that, in a barter economy, an individual in country A owns wheat. He exports wheat to feed workers in country B who make an investment in a company of which the individual of country A becomes a shareholder. This individual, instead of owning wheat in country A, has become an owner of labour services in country B. He will later receive a portion of the return of this work in country B and possibly decide to repatriate the resources thus obtained. Entries in the balance of payments account will be in the opposite direction to those made in the current period: repatriating in country A the return of the capital invested in country B is the equivalent of a sale of property rights. The purchase by the individual of country A of property rights in country B in the first period is followed, in a subsequent period, by a sale of property rights located in country B. These are called 'movements of capital' or 'capital flows', but this terminology can be confusing, so it will be considered later. The above reasoning can be presented in a more formal form by distinguishing, as is often done, total production (or total income) and total demand.[9] We can thus write (not distinguishing, for the moment, equity capital and loanable funds):

---

[9]    This traditional presentation is hazardous insofar as it could imply that aggregate demand and aggregate supply are determined independently from one other. However, we know that there is no demand without supply, and no supply without demand, and this is also why there is equality between supply and demand, both at the level of an individual and at the level of a set of individuals, for example those who represent a country. The distinction between aggregate demand and aggregate supply is obviously drawn from the Keynesian tradition. It unfortunately leads to the belief that it is possible to increase overall demand at will (and then, as a result, to obtain an increase in the aggregate supply), which can only be an illusion.

$$y = c + s \tag{9.2}$$

where $y$ is the total production (or total income) in a country, $c$ is total consumption and $s$ is total savings;

$$z = c + i + (x - m) \tag{9.3}$$

where $z$ is total demand, $c$ is consumption, $i$ is domestic investment and $(x - m)$ the trade balance (where $x$ is exports and $m$ is imports).

From the equality between $y$ and $z$ (production and demand), one thus derives:

$$x - m = s - i \tag{9.4}$$

which implies that the balance of the trade balance is equal to the difference between domestic savings and domestic investment. If savings are greater than investment, there are exports of savings to the outside and there is a trade surplus ($x > m$): this surplus means that the country gives away more commodities than it receives. It provides the means by which the real savings are transferred outside.

Now, if there are equity capital and loanable funds, we can write:

$$y = c + s_{owni} + s_{owna} + s_p \tag{9.5}$$

where $s_{owni}$ represents own savings invested inside the country, $s_{owna}$ own savings invested abroad, and $s_p$ savings lent outside: the income obtained from the production is either consumed or saved (in the form of equity or loanable funds, used indoors or outdoors).

Total demand can be written as follows:

$$z = c + i_{owni} + i_p + i_{owna} + (x - m) \tag{9.6}$$

where $c$ is the demand for consumer goods, $i_{owni}$ own domestic investment, $i_p$ domestic investment from loanable funds, and $i_{owna}$ investment from foreign equity capital.

Equality between total demand and total income gives:

$$s_{owni} + s_{owna} + s_p = i_{owni} + i_p + i_{owna} + (x - m) \tag{9.7}$$

or:

$$(x - m) = s_{owni} + s_{owna} + s_p - i_{owni} - i_p - i_{owna} \tag{9.8}$$

Given that $s_{owni} = i_{owni}$ (own domestic savings is necessarily equal to own investment in domestic equity capital), we get:

$$(x - m) = (s_{owna} - i_{owna}) + (s_p - i_p) \qquad (9.9)$$

which implies that the balance of the trade balance is equal to the sum of two differences: on the one hand the difference between own savings financing own investments abroad and own investment funded on foreign equity capital and, on the other hand, the difference between domestic loanable funds and domestic investment financed by loanable funds. There will be a surplus of the trade balance ($x > m$) if domestic savings (in equity capital or loanable funds) are greater than domestic investment (financed by equity capital or loanable funds).

Finally, it may be useful to clarify the role of the public budget.[10] There is indeed a net demand for goods by the state which can be written as follows:

*balance of the budget (g) = public expenditures – revenues (taxes and various recipes)*

The equation for aggregate demand (9.3) above can therefore be rewritten as follows by distinguishing private demand and public demand:

$$z = c + i + (x - m) + g \qquad (9.10)$$

that is, total demand is the sum of the demand for consumption goods, the demand for investment goods, the net external demand (exports minus imports) and the public net demand (public spending less public revenues). By equating aggregate demand (equation 9.10) and aggregate income (equation 9.2), we obtain:

$$x - m = s - i - g \qquad (9.11)$$

that is, an increase in the public deficit, all other things being equal, results in a negative change in the trade balance (the trade surplus decreases, or there is an increase of the trade deficit). This means very clearly that an increase of one component of total demand – the public deficit – translates

---

[10]   The balance of the public budget can be defined not only as the balance of the budget of the state, but also as the sum of the budgetary balances of the state, local communities and public agencies, such as the social security administration.

into a decrease of the same amount in another component of the aggregate demand, in this case the trade balance.

### 9.2.4　Fourth Step: Reintroduction of Money

Let us now assume that money exists and that it can be traded internationally. The balance of payments therefore now has three main items: the trade balance (or balance of goods and services), the capital balance (or balance of financial assets), and the money balance, to which is given, unfortunately, the term 'balance of the balance of payments'. Indeed, strictly speaking, the balance of the balance of payments is, as is the case for the balance of any account in accounting, the balance of all the items of an account, and it is necessarily equal to zero. By calling the net balance of currency exchanges the 'balance of the balance of payments', it suggests implicitly that this balance is purely 'compensatory' and that it is used to finance the two other items (trade balance and capital balance), which are supposed to be determined independently from one another. However, as we know, individuals are not indifferent to their amounts of money cash balances and they exhibit active behaviour in this regard. Certainly, in a monetary economy, all transactions are processed by using a currency and, for example, someone will agree to receive money against commodities even if he does not want to keep these money cash balances. But he knows that he will spend them, more or less quickly, against the commodities or the financial assets which he wants to buy. This is exactly what was previously represented in Figure 4.1 in Chapter 4, which represented the evolution over a period of the amount of real balances of an individual. What is true for an individual is true for a set of individuals: the amount of cash balances held at a given time by residents of a country is desired in the short term (otherwise it would not have been bought), but not necessarily in the longer term (one may desire to hold on average more or less cash balances than what is owned at a given point of time).

There is thus, as regards money, a process of specialization between countries quite similar to the one we met for goods and services or financial assets. Different countries have different abilities to produce money, and different currency needs. Money flows will therefore on average go from countries relatively specialized in the production of money to countries relatively specialized in other goods and therefore relatively demanding money. This will be one of the main objects of the subsequent chapters of this book, to specifically analyse the determinants of these money flows (evaluated in real or monetary value).

If a country is a seller of money over a period this will result in an entry with a plus sign in the balance of payments. In return, this country will necessarily be importing goods and services and/or financial assets. On the other hand, the country which is a buyer of money will necessarily have a surplus in its trade balance and/or in its balance of financial assets.

The United States provides a particularly obvious example of a seller of money to other countries. Indeed, for various reasons, the dollar has been for decades one of the most desirable currencies in the world and it is in demand to undertake international transactions and, eventually, as a store of value. However, although the United States (US) is obviously relatively specialized in the production of dollars, dollars can also be created by financial institutions outside the US (they are called 'euro-dollars'). So it is normal that the United States exports dollars, especially since there is an almost steady growth in international trade and thus an increasing demand for dollars. The US balance of payments thus records a surplus in the money balance and, in return, there must be an accounting deficit in the trade balance and/or the balance of financial assets. However, the US has a low saving rate so that it imports a portion of the savings needed for its investments. It is therefore an exporter not only of money, but also of financial assets, which means that it necessarily has a trade deficit. There has been one for decades, despite the efforts of politicians who – not understanding this process – claim constantly that they will delete or reduce this deficit, because they are unfortunately convinced by the precepts of Keynesian origin according to which it is good to have a trade surplus to stimulate domestic production. But this trade deficit is the result of desired behaviours as regards the sales of financial assets, as well as the sales of money, so that it is absolutely impossible to make this deficit disappear. The trade balance is not determined independently of the other items of the balance of payments: it reflects the desired equilibria of the balance of financial assets and of the monetary balance, and the trade deficit will persist as long as the outside world wants dollars and as long as the Americans need external savings to finance their development. Moreover, and contrary to what Keynesians believe, the United States should have no reason to complain about this state of affairs: thus it exports a good – money – the production cost of which is virtually zero, and gets in return goods and services which would be expensive for it to produce if they could not be obtained this way. Unlike the usual bias in ideas according to which the trade deficit is necessarily an economic disequilibrium, the trade deficit of a country like the United States is an 'equilibrium deficit', since it corresponds to what is desired by all partners in exchanges, and since 'equilibrium' has previously been defined in this book as a situation in which all concerned persons are satisfied. The name 'seigniorage' is sometimes given to the difference between the sale price and the cost of production of money. Assuming, for simplicity, that the cost of production of the currency is zero, the seigniorage received by American producers of money is equal to the balance of the money item which is equal to the sum of the trade balance and the financial balance. If the financial balance was in accounting equilibrium, the trade balance would be just equal to the monetary balance and it would therefore represent the amount of seigniorage received by the American producers of money.

Ultimately, from the distinction between three types of accounts in the balance of payments, corresponding to the three types of goods (commodities and services, financial assets, money), 13 possible structures of the balance of payments can be identified, none of which can be regarded as preferable to any other:

| | 1 | 2 | 3 | 4 | 5 | 6 | 7 | 8 | 9 | 10 | 11 | 12 | 13 |
|---|---|---|---|---|---|---|---|---|---|---|---|---|---|
| trade balance | + | + | + | − | − | − | 0 | 0 | 0 | − | + | + | − |
| financial balance | + | − | − | + | + | − | 0 | − | + | 0 | 0 | − | + |
| money balance | − | − | + | − | + | + | 0 | + | − | + | − | 0 | 0 |

Except in the case where the balance of each item is equal to 0 (case 7), it is impossible for the three accounts to be affected by the same sign, since the total of the balances must be equal to zero.

Each of these structures of balance of payments can easily be interpreted. For example, in case 4, the country is a net buyer of commodities and services and of money, and it funds these purchases by sales of financial assets, which means that it goes into debt. It promises to sell products and services in the future.

# 10. Lessons from the analysis of the balance of payments

Many lessons can be drawn from the analysis of the balance of payments which has just been made, but it is impossible to give a comprehensive set of statements about such a topic. Therefore, I will select some of these lessons, to focus on those which seem the most important, in order either to understand existing problems or to correct frequent errors of interpretation.

## 10.1 THERE IS NO A PRIORI REASON TO PREFER A DEFICIT OR A SURPLUS OF THE TRADE BALANCE

The traditional Keynesian approach rooted in people's minds the idea that a trade deficit is regrettable and that a trade surplus is desirable (so that one ought to try to act in order to achieve it). In fact, the justification for this idea consists in believing that a trade deficit reduces aggregate demand (and therefore the production which it determines), whereas a trade surplus increases total demand. I will later discuss the role thus assigned to 'total demand' (and therefore to the trade balance). But we have already seen that the balance of the trade balance is determined simultaneously with the balances of the balance of financial assets and the monetary balance, and it is not determined 'independently'. Recall also that a trade deficit represents an inflow of savings and a trade surplus an outflow of savings. In other words, if a country has a trade deficit, it receives more commodities and services than it provides to foreign countries. It therefore has more abundant real resources, which makes it possible to increase domestic investment correspondingly: the balance of the trade balance is equal to the difference between domestic investment and domestic savings.

### 10.1.1 Resource Planning over Time (in the Absence of a State)

In order to reason progressively, let us assume first that there is no state, or at least that the state budget has a zero accounting balance (public expenditures are equal to revenues). Questioning whether a deficit of the trade balance is desirable is to question whether it is desirable to obtain more resources that one has produced, which is the case when there is a 'trade deficit', which means that the market value of imported goods is greater than the market value of exported goods. No doubt, the answer will appear obvious if one refers to an individual's rational behaviour. Thus, it is possible to ask the question in the following way: is it desirable for an individual to have, during the current period, a quantity of available resources greater than what he has produced? Everything depends on the assessment made by the individual. Indeed, saying that he has more resources than he has produced is saying that he borrows. Rationally, an individual borrows, in particular, if he believes that the expected return of the resources which he has borrowed is higher than the interest rate. More specifically, he can borrow to consume the surplus of borrowed resources immediately, or he can invest these resources in order to get a future return (and therefore future consumption). In the first case, he compares the subjective value of this additional consumption with the future sacrifice which he will have to make to pay interest and repay his debt. Now, it can be quite rational on his part to do so if, for example, he anticipates strong growth of his future income or if he faces in the present an exceptional expense, such as the marriage of one of his children. In the second case – where the borrowed resources are used to finance an investment – he compares the expected return of this investment and the interest rate. It is justified for him to borrow if the present value of the interest paid (and the repayment of his loan) is smaller than the present value of his investment yields. In other words, he borrows so as to allocate his resources over time in a way which gives him the highest satisfaction, even if he has to pay interest. Of course, because we are always in a world of uncertainties, it may transpire that the expectations of the individual are not met, so that in the future he will regret his past decision to borrow. But at the time at which he took this decision it brought him an additional satisfaction for reasons which are specific to him and which an outside observer cannot know perfectly.

If the individual is acting freely – and not under coercion – we know that he is necessarily satisfied when borrowing (otherwise, being rational, he would not borrow), that he wishes what may be termed a 'deficit of his balance of transactions'. It is therefore wrong for an outside observer to say that this individual is in a situation of disequilibrium because he has a 'trade deficit' (he buys more commodities and services than he sells during a period).

What is true for an individual is true for a set of individuals, for example the residents of a country. For given values of interest rates (determined by the global financial markets) there are very probably economic agents who wish to borrow and others who wish to lend. If, as a whole, residents of the countries are borrowers rather than lenders, they sell financial assets outside and buy actual resources as a counterpart, which means that there will be a trade deficit (imports higher than exports), which means an inflow of savings. As is the case for an individual, it would be totally wrong to consider that this deficit corresponds to a macroeconomic disequilibrium. Insofar as it corresponds to the free choices of economic agents (in the country and outside), this trade deficit is an equilibrium deficit. It is the consequence of the relative time preferences between the residents of the country and those of other countries. Thus, if the propensity to save is low in the country compared to the rest of the world, and/or its ability to invest resources in an efficient way is high compared to the rest of the world, this country will be purchasing savings (trade deficit) and selling future assets (surplus of the balance of financial assets). We find here simply an application of the principle of exchange we have previously met: the inhabitants of the country specialize in the production for which they have a comparative advantage. In the case which we have just seen, the country which has a trade deficit has a relative advantage in future goods and the rest of the world in present goods. Thus they exchange present goods against future goods at a relative price of $1/(1 + r)$ (that is, a unit of present goods is traded against $1 + r$ units of future goods, $r$ being the interest rate). Of course, there are all sorts of practical reasons for the propensities to save or invest, as well as individual time preferences, to differ between countries. These include cultural differences, differences in the capacity to innovate and to invest, and so on. But there are also institutional reasons. Thus, if in a country there is a tax system which discourages savings – that is, the choice of the future – the residents of the country will be encouraged to buy savings abroad to finance their investments. This relative lack of savings is a common situation nowadays and it is compensated by capital imports (but also, quite often, by a monetary creation, the consequences of which there will be the opportunity to see later, especially in Chapter 22). Still, in this case, what is regrettable is not the fact that there is a trade deficit, but the fact that there is a punitive taxation of savings: the situation of the trade balance is nothing but a reflection of this deeper situation, and it is pointless to want to correct it without changing the factors which explain it.

In the same way, if a developing country has good prospects for development, it will attract foreign capital and it will therefore have a surplus in its balance of financial assets (excess supply of national assets) and a trade deficit which will allow the country in question to obtain more resources than it actually produces itself, and therefore to invest more. It would be absurd to want to fight this trade deficit, and in reality it would not be possible to succeed.

Since the trade deficit – when it is the result of free exchange – corresponds to a situation of equilibrium, one might question why it is so generally considered that one ought to deplore a trade deficit and try to remove it, or at least reduce it.[1] There may be two reasons. First, it may be a simple problem of language: the term 'deficit' has a negative tone and it therefore leads to considering that a trade deficit is necessarily bad. But more deeply, in this prejudice may be seen the negative influence of Keynesian theories according to which, to increase the employment rate and/or the level of production, aggregate demand should be increased. The balance of the trade balance being considered as a component of aggregate demand, a deficit is supposed to have a negative influence, and a trade surplus a positive influence. But this theory is flawed, for reasons that will be considered later: both because it is an illusion to think that the trade balance may evolve independently of other economic variables, and because, generally speaking, the concept of aggregate demand is devoid of any meaning.

## 10.1.2    The Role of the Public Budget in a Closed Economy

The role of the public budget will now be analysed, but to reason progressively, we will first consider the country under review to be a closed economy, which means that there are no economic relations with other countries (and therefore no balance of payments). In Figure 10.1, supply and demand for loanable funds are represented as a function of the interest rate. If the state budget is in accounting equilibrium, public expenditures are equal to the revenues of the state and there is no net demand for loanable funds by the state. The equilibrium interest rate, $r_0$, is then determined by the private supply and demand for loanable funds which determine a market equilibrium for an amount of loanable funds equal to $F_0$.

Now suppose that a public deficit equal to $g$ appears. The total demand for loanable funds (private demand + public demand) is then represented by the curve $D_1$ (obtained from the curve $D_0$ thanks to an horizontal translation equal to $g$). This increased demand for loanable funds translates into an increase of the interest rate shifting from $r_0$ to $r_1$, so that the new equilibrium point in the market for loanable funds is point $V$ (equality between the supply and the total demand for loanable funds). The public deficit is represented by the $TV$ segment and Figure 10.1 shows that it is funded by two means:

---

[1]    The fact that so many people think so can be considered as a proof of the fact that most people – even those who claim to be economists – are unaware of economic science (or at least that which is based on rigorous and consistent foundations).

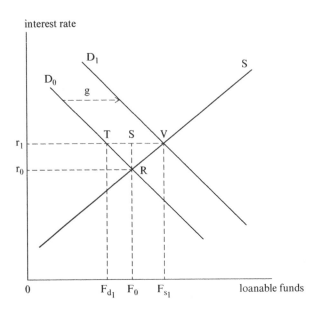

*Figure 10.1    The market for loanable funds and the public deficit in a closed economy*

- There is an increase in the supply of loanable funds because of the increase in the interest rate. The supply is increased by an amount equal to $SV$ (or $F_0 F_{s1}$).
- There is also a decrease in the demand for loanable funds, represented by the $TS$ ($= F_{d1} F_0$) segment. Indeed, the private demand for loanable funds is represented by the curve $D_0$ and the increase in the interest rate causes a decrease in this demand. This is what is known as the 'eviction effect', which means that the financing of the public deficit is partially made at the expense of the financing of private investment.[2]

At this point, some valuable teachings may be drawn from this analysis. According to the Keynesian tradition, an increase in the public deficit is assumed to increase total demand and thus to encourage producers to increase their production. In fact, nothing similar occurs, and it is necessary to finance this deficit. But its funding is obtained, on the one hand, by a decrease in the financing of private investment, and on the other hand,

---

[2]    But we will see later on that it would be more justified to call this effect the eviction effect in a narrow sense since we will meet an eviction effect in a broader sense.

by an increase in the supply of loanable funds. The latter is necessarily either at the expense of savings into equity capital – so that own investments decrease by the same amount – or at the expense of consumption. Therefore, the increase in the public deficit is fully compensated – as regards the so-called total demand – by a decrease in private investment, consumption and own investments. The increase in the public deficit cannot increase total demand, because this is impossible; it only changes the structure of savings and investment and the structure of production.

As the public deficit cannot play the role with which it is generally credited, namely to stimulate economic activity, its possible consequences can be considered. We have seen that the financing of the government deficit necessarily implies an eviction effect in the broad sense: that is, it not only causes a reduction in private investment (which might be called the eviction effect in the restricted sense), but it also causes a decrease in own investment (equity capital) and in consumption. The only question remaining is then to assess to which extent public expenditures thus funded could be more 'useful' than the spending which has thus been suppressed. It is sometimes argued that the public deficit is justified insofar as it allows the financing of public investments and not current expenditures. But this criterion is not satisfactory. In fact, what should be known is whether the future performance of these investments is higher than that of the private investments which were sacrificed. But there is no way of knowing.

In fact, the assessment is even more difficult, for the following reason. As we know, an individual compares the marginal utility of his consumption, the marginal utility of resources obtained in the future by savings and investments via loanable funds, and the marginal utility of future resources obtained through savings and investment via equity capital, taking into account the interest rate. This is a purely subjective assessment. But it is absolutely impossible to aggregate the individual utilities and to compare, for example, the marginal utility of current consumption for all residents of a country to the future marginal utility for these same people of resources obtained by public investment or private investment. In fact, the decision to have a public deficit meets other considerations, in particular those which are linked to the working of what is sometimes called the 'political market' (which has no similarity to a real market). Indeed, insofar as the rulers have a short-term decision horizon – mainly the horizon of the next elections – they are encouraged to distribute resources in the present, but to leave the burden of the corresponding payment (in the form of the repayment of loans and the payment of the corresponding interest) to the voters of their successors.

To understand the mechanisms involved, let us imagine the extreme situation of a country made up of two people, called 'the state' and 'the citizen'. If the state wants to fund current expenditures or investment expenditures by borrowing, the citizen, potential lender, will be well aware that he will be in the future the taxpayer to reimburse the loan. He will refuse to lend to the state if he feels that the expenditures by the state will be less useful than those he could have made. But let us assume now that there are a large number of citizens and that each is aware of the fact that the state uses borrowed resources wrongly, and that he may well be one of the taxpayers who will have to repay the loan tomorrow. He may however be inclined to lend to the state because he will make the following reasoning: 'To get its desired financing the state is obliged to propose an interest rate higher than that which existed previously (it offers $r_1$ instead of $r_0$). Given that the state will find lenders anyhow, I will necessarily have to repay its debt as a taxpayer. So, why not enjoy the higher interest rate offered by the state?' If a large number of citizens are reasoning in this way – which is rational – the public deficit will be funded by citizens who, as a whole, would not gain from it. But now let us see what happens in an open economy.

### 10.1.3    The Role of the Public Budget in an Open Economy

Let us suppose now that there are flows of goods and financial assets between the inhabitants of a country and the rest of the world. And let us suppose also that the country is small compared to the rest of the world, in such a way that the decisions of its inhabitants have no influence on the determination of prices, in particular on the price of time, namely the interest rate. We can therefore consider that the interest rate is exogenous – determined by the supply and demand for loanable funds in the rest of the world – and for simplicity we will assume that it is constant, $r_w$. Let us suppose, on the other hand, as we have done in the case of a closed economy, that there is no public deficit initially; but let us suppose in addition, to simplify the reasoning, that for this world interest rate $r_w$, the domestic demand for loanable funds is exactly equal to the domestic supply of loanable funds. This situation is shown in Figure 10.2. It implies, as regards the balance of payments, that the balance of financial assets is in an accounting equilibrium (there are no net sales or net purchases of financial assets with the rest of the world) and therefore the trade balance is also in an accounting equilibrium.

Let us now suppose that a public deficit appears in the country under review. It is represented, as previously, by a translation of the $D_0$ curve which becomes $D_1$. As the interest rate, $r_w$, is constant, the private demand and the private supply of loanable funds inside the country do not change and remain equal to $F_0$. But there is a supply of foreign loanable funds

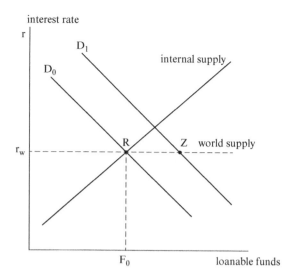

*Figure 10.2    The market for loanable funds and the public deficit in an
open economy*

which can be considered as infinitely elastic in relation to the world interest
rate $r_w$ (which corresponds to the $r_wZ$ line). The financing of the government deficit is entirely by borrowing from abroad, which is represented by
the $RZ$ segment. There is, therefore, in the balance of payments, an export
of financial assets and a trade deficit in return. This deficit means that the
country receives more resources than it actually produces, thus allowing
the financing of the public deficit. We can see therefore that there is a strong
link between the public deficit and the balance of payments. Contrary to
the usual ideas, the trade deficit does not reflect a 'lack of competitiveness' on the part of the country; it is the necessary counterpart of an excess
supply of financial assets due, in our example, to the budget deficit.

An additional piece of information may be useful for a proper understanding of this process. The equality which exists between the public
deficit on the one hand, and on the other hand, the trade deficit and the
surplus of the balance of financial assets (under the assumption that there
was no trade deficit initially), does not mean that there is an export of
government bonds equal to $RZ$ (surplus of the balance of financial assets).
It may be that all or part of the supply of public bonds was purchased
by national agents, in which case a corresponding share of the private
supply of financial assets (demand for loanable funds) will be sold outside.
Similarly, the trade deficit does not imply that it corresponds exactly to the
demand for goods and services by the state. It may be that all or part of

the additional demand for goods and services corresponding to the deficit is met by domestic producers. But they correspondingly decrease their production of goods desired by the national private sector, and they move the factors of production towards the production of the goods requested by the state (if they are different from those which were demanded by the private sector). The private demand for goods and services of the inhabitants of the country is then met by imports, which thus replace domestic products.

As in the case of a closed economy, we can evaluate this situation of public deficit and trade deficit. We have seen that an increase in the public deficit necessarily resulted in an equivalent increase in the trade deficit. But it is sometimes wrongly referred to as the 'twin deficit' (an expression, in particular, often used in relation to the United States), which suggests that there are two independent problems to solve. In fact, there is no reason to worry about the trade deficit. If a public budget deficit is desirable for some reason or another, the corresponding trade deficit is also desirable because it is a necessary consequence. If the budget deficit is regrettable, the trade deficit is also. But by itself the equilibrium of the balance of trade is neither desirable nor unfortunate. If a judgement is to be made, it must involve the public deficit and not the trade balance. The criterion of evaluation is an internal one and not an external one. From this point of view, the assessment which can be made of the public deficit is identical to that mentioned above in the case of a closed economy. However, the eviction effect is different in each case. In the case of a closed economy, an increase in the public deficit determines a decrease in present consumption or in present investment. In the case of an open economy, it is not necessary to reduce present consumption or investment, as the resources corresponding to the increase in the public deficit can be obtained by borrowing abroad. But there will be a reverse situation later on: when interest has to be paid on the external debt and the repayment of loans, there will clearly be a need to have a trade surplus, which means that the corresponding resources will not be available for consumption or domestic investment. There is a future eviction effect.

In any case, it is logically undeniable that it is wrong to consider the trade balance as a target of economic policy, as is the case quite often. The idea of an 'external equilibrium' to be achieved is a misconception. From this point of view, it might therefore be questioned whether, at the limit, it would be wise not to present balance of payments statistics since, in any case, they cannot give useful information, but may be misleading in terms of creating unjustified economic policies. Moreover, these policies are necessarily doomed to failure, since they are unable to meet their alleged targets: if a trade deficit is the result of a public budget deficit, it is impossible to reduce this trade deficit as long as the budget deficit persists. The so-called 'external equilibrium' target is therefore both unjustified and necessarily doomed to failure.

But, furthermore, and as is the case in a closed economy, it may be noted that a recovery policy based on an increase of total demand also rests on a serious conceptual error. Let us suppose that a government thinks it can revive economic activity by increasing the budget deficit. We have seen that in an open economy, this increase in the deficit necessarily implies an equivalent increase in the trade deficit, that is, an equal decrease in total demand. As we know, total demand, $z$, can be defined as follows:

$$z = c + i + (x - m) + g$$

In a closed economy, an increase in the public deficit ($g$) translates into an equal decrease in consumption and/or investment ($c$ and $i$). In an open economy, it translates into an equal decrease in the trade balance ($x - m$).

## 10.2   CAN THE BALANCE OF PAYMENTS BE IN DISEQUILIBRIUM?

The very idea of a disequilibrium in the balance of payments must be considered a priori as strange. In fact, as we know, the balance of payments is an account and it is necessarily in accounting equilibrium. Therefore, it is an abuse of language to speak of a deficit or a surplus of the balance of payments. In fact, when using these expressions one establishes a priori a separation between the items of the balance of payments which, it is believed, should be in an accounting equilibrium. Specifically, if we consider a balance of payments consisting of three main items – the trade balance, the balance of financial assets and the monetary balance – what is generally called a balance of payments deficit is a situation in which purchases of goods and services and financial assets are more important than sales (there is a deficit of the sum of the trade balance and the balance of financial assets). This obviously implies that in return the monetary balance – which records the purchases and sales of money – is in surplus. Thus, what is called a 'deficit of the balance of payments' is a situation in which a country is a net seller of money, which is also sometimes called a 'loss of currency' or a 'loss of monetary reserves'. These different expressions are sometimes used in a more restricted sense to refer to a situation where, under a fixed exchange rate regime, there are sales of money by the central bank to foreign countries. There will be the opportunity to analyse these processes later on.

As we have seen, there are no reasons to regret or wish a certain balance of the trade balance. Similarly, there are no reasons to deplore or to wish a certain 'balance of the balance of payments'. If, to use the usual terminology, a country has a 'balance of payments deficit', which implies that it has a surplus in its monetary balance, this simply means that it is a seller of money, which can be explained by a variety of reasons. In general, if exchanges take place freely and the inhabitants of a country are sellers of money (and thus buyers of goods and services or financial assets) it is because they wish it and they can thus increase their well-being, as is the case for any exchange. This means that a 'balance of payments deficit' corresponds to a situation of equilibrium and there is obviously no reason for anyone to want to change an 'equilibrium deficit'. Many kinds of situations where there is a balance of payments deficit will be introduced later on. This will be the case, for example, if in a fixed exchange rate regime, the central bank of a country is undertaking a too-expansionary monetary policy. The inhabitants of this country have money cash balances greater than what they want and they sell part of their excess holdings of money outside. It is in a sense a good deal for the country in question since money does not cost anything to produce, but it is sold against real commodities or financial assets. Certainly, this excess of money creation is to be regretted, as it is a source of inflation and of economic distortions, as will be seen later on. But what we must deplore is not that there is a 'balance of payments deficit', but that there is an excess of money creation and that the existing institutional system does not prevent this excess. The situation of the balance of payments is only the reflection of a deeper problem, which consists in creating too much money.

Let us take another example. Let us assume that a currency is particularly demanded in the world, and it is especially produced in one of the countries of the world. Such is the case with the dollar and the United States. It is quite normal that this country should be a seller of money, since it is relatively specialized in this activity, and therefore it constantly has a deficit of its balance of payments (that is, a surplus of its monetary balance). It is not surprising that, for decades, a country like the United States has had a 'balance of payments deficit'. This has often been considered as regrettable and efforts have been made to try to suppress this deficit; without ever succeeding, since this deficit is an equilibrium deficit: it corresponds to the desire of producers of the American currency to sell dollars, and the desire of the people of other countries to buy dollars as a means of international exchange or as a store of value.[3] Of course, if we

---

[3]    This is why I have been explaining for a long time (since 1969) that the deficit of the US balance of payments was not regrettable, and that it would persist for a long time. The sequence of events has proven that this reasoning was correct.

were in a totally stationary world, the United States would not be a seller of dollars once the holders of dollars in the rest of the world had accumulated exactly the amount of dollars they wanted. But such is not the case, since there is a continuous growth of international transactions, so that the demand for dollars is also growing; and since, moreover, there is an excess of money creation, and therefore inflation, so that foreign holders of dollars must continuously restore the real value of their cash balances – according to processes we have already met – and therefore they must buy dollars for this purpose.

The rate of savings is low in the United States and the inhabitants of the country are net buyers of savings from outside, that is, they are sellers of financial assets. The structure of the balance of payments of the United States thus becomes very clear: Americans are sellers of financial assets and money and, in return, they are purchasers of real commodities and services, which means that there is a deficit in the trade balance (and a so-called 'deficit of the balance of payments'). Using the conventional accounting signs, the structure of the balance of payments of the United States is as follows:

| | |
|---|---|
| trade balance | – |
| balance of financial assets | + |
| monetary balance | + |

At the microeconomic level it is of course normal that a bank sells money and that non-bank economic agents are purchasers of money. Similarly, if a country is relatively specialised in the production of a currency, it is normal that it is a seller of this currency and that the inhabitants of other countries are buyers.

Finally, there is a problem of terminology to which we should pay attention. The expressions 'capital exports' and 'capital imports' are frequently used. But it is appropriate to clarify their meaning in order to avoid possible misinterpretations. What are called 'capital exports' of a country are imports of foreign financial assets. This might seem problematic insofar as purchases of financial assets are given a minus sign, and a minus sign means imports, not exports. If one is talking in this case of exports of capital, it is because one thinks in reality of the possible counterpart of the imports of financial assets, namely the exports of commodities (trade balance surplus). The trade surplus is precisely the means by which the country transfers real resources abroad. Of course, these resources do not necessarily consist of investment goods (or capital goods), but by freeing the resources available, they make possible a greater accumulation of capital in the countries benefiting from these flows. In other words, when speaking of exports of capital, it is not the 'financial capital' which is considered, but the real capital which is its counterpart.

## 10.3    THE SO-CALLED 'EXTERNAL EQUILIBRIUM' POLICY

As a result of what we have just seen, a balance of payments policy or an external equilibrium policy is meaningless and necessarily doomed to failure. If, for instance, there is a situation similar to the one just mentioned in respect of the United States, the external equilibrium policy consists in considering that a 'balance of payments deficit' is a symptom of macroeconomic disequilibrium, although it is an equilibrium deficit. Adopting a piecemeal approach which does not take account of the interdependence of all markets, efforts will therefore be made, for instance, to increase exports and/or to reduce imports, by subsidizing exports or by imposing tariffs on imports. But to the extent that the sale of financial assets and money by Americans is desired by them as well as by their purchasers, it necessarily follows that the trade deficit will last indefinitely. Thus, a policy of restriction on imports will not alter the balance of the trade balance, but it will probably reduce both imports and exports without changing the balance of the trade balance.

In general, the so-called external equilibrium policy is doomed to failure because it is based on an a priori and arbitrary definition of equilibrium and disequilibrium. As we have seen, a negative trade balance, for example, is not representative of a situation of disequilibrium if it is the result of exchanges freely made by individuals and of their choices between present goods, financial assets (future goods) and money. Since this balance – just as the other balances – is desired, it cannot be modified, except by exercising coercion. Thus, if exchange control measures are introduced to prohibit or to limit the international exchange of financial assets, a compulsory change in the balance of the balance of financial assets can be created, and therefore in the balance of the trade balance. But, in so doing, this creates a disequilibrium since it is forbidding individuals to allocate their resources over time in a way which would be optimal for them. And furthermore, it wastes resources since controls necessarily have a cost (the cost of bureaucratic measures, but also the loss of time for those who must bear these control measures). It would be absurd to prohibit an individual from going into debt under the pretext that it would create a deficit in his balance of transactions (his 'trade balance'). It is equally absurd to impose such measures on all the inhabitants of a country. Of course, the justification which is given to such a policy consists in claiming that one can increase overall demand by reducing a trade deficit or even by creating a trade surplus. But this is only an illusion.

Let us consider again the assumption which has been examined above, in which there is a public budget deficit, wholly or partially funded by the sale of financial assets abroad. Reducing these sales, and therefore the corresponding trade deficit, the financing of the budget deficit will have to be done within the country, so that nationals will have to reduce their consumption or their investments to finance the public deficit. The increase in demand corresponding to the positive change in the trade balance is therefore totally offset by the decrease in total demand due to the decline in the demand for consumer goods and investment goods. This allows me to emphasize once again that the economic policy prescriptions inspired by the Keynesian tradition are based on a serious intellectual error.

An external equilibrium policy is also based on another intellectual mistake, which consists in thinking that the balance of payments is the result of the summation of entries which are totally independent one from each other. Thus, it would be necessary to record imports, exports, sales of financial assets, purchases of financial assets, calculate the sum of all these items, and thus obtain a 'balance of the balance of payments'. Then, any item could be modified, for instance by subsidies, customs duties or prohibitions, without affecting other items in the balance of payments. This ignores that all human decisions consist in choosing among different options, and that an exchange always includes a purchase part and a sale part, inseparable one from the other. The complementarity between the different balances of a balance of payments reflects the fact that individuals choose between holding present goods, future goods (financial assets) or money.

In reality, an external equilibrium policy is a convenient justification for politicians when they attribute specific benefits to certain categories of people. Thus, they will say that by subsidizing exports of this or that product, protecting certain domestic producers from competition from foreign producers, they make it possible to re-equilibrate external trade. In reality, they introduce disequilibria by pushing individuals away from the situations they prefer.

## 10.4   THE EXCHANGE RATE AND THE TRADE BALANCE

So far we have more or less implicitly assumed that there is a single currency in the world we are analysing. But let us now assume that there are two countries in the world with a different currency in each of them.

It is generally accepted that there is a relationship between the balance of the trade balance and the exchange rate. Thus, in the case of a floating exchange rate regime – that is, exchange rates freely determined on markets – it is believed that, the trade deficit being a symptom of disequilibrium, it will cause a depreciation of the national currency against the foreign currency. It is estimated that a depreciation or a devaluation of the national currency will result in a positive change of the balance of the trade balance.

The relations thus established are a priori questionable. Indeed, the exchange rate is a price: the price of one currency relative to another. As with any price, it influences the supply and demand of the goods involved, in this case the two currencies. But the exchange rate is not the price of the balance of the trade balance, which would obviously be meaningless. For example, we have seen that the trade balance is a counterpart of the balance of financial assets and of the monetary balance, but that a deficit is not a symptom of disequilibrium, and it therefore has no reason to cause a change in the exchange rate. It is the existence of an excess demand or an excess supply of one of the currencies against the other which will determine exchange rate variations. However, it is likely that a change in the exchange rate will have – quite often temporarily – an influence on the monetary balance, and therefore, indirectly, on the balance of trade, to the extent that, for instance, real commodities are exchanged against money cash balances. I am not going to explore these potential effects at the moment, but we will meet them again later on.

# PART III

# International monetary equilibrium in modern monetary systems

Part III looks at things only in the context of the monetary systems of our time, but later I will analyse and evaluate the working of other monetary systems. Modern monetary systems are characterized by the fact that they are usually hierarchical, national and monopolistic. They are hierarchical because a bank – the central bank – can take decisions which apply to other banks, the commercial banks, sometimes referred to as second-rank banks (the central bank being the first-rank bank). They are national because each nation (or group of nations, as is the case for the European monetary union, sometimes called the eurozone) has its own monetary system and its own central bank. They are monopolistic because each state prohibits competition from other monetary systems on the national area it controls, although this monetary area can combine several nations in the case of a monetary union. The monopolistic character is often reinforced by a number of regulations, for example the existence of legal tender laws, that is, the obligation made to residents of a country to use the national currency for internal transactions; or exchange controls, that is, the existence of provisions restricting or banning the use of currencies other than the national currency. These three characteristics – hierarchical, national and monopolistic – are obviously linked together: in fact, generally speaking, the state benefits from a monopoly of legal coercion on its national territory. In the monetary field it uses this power to impose the national currency it controls through the central bank. The monopoly position is obviously the result of a public decision and it is attributed to a central bank which is most often a public institution, but which sometimes may be a private institution. This is the case, for example, of the Federal Reserve in the United States (generally called the Fed), but it is no less true that the appointment of the Governor of the Fed is the outcome of a political decision.

As we will see later, these three features of modern monetary systems – hierarchical, national and monopolistic – are not necessary for the working of a monetary system and it is easy to imagine other systems or find multiple examples in monetary history. But it is only the operation of modern monetary systems that will be analysed in this Part III of this book. Although there is an obligation to use the 'legal tender' in internal transactions, the existence of international transactions makes it necessary to shift from one national currency to another by using the exchange rate, which is the relative price between two currencies (that is, more precisely, the relative price between the currency units issued by different national monetary systems). But before studying how this exchange rate is determined and the role it can play, I will begin with a few essential reminders concerning the working of a monetary system (that is, the relationship between the central bank and second-rank banks), as well as the analysis of inflation.

# 11. Money creation in hierarchical systems

Let us consider a nation in which a national currency is circulating and let us be unaware, for the time being, of the existence of other national currencies (which will subsequently be reintroduced in the reasoning). During the greatest part of monetary history, monetary units consisted of real commodities, such as gold or silver coins. But nowadays the monetary units are mostly claims on banks (apart from coins of small denominations). These claims may take one of two forms.

Firstly, they can be dematerialized – that is, they are simple accounting entries – and they are named (bank) deposits. The term 'deposits' is a legacy of a past time in which money-holders deposited gold – or another precious metal – into the coffers of a bank[1] and in return held claims on their bank, which had an equivalent value and which were redeemable into gold.[2] Nowadays, these deposits do not result from the 'deposit' of a precious metal, but from a credit operation by which a commercial bank exchanges a monetary debt (money) that it issues against a claim (credit supplied to a customer of the bank). As is well known, there are different kinds of bank deposits, notably demand deposits and savings deposits. As their names indicate, demand deposits are redeemable (against banknotes or against bank deposits in another bank) at any time, whereas savings deposits are redeemable only at maturity. In the economic literature there is a broad debate to determine to what extent savings deposits should be taken into account in the evaluation of the quantity of money, that is, the amount of currency units existing at a given time. I will not enter into this debate and will adopt instead the simplifying assumption that all deposits are demand deposits, that is, perfectly 'liquid' deposits.[3]

---

[1] As will be explained later, at the origin of paper currencies (now called banknotes), deposits were not made in a bank, but, for instance, at a goldsmiths.

[2] The evolution over time of these banking practices will be examined later.

[3] If the relative proportion of demand deposits and savings deposits remains roughly constant, this simplifying assumption has no consequence on the working of monetary systems. On the other hand, when there are transfers of deposits from a bank to a deposit account of another bank (for example by cheque or bank transfer), this is only a technical banking problem and has no impact on the working of monetary systems.

Secondly, monetary claims can take a materialized form, in the form of printed papers (and not of precious metals). They are then called banknotes. Nowadays the central banks have a monopoly on the issuance of banknotes, except for some rare exceptions (for example, in Hong Kong where several private banks issue notes and where, moreover, there is not really a central bank). This situation can be considered as paradoxical, since banknotes were invented by commercial banks – or even by private producers, such as goldsmiths – at a time when central banks did not exist.

Finally, there is a particular form of monetary claims, the claims of commercial banks on the central bank, to which is given the name of 'reserves'. This term is also a relic of the past: when deposits or banknotes were created in exchange for a deposit of gold (or other precious metals), gold placed in the vaults of the bank constituted a reserve, which meant that it was kept as a reserve while waiting for customers of the bank to possibly request the conversion of their monetary claims against the gold in question.

These clarifications being made, the following definitions can be given. The quantity of money – also called 'money supply' – is the set of all the monetary units, that is, monetary claims held by the non-banking sector on the banking sector, for instance in a country (or a group of countries, as is the case with the eurozone). It is composed of two elements – deposits and banknotes – and it can therefore be written as follows:

$$M = D + C \qquad (11.1)$$

where $M$ is the amount of monetary units, $D$ is the total amount of deposits in the monetary system, $C$ is the total amount of banknotes.[4]

The monetary base is the total of the balance sheet of the central bank. By evaluating it from the liabilities side of the balance sheet (that is, the central bank's liabilities, themselves equal to claims on the central bank held by the public and by commercial banks) the monetary base is equal to the following amount:

$$B = C + R \qquad (11.2)$$

where $B$ represents the monetary base (in nominal terms), $C$ the total amount of banknotes and $R$ the reserves of commercial banks with the

---

4   In accordance with convention, uppercase letters are used to denote variables measured in terms of monetary units ($M$ is then, for instance, the value in euros or dollars of the quantity of money) and lowercase letters to denote variables measured in real terms ($m$ is the real value of the quantity of money in terms of commodities, that is, with a real numéraire).

central bank (which could possibly be called deposits of commercial banks with the central bank).

The balance sheets of the central bank and of commercial banks can therefore be represented as follows:

Balance sheet of the central bank

| assets | liabilities |
|---|---|
| financial claims | C  banknotes |
|  | R  reserves |

Balance sheet of commercial banks

| assets | | liabilities |
|---|---|---|
| financial claims | | D  deposits |
| reserves | R |  |

Claims listed on the asset side in the balance sheet of the central bank and commercial banks can be claims on the private non-bank sector or claims on the state (treasury bills). In order to simplify the analysis, and by taking into account the needs of the subsequent demonstrations, only monetary variables have been included in the balance sheets above. But to give a more complete picture of reality, other elements should of course be added. Thus, as regards commercial banks, one should add the amount of equity capital to the liability side and add financial and material investments to the asset side. Furthermore, to the extent that banks also – and even primarily – have a financial intermediary role, as mentioned previously, one should write on the liability side, in addition to equity capital, borrowed funds; and on the asset side the corresponding claims and investments.[5] Furthermore, when the existence of other currencies is introduced, one will find on the asset side of the balance sheets of banks their holdings of foreign currencies, and this variable will also play a very important role in the analysis of the working of monetary systems.

To analyse the relationship between the above variables and, more specifically, the relationship between the monetary base and the money supply, we need to add two behavioural assumptions. The first assumption relates to money-holders as regards the sharing of their cash balances

---

[5]   It is this financial intermediary role and not the role of producer of money which characterizes a bank. Historically, the first role appeared well before the second: there are lending and investment operations in societies which use only real currencies, that is, for instance, gold or silver coins which are not produced by banks.

between banknotes and deposits. We can write the behaviour equation in the following simple form:

$$C = cM \qquad (11.3)$$

where it is assumed that money-holders always wish to hold a fraction – equal to $c$ – of the quantity of money in the form of banknotes. For simplicity, we will retain the hypothesis that $c$ is constant. But it is obvious that this assumption does not exactly correspond to the reality. Indeed, firstly, there are fluctuations in this ratio over time (for example, during holiday periods). Secondly, there may be a long-term evolution of this coefficient. Thus it has been found, in general, that the share of banknotes is high in low-income countries and that this proportion decreases as economic development occurs until it reaches a roughly stable value (for instance, located at a level close to 20 per cent). To simplify the subsequent presentations without altering their meaning, we will suppose that we are in the period of 'maturity' in which this coefficient can be considered as roughly stable, and we will not take into account its possible short-term fluctuations.

Given that, from equation (11.1), $D = M - C$, we can write equation (11.3) in the following form:

$$D = (1 - c) M \qquad (11.4)$$

The second assumed behaviour function concerns banks and it can be written as follows:

$$R^d = rD = r (1 - c) M \qquad (11.5)$$

where $R^d$ is the desired level of reserves of commercial banks and $r$ is the 'reserve coefficient' which, as we will see, plays a very important role in the working of any monetary system. In fact, a commercial bank should strive to deal with possible requests by its customers for conversion of their deposits into banknotes. However, as banknotes are issued by the central bank, by virtue of its monopoly in the production of banknotes nowadays, a commercial bank must apply to the central bank to make this conversion, which implies that it exchanges a part of its reserves against the amount of banknotes which is necessary to meet the needs of its customers. The reserve coefficient in equation (11.5) is a desired coefficient since it indicates the amount of reserves desired in relation to deposits. How does the bank determine this ratio? If the reserve coefficient is too low, it may not be able to meet the demands of its customers for conversion of deposits into banknotes, and from this point of view it has an interest in having a high coefficient. But, on the other hand, it must incur higher costs, the higher is this coefficient. In order to obtain reserves from the central bank, a bank must in return give financial claims (on the private sector or the state) which would have earned it interest. The unit opportunity cost of the holding of reserves is therefore equal to the difference between the market interest rate and the rate of interest paid by the central bank on reserves. However, taking advantage of its monopoly status, the central bank most often imposes a zero rate of return on reserves held with it by commercial banks. Thus, each bank must decide an optimal amount of reserves, taking into account the fact that the increase in its reserves decreases the risk of not being able to meet the demands for banknotes of its clients – which would create a risk of it losing clients – but it decreases its profitability. As in many human decisions, there is an arbitration between performance and risk. Each bank having its specificity and probably having clients with different habits, it is very likely that all the banks belonging to the same monetary system will choose different desired reserve coefficients. However, to simplify the subsequent reasoning – without altering its scope – we will assume implicitly that all banks of a monetary system have the same desired coefficient, or that we calculate and use the average of the desired reserve coefficients of all these banks.

However, the reserve coefficient has become an instrument of monetary policy, insofar as the central bank may impose on the commercial banks the obligation to maintain a minimum reserve ratio. The reserve coefficient is then no longer a desired coefficient, but a mandatory coefficient. By increasing its requirements concerning the reserve coefficient, the central bank induces commercial banks to perform less money creation. When a commercial bank provides a credit, it buys a claim on its client and in return it credits his deposit account. But it will not be able to keep an amount of claims equal to the amount of new deposits, since a portion of its assets must necessarily consist of required reserves instead of claims. It must therefore refinance itself with the central bank, that is, increase its reserves (against a remittance of claims). Insofar as claims earn an interest rate higher than reserves, the profitability of a credit supplied by a bank is lower, the higher is the reserve ratio. It therefore has less incentive to make an expansion of credits and deposits, the higher is the minimum reserve coefficient.

The coefficient $r$ contained in equation (11.5) represents the required reserve ratio if it is higher than the desired reserve ratio. It represents the desired reserve ratio insofar as it is greater than the required ratio. Of course, the changes in the required coefficient decided by the central bank can have effects on the decisions of banks concerning monetary creation and the corresponding supply of credits when the required coefficient is higher than the desired coefficient.

We can now write the relationship between the monetary base and the money supply from the equations above. From equation (11.2) we know that $B = C + R$. Replacing $C$ and $R$ in this equation by their values given by equations (11.3) and (11.5) gives:

$$B = \{c + r(1 - c)\}\, M \qquad\qquad (11.6)$$

which can be written:

$$M = B\, /\, \{c + r(1 - c)\} \qquad\qquad (11.7)$$

which implies that the money supply is a multiple of the monetary base. To simplify we will generally assume subsequently that the coefficients $c$ and $r$ are constant.

Equation (11.7) is the – simplified – expression of monetary policy, that is, the policy which determines the quantity of money ($M$). The central bank obviously cannot modify the coefficient $c$, since it corresponds to the monetary behaviour of economic agents. But it can determine the monetary base or the required coefficient of reserves (provided that it is greater than the desired coefficient). Assuming that the coefficients $c$ and $r$ are constant, an expansion of the monetary base causes a proportional expansion of the money supply. Moreover, as we have seen, for a given monetary base, variations in the required reserve ratio cause variations in the money supply, except in the case where this ratio becomes lower than the desired coefficient. As seen in equation (11.7), an increase of the minimum required reserve ratio $r$ translates into a growth in the money supply which is lower than that of the monetary base (restrictive monetary policy), while a decrease in this rate obviously translates into an expansionary monetary policy (at least if commercial banks do not wish to maintain a desired reserve ratio higher than the required reserve ratio).

However, these two policies – the policy concerning the monetary base and the policy concerning the reserve ratio – cannot play the same role and they are therefore not substitutable. Indeed, one can easily imagine – as this is usually the case – that the central bank has a policy of steady long-run growth of the monetary base (and therefore of the supply of money), or possibly even a policy of steady decline of these quantities. But we cannot imagine a policy to increase or to lower the minimum reserve ratio continuously. Indeed, the increase is not possible insofar as a coefficient equal to 100 per cent has been reached, and the decrease has no more effects as soon as the required reserve coefficient becomes smaller than the desired coefficient.

It can also be specified that a policy of expansion of the monetary base can be carried out in various ways. The central bank may have a quantity policy, that is, it determines the amount of claims which it agrees to buy or to sell in return for reserves, or it decides the amount of loans it grants to the banks. This results, in both cases, in a certain rate of interest. It can also have a pricing policy, that is, it announces an interest rate at which it is prepared to lend without limits to banks (and therefore to buy claims on them and to credit their reserve accounts). What is very important in modern policies of money creation is that the creation of monetary units is always made with a corresponding distribution of credits (purchases of claims by the central bank and commercial banks). This has extremely important consequences which we will encounter later.

# 12. Inflation, a monetary phenomenon

In accordance with modern terminology, we can define inflation as the increase in the monetary prices of goods.[1] On the other hand, deflation is the situation in which the monetary prices of goods are decreasing. To analyse the process of inflation (or deflation) we will start with a simple assumption, namely that there is a single commodity, which we call wheat. If we choose money as the numéraire and if we call this currency the Ecu, the price of wheat represents the amount of currency units (of Ecus) redeemable against a unit of wheat. Thus, saying that 1 pound of wheat costs 2 Ecus means that 1 pound of wheat can be exchanged against 2 Ecus. Inflation corresponds to the fact that the quantity of money needed to obtain 1 pound of wheat increases over time. From a given date, the price of 1 pound of wheat will be, for example, 4 Ecus a year later, 8 Ecus two years later, and so on.

Although it is thus usual to define inflation by a steady increase in the monetary prices of goods, it may be more useful to use the symmetric definition, which consists in defining it by referring to the real price of money, that is, by taking wheat as the standard of value. Inflation is then defined as the decrease in the price of money in terms of goods (in this case wheat). Thus, in the example above, 1 Ecu obtained half a pound of wheat initially, then one-quarter of a pound after one year and one-eighth of a pound two years later. This definition – unusual, unfortunately – is important: it shows, in an undebatable way, that inflation represents a deterioration in the purchasing power of money (this purchasing power representing the quantity of goods – of wheat – which can be obtained against a unit of currency). We can and must draw from this definition an absolutely indisputable idea, namely that inflation is necessarily bad and undesirable. In fact, because of inflation a currency loses what constitutes the very justification for its existence, since we have defined money as a pending purchasing power. It follows from this

---

[1]   Not all economists use this term in exactly the same way. Thus, Ludwig von Mises preferred to define inflation as the increase in the quantity of money, the increase in prices being a consequence. But to the extent that he stressed – as will be seen later – that all prices do not increase at the same rate in such a situation, he considered that the expression 'increase in the general level of prices', which is the traditional definition of inflation, was meaningless.

statement that a monetary system is better, the less inflationary it is. And one must even admit – contrary to a common, but wrong, idea[2] – that deflation is desirable, since it means the increase in the price of money in terms of goods, that is, an increase in the purchasing power of money. Of course, one might say that, even if inflation is deteriorating the purchasing power of money, it can have desirable consequences, so that an arbitration can be made between these two aspects in order to obtain what might then be called an 'optimal inflation rate'. We will see later why there is no such possibility.

This having been said, one must obviously ask what causes inflation. The answer is very simple, since it is sufficient to apply the general theory of prices. This teaches us that the evolution of the price of one good (wheat) relative to another one (money) is determined by the evolution of the relative scarcity of these goods: the price of the good which becomes relatively scarcer increases relative to the other. Now the relative change in scarcities depends on the relative evolution of supply and/or demand: if, for example, one assumes that demand functions do not change, the price of one good decreases relatively to the other one if its supply increases at a rate higher than that of the other good. Therefore, an increase in the quantity of money which is faster than that of real commodities (the quantity of wheat in our example) determines a decrease in the relative price of money – the relative scarcity of which decreases – that is, an increase in the monetary price of wheat (inflation). In this sense it can be said that inflation is always and everywhere a monetary phenomenon: there is no inflation without an increase in the relative abundance of money (that is, a decrease in its relative scarcity).

Let us take the equation of the demand for money (obtained easily by combining equations 4.5 and 4.6 from Chapter 4):

$$M^d = k(\ )Py \qquad (12.1)$$

and let us write the equality between the demand for money and the supply of money which corresponds to the amount of money, $M^\circ$, which exists at a given time. By assuming that $k(\ )$ is constant, that is, that the form of the demand function does not change, so that we can write a constant coefficient, $k$, instead of the function $k(\ )$, we obtain:

$$M^\circ = kPy \qquad (12.2)$$

---

[2]   We will see later that this error may be the result of a confusion, deflation often being interpreted to mean an economic depression.

By differentiation, as seen in Chapter 4, we get the following expression:

$$\mu = \pi + \rho \qquad\qquad (4.15)$$

where $\mu$ is the rate of change in the quantity of money, $\pi$ the rate of inflation, and $\rho$ the real growth rate.

We have assumed above that there is a single good apart from money, namely wheat. But obviously this does not correspond to reality. When there are a large number of goods, the evolution of the purchasing power of money should be evaluated against a set of goods, what is generally called a 'basket of goods'. What interests each individual is the evolution of the purchasing power of money in terms of the basket of goods he is likely to buy. Of course, nobody measures absolutely precisely the evolution of the monetary value of such a basket and it can be considered that this basket is rather implicit, each individual having a fairly general idea of the evolution of the value of the basket which concerns him. As we know, in practice, statisticians define a basket of goods intended to be representative of the buying habits of the people in the society they are considering (for example, a country for which they want to measure the rate of inflation). This index is obviously arbitrary and it does not correspond to the basket of each of the members of the society. But it gives an idea of the evolution of the overall evolution of the prices of commodities and therefore of the purchasing power of money. This approach would not be questionable if all monetary prices were to change in an absolutely homothetic manner, so that any price index would measure the rate of inflation (or deflation) in the same way. This is obviously not true in reality, and the price index is therefore an approximation. But, for the sake of simplification and to be concerned only with the basics, we will assume later – with possible exceptions which will be indicated – that the evolution of monetary prices is the same for all commodities. The $P$ variable, which represented, above, the monetary price of 1 pound of wheat, will now represent the monetary price of the representative basket of goods.

As an illustration of this problem, see Figure 12.1 in which it is assumed that there are only two goods (apart from money): wheat and oil. Initially one lies at point $A$. The $i_1$ index represents the different combinations of wheat and oil prices for which the monetary value of a basket consisting of a given quantity of wheat and a given quantity of oil is equal to 1. The $i_2$ index indicates also a value equal to 1, but for a basket composed differently, that is, in which the weights of wheat and oil are different from those used for the $i_1$ index. If there is an homothetic increase in prices, one will move, for instance, from $A$ to $B$: the prices of both commodities are doubled and an inflation rate of 100 per cent is therefore recorded regardless of the chosen price index (the relative weights of each item in the index do not change

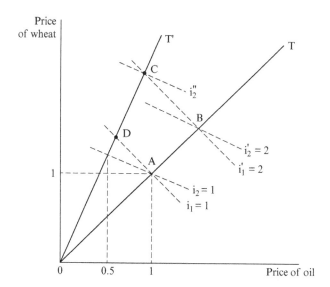

*Figure 12.1   Variations of monetary prices and relative prices*

the measurement of inflation in this case). But let us suppose that one is going from *A* to *C*, that is, that there is both an increase in the monetary price of both commodities and a change in their real relative prices (that is, the price of wheat in terms of oil or the price of oil in terms of wheat). The index $i_1$ indicates a doubling of the value of the representative basket, but the index $i_2$ indicates higher inflation. There is obviously no a priori reason to prefer one index or the other. But it is important to distinguish carefully between changes in monetary prices and changes in relative prices. The latter is represented by the pivoting of the line *OT*, which becomes *OT'*, whereas inflation is represented by a shift upward of a line representative of an index. We can say, in other words, that a monetary shock creates a shift of a line representative of a given price index parallel to itself, and a real shock is represented by the pivoting of the line of relative prices. We will see later that there are usually both real relative price changes and changes in nominal prices during an inflationary process, especially because inflation disturbs in a differentiated way the information of economic agents and therefore supply and demand behaviours. We will also see later that it can be very important to pay attention to the variations in real relative prices.[3]

---

[3]   Moreover, we considered above the evolution of the purchasing power of money in terms of commodities – wheat and oil – but this could possibly reflect the evolution of the price of financial assets, that is, future commodities.

The above equation (4.15) is a fundamental equation for monetary theory and the theory of monetary systems. It underlines the undeniable fact that inflation is always and everywhere a monetary phenomenon. This means that there cannot be inflation if there is not – at one time or another – a growth in the quantity of money which is greater than the real growth (assuming, of course, that there is a 'satisfactory' price index and that the $k$ coefficient is constant). But this relationship of compatibility between growth rates (monetary growth and real growth) does not imply a single causality: it can be assumed that it is the increase of the money supply which causes inflation, or that it is the increase in prices which is at the origin of an increase in the money supply.

Let us initially consider the first case, that is, where monetary growth has a causal role in the inflationary process. Let us assume for simplicity that real income is constant ($\rho = 0$) and economic agents have initially the nominal and real amounts of money cash balances which they desire, given their real income levels and the existing price levels. Let us imagine now that the money supply increases as a result of an expansionary monetary policy. Economic agents therefore have excess nominal cash balances and they prefer to exchange them for other goods rather than to keep them (the marginal utility of cash balances has declined compared to the marginal utility of these other goods). As there are no economic agents demanding money balances (which would imply that their cash balances are too low), there is a global excess supply of money against goods. By a simple application of the theory of prices, the monetary price of goods will increase, meaning that the real value of money will decrease. This process will continue until all individuals have exactly the amount of real cash balances which they desire. As already mentioned, this is what is called the 'real cash balance effect'. In this case, causality has therefore been from the quantity of money to monetary prices. Can we then assume that causality plays in the other direction, that is, that a price increase causes an increase in the quantity of money? To this end we will consider two assumptions.

The first assumption is of a closed economy (or, as will be seen later, a regime of flexible exchange rates), with a given quantity of money which exactly meets the monetary needs of individuals. Let us then imagine that the prices of commodities are increasing. To illustrate this assumption let us assume for instance that the state decides upon an increase in compulsory social contributions paid by firms, which increases the costs of production of producers. They will try to shift this increase in costs onto the buyers of their products in order to avoid too sharp a drop in their profits. But to the extent that the monetary purchasing power of individuals has not been changed (assuming a constant real income and a constant money supply), the producers cannot sell all their production at higher prices. So they will probably try to shift the increase in social contributions onto wages, but it is well known that there is a certain downward rigidity of wages, which makes this kind of adjustment difficult. As they cannot reduce their production costs, they will then record a decline in their profits, and some of them will perhaps go bankrupt (which implies a creation of unemployment). To avoid such consequences, monetary authorities may be tempted to increase the money supply, which makes it possible to obtain the desired increases in nominal prices. We thus see that, in this case, the causality 'from the rise in prices to the increase in the quantity of money' does not result from a 'natural' adjustment process (as was the case in the symmetric case in which money creation had a causal role), but that it depends on the discretionary decisions of monetary authorities. Thus, we can only say that the initial (tentative) price increase creates an incentive for monetary authorities to increase the money supply.

The second assumption is that of a fixed exchange rate regime and an increase in the prices of imported goods in a country, which is communicated through a substitution effect – or contagion effect – to the prices of all goods. This is the so-called imported inflation. Later on, we will see that, in this case, there is an adjustment process which necessarily leads to an increase in the money supply (through imports of money cash balances). In this case, there is a causality which runs from prices to the money supply.

Thus the processes which make the monetary growth and the growth of prices compatible can be different, but the fact remains that there cannot be sustainable inflation without having corresponding monetary growth at one time or another. The monetary growth may come before the increase in prices or it may follow it, but it has to take place at one time or another to make inflation actually happen (otherwise, a momentary increase in monetary prices is followed by a drop in prices which brings them back to their original values).

These arguments challenge a distinction which is often made between what is called demand inflation and cost inflation. Indeed, it is not sufficient that some costs increase for an inflationary process to exist. As we have seen, this cost pressure can create sustainable inflation only when corresponding money creation takes place. But an increase in some production costs is a real phenomenon and not a monetary phenomenon. Conversely, inflation is a monetary phenomenon – it is the increase in the prices of goods in terms of money – and it necessarily involves a monetary growth rate higher than the real growth rate.

The above remarks also have a significant implication for policies aiming at fighting inflation. In fact, insofar as inflation is a monetary phenomenon, there cannot be a successful fight against inflation without adopting a restrictive monetary policy. More specifically, the excess of money creation was the *sine qua non* condition for the inflationary process to develop, and obviously it is not possible to put an end to this process without ending the excess of money creation. In this sense it would be more correct to speak of a 'policy of ending inflation' rather than a 'policy against inflation' (as if inflation was an exogenous phenomenon which ought to be thwarted). Furthermore, the 'fight against inflation' may have several meanings: a slowdown of inflation, stability of prices (as long as this can be properly defined), deflation (in which case the drop in monetary prices more or less compensates their previous increase).

Deflation – falling monetary prices – is much often negatively considered and it is frequently believed that it is linked to an economic recession (which constitutes a statement symmetrical to that which consists in thinking that inflation stimulates economic activity). This idea is necessarily questionable since, as we have already seen, deflation is desirable, insofar as it means an increase in the purchasing power of money, so that money plays its role efficiently as a pending purchasing power. To illustrate this idea, let us suppose that there is a single currency in the world and that the quantity of money is constant. If there is technical progress in certain activities, the sale price of the corresponding goods will decrease and there will be, on average, deflation. If nominal wages are constant, real wages will increase because of this fall in prices. Insofar as this deflation is at a (roughly) constant rate, each individual has stable information and can correctly forecast the rate of deflation. It is on the basis of these expectations of deflation that people will determine, for instance, nominal wage rates or interest rates.

But suppose now that there is a period with a rate of inflation that is more or less important, and that this rate is considered as a steady rate by economic agents. It is on the basis of their inflation expectations that they will determine, for example, nominal wages or nominal interest rates. However, imagine that, suddenly, monetary authorities decide upon a very restrictive monetary policy which leads to a decrease in the quantity of money. There will be a fall in prices, not due to some progress in productivity, but due to monetary policy. The resulting deflation was not forecast and it therefore has real consequences. Thus, nominal wages had been determined on the basis of the forecast steady rate of inflation, and they would have been lower if the deflation had been foreseen. Thus, producers are 'sandwiched' between nominal wages which are constant (or even increasing) and selling prices that are decreasing. Their profits decrease and some of them even suffer losses and go bankrupt. The result is a decline in economic activity and rising unemployment. However, it is clear that it is not deflation by itself which creates the recession and the unemployment, but the fact that this deflation had not been anticipated. This is exactly the scenario that occurred during the Great Depression (in the 1930s) and it has left in people's minds the (questionable) idea that deflation should be associated with recession. But, on the other hand, this consequence of an unexpected deflation would not occur if there was perfect flexibility of all nominal variables, especially nominal wages. Thus, the phenomenon described above would not occur if wages could be instantly changed depending on the observed variation in prices.

# 13. The formation of international prices

## 13.1 PRICES AND INFLATION RATE

Let us consider a country assumed to be relatively small compared to the rest of the world, and let us assume for the time being that there is a single currency in the world, so that all prices are expressed in this currency. We use the index $j$ to designate a variable concerning the country in question, and the index $w$ for variables concerning the rest of the world. As far as there is a price arbitration between countries it means that the price of a commodity $a$ in country $j$ is related to the price of the same commodity in the rest of the world. We can thus write:

$$P_{aj} = (P_{aw} + r_{aj})(1 + t_j) \tag{13.1}$$

where $P_{aj}$ represents the price of good $a$ in country $j$, $P_{aw}$ is the price of this same good in the rest of the world, $r_{aj}$ is the unit cost of transportation of good $a$ to country $j$ from the rest of the world, and $t_j$ is the rate of customs duties (if they exist).

Assuming, to simplify the reasoning, that the rate of change of the price of transportation is equal to the rate of change of the price of good $a$ in the rest of the world (which means that there is a variation of nominal prices, but not of real relative prices: in Figure 12.1 one is going from $A$ to $B$ and not from $A$ to $C$ or $D$[1]) the following relationship is obtained between the rates of change:

$$\pi_{aj} = \pi_{aw} + \tau_a \tag{13.2}$$

---

[1]  Insofar as this simplifying assumption is maintained later, a perfectly accurate description of the studied processes is not given. But this is without important consequences since the focus in this book is on monetary variables and it is therefore more important, for example, to know the effects of the variation of a monetary price or of the quantity of money rather than to know the effects of possible variations in relative real prices.

in which $\pi_{aj}$ represents the rate of change of the price of good $a$ in country $j$, $\pi_{aw}$ the rate of change of the price of this good in the rest of the world and $\tau_a$ the rate of change of customs duties on good $a$. However, taking into account the aims of this book, we can legitimately assume that customs duties do not change,[2] so that we can write:

$$\pi_{aj} = \pi_{aw} \qquad (13.3)$$

Thus, under the simplifying assumptions which have been made, the rate of change of the price of a good in terms of the world currency is the same in country $j$ and in the rest of the world. This is true for all goods, so that we can write:

$$\pi_j = \pi_w \qquad (13.4)$$

where $\pi_j$ represents the rate of change of a price index (that is, the price of a representative basket of goods) in country $j$, and $\pi_w$ represents the rate of change of the same price index in the rest of the world. In other words, the rate of inflation is the same in the small country studied and in the rest of the world in terms of the world currency, thanks to price arbitration: if the price of a good was to change differently in the country and in the rest of the world there would be shifts in supply and demand which would restore the equality between the rates of change.

Now suppose that there are two different currencies in the small country and in the rest of the world. The exchange rate, $E$, is defined as the number of units of the currency of the small country which can redeem one unit of currency in the rest of the world. Equation (13.1) then becomes:

$$P_{aj} = E(P_{aw} + r_{aj})(1 + t_j) \qquad (13.5)$$

Thus, one moves from a price expressed in terms of the currency of the rest of the world to a price expressed in terms of the currency of the small country by using the exchange rate, $E$. If, for instance, one uses a currency called the franc in the small country and a currency called the Ecu in the rest of the world and 1 Ecu can be exchanged against 2 francs, a good which is worth 1 Ecu in the rest of the world, will be worth 2 francs in the

---

[2] Similarly to the previous footnote: the objective of this book is not to study the effects of a change in customs duties, but the effects of monetary phenomena. The relationship between the significant variables is studied under the assumption of 'all other things being equal'. But, of course, it would not be difficult to abandon these simplifying assumptions and the bulk of the demonstrations would not be modified.

small country, if $E = 2$. Using the same simplifying assumptions as above (according to which the variations in the costs of transportation are identical to the changes in the nominal prices in the rest of the world and there are no changes in tariffs), we get the following equation:

$$\pi_j = \varepsilon + \pi_w \tag{13.6}$$

where $\varepsilon$ represents the rate of change of the exchange rate, $E$. We thus obtain a relationship of compatibility between these three variables: the rate of inflation in the small country, the rate of inflation in the rest of the world and the rate of change of the exchange rate.

We have seen previously that there is a relationship of compatibility between the inflation rate and the rate of change of the quantity of money, and that various assumptions of causality can be made. Similarly, different causal assumptions can be made about the relationship of compatibility (13.6): we can imagine, for example, that there is a gap between the inflation rates of the two parts of the world (the small country and the rest of the world) and the result is a variation of the exchange rate; or we can imagine that a change in the exchange rate causes a gap between inflation rates. But, as has just been pointed out, there is a relationship of compatibility between the inflation rates and the rates of change in the quantity of money, and we will subsequently have to study the relationships and causalities which may exist between all these variables: the changes in the quantities of each currency, the changes in prices (inflation rates) and the changes in exchange rates.

## 13.2   PURCHASING POWER PARITY

Many empirical studies have validated the assumption according to which there are international price arbitration processes. In this respect the expression 'purchasing power parity' is often used to express the idea that the purchasing power of a given quantity of money is (roughly) the same if one is using this currency in the country in which it is normally circulating or if one exchanges it against another currency, via the exchange rate, and one obtains the corresponding goods outside. But the fact remains that this equivalence is not perfect in reality. First of all, in general, the same price indices are not used in different countries or in different currency areas, which has an impact on the measurement of the purchasing power if relative prices between commodities change, as we saw previously (Figure 12.1 in Chapter 12).

Furthermore, even if the same price indices could be used in all countries, there may be deviations from the theoretical purchasing power parity, that is, the purchasing power calculated by using the exchange rate to convert the price of a certain basket of goods in terms of another currency. Indeed, we have assumed until now that there is an arbitration process for all goods because of international competition. But all goods are not similarly tradable and it is possible, by simplifying, to distinguish tradable and non-tradable goods. Certainly, in reality, goods are more or less tradable and there are degrees in the tradability of goods. Thus, it is excessive to say that a house is non-tradable since it is possible to demolish it, transport the materials abroad and rebuild it.[3] In this sense a house is only relatively less tradable, for example, than a tonne of steel. But, for the sake of argument, let us assume simply that there is a clear-cut distinction between tradables and non-tradables. If this is so, and if the price index which is used to measure the purchasing power parity contains both tradable goods and non-tradable goods, changes in relative prices between these goods will give a different evolution of the price indices (taking into account possible changes in the exchange rate) in different countries. This will be so even when using the same price index, because changes in relative prices between the two types of goods may be different in different countries.

The index of the difference between the actual exchange rate between two currencies and the theoretical exchange rate which would exactly match the purchasing power parity may then be called the 'real exchange rate'. One is generally inclined to consider that a change in the real exchange rate means that the nominal exchange rate (which can be observed on the exchange rate market) does not correctly reflect the relative change in nominal prices expressed in terms of both the currencies concerned: one currency is undervalued or overvalued relative to the other. But it may well be that the gaps thus revealed by the changes in real exchange rates correspond to changes in relative prices between tradable and non-tradable goods, for the reasons mentioned above. This difficulty is avoided by using price indices which exclude the prices of non-tradables, and by thus measuring only the changes in the prices of tradable goods (as far as such a distinction between goods can properly be made).

---

[3]   For example, this is precisely what has been done to develop the Cloisters museum in New York City, since European cloisters have been transported and reconstructed.

# 14. General principles about the working of fixed exchange rate systems and flexible exchange rate systems

We have just seen in Chapter 13 the equation which expresses the relationship between inflation rates in two countries and the variation of the exchange rate between their two currencies, namely:

$$\pi_j = \varepsilon + \pi_w \qquad (13.6)$$

On another hand, we have seen previously in Chapter 4 that there is a relationship between changes in the quantity of money, inflation rates and growth rates in each country, namely:

$$\mu = \pi + \rho \qquad (4.15)$$

which can be written in the following form:

$$\pi = \mu - \rho \qquad (14.1)$$

which means that the rate of inflation in a country is equal to the difference between the rate of growth of the quantity of money and the real growth rate: inflation is higher, the higher is the monetary growth or the weaker is the real growth. By replacing the rate of inflation in each country in equation (13.6) in Chapter 13 by its expression in equation (11.1) in Chapter 11, we get:

$$\mu_j - \rho_j = \varepsilon + \mu_w - \rho_w \qquad (14.2)$$

or:

$$\varepsilon = (\mu_j - \rho_j) - (\mu_w - \rho_w)$$
$$(14.3)$$

which means that the rate of change of the exchange rate is equal to the difference between the 'inflationary gaps' of each country, an inflationary gap being defined as the difference between the monetary growth rate and the real growth rate.

The exchange rate $E$ has been previously defined as the number of units of the currency of country $j$ needed to get a unit of currency of the rest of the world (country w). An increase of $E$ – that is, a positive value of the rate of change of the exchange rate, $\varepsilon$ – thus indicates a depreciation of the currency $j$. And according to equation (14.3) the depreciation of the currency $j$ will therefore be all the more important that the monetary growth in country $j$ will be higher compared to the rest of the world, and the real growth rate in country $j$ will be lower compared to the rest of the world.

Actually the equation (14.3) can be regarded as a simple application of the general theory of prices. In fact, the real growth rate has been introduced in this equation because it is assumed that the demand for money is higher, the higher is the level of real income. As indicated in equation (14.3) the variation in the relative price between the two currencies is a function of the differences between the growth rate of demand (represented by the real income) and the growth rates of supply for each of these two currencies. The price of one good (of a currency) relative to another one increases, the more the demand for this good increases (compared to the demand for the other good) or the less the supply of this good (of this currency) increases (relative to the supply of the other good). Equation (14.3) can therefore be considered to be a simple and necessary application of the best established principles of economic theory.[1]

Equation (14.3) may be considered to be at the core of monetary policy or exchange rate policy, and it therefore plays a fundamental role in the study of the working and the role of monetary systems. This equation provides a relationship between five variables, but it is well known that only one of these variables may be endogenous, the other four being determined exogenously, that is, by other processes. However, it is legitimate to consider only the two following possibilities.

Firstly, under flexible exchange rate regimes (or floating exchange rates) the rate of change of the exchange rate, $\varepsilon_-$, is the endogenous variable. This rate is determined by the rates of monetary growth and real growth in both countries. Real growth rates are determined by a variety of factors which are analysed by the growth theory (for example, technological

---

[1] Of course this expression cannot be perfectly consistent with what we may see in reality, taking into account the simplifying assumptions that had to be made, for example about the price indices or the stability of certain behaviour coefficients. But it at least gives qualitative information about the relations between the variables involved.

progress, the institutional environment which determines the incentives of productive economic agents, and so on). Monetary growth rates, meanwhile, are determined by monetary policies and we have previously studied how this determination takes place. In particular, we have seen that there is a relationship between the money supply and the monetary base, so that changes in the monetary base decided by monetary authorities are one of the determinants of the variation of the exchange rate. It is important to emphasize at this point that under flexible exchange rates the monetary policies made in the different countries which are suppliers of currencies are independent. Monetary authorities in each country decide the monetary policy which they want and, as a result, there are changes in the exchange rates on foreign exchange markets.

Secondly, under a system of fixed exchange rates, the rate of change of the exchange rate is zero by definition ($\varepsilon_- = 0$), which means that the exchange rate is determined exogenously (that is, it is determined outside the model which we are analysing). We will later see specifically how this exogenous determination occurs. Another of the five variables in the model can therefore be endogenous. It is legitimate to consider that one of the money supplies is endogenous. In other words, if one accepts – as is usual – that real growth rates are exogenous (determined by other non-monetary factors, not represented here) and that one of the money supplies is exogenous (for example, the money supply of country $w$), the other quantity of money – of country j – is endogenous, which means that it is determined by the model in consideration and it cannot be determined independently by monetary authorities. In other words, under fixed exchange rates monetary authorities cannot implement an independent monetary policy. However, in the model with two countries which we are considering for the time being, one of the countries can implement an independent monetary policy (and it determines the monetary growth in the other country). In a system with $n$ countries, the monetary authority of one of these countries can implement an independent monetary policy, which is not the case for the $n - 1$ other countries. We will later see how this interdependence between monetary growth rates actually takes place. But here I will mention the special case in which there is a system with $n$ currencies – therefore $n$ quantities of money – and an exogenous monetary asset, such as gold in a gold standard. The growth of the stock of monetary gold is exogenous, therefore not determined arbitrarily by monetary authorities. It determines the monetary growth in all countries belonging to this system of fixed exchange rates (in which the exchange rate between the $n$ currencies and gold is fixed).

Finally, the question arises of why it would not be possible to choose one of the real growth rates as the endogenous variable, if all other variables were exogenous, that is, the exchange rate variations (decided by one monetary authority), the quantities of money and the real growth of the other country. We must recognize here the often-expressed idea according to which the depreciation or the devaluation of a national currency would increase a country's growth. We will see later why this idea is erroneous.

A last important general note must finally be made at this point. We have logically deduced above a relationship between, on the one hand, the variation of the exchange rate and, on the other hand, the rates of monetary growth and the rates of real growth. However, it is usual to consider a priori that there is a relationship between a variation in the exchange rate, on the one hand, and a change in the balance of the trade balance, on the other hand. One thus thinks that a depreciation (appreciation) or a devaluation (re-evaluation) of the exchange rate results in a positive (negative) change in the trade balance. Likewise, a trade deficit (surplus) is supposed to lead to a depreciation (appreciation) of the exchange rate or requires – to be corrected – a devaluation (re-evaluation). These mainstream ideas are necessarily questionable since, as has been rigorously demonstrated in Part II of this book, there is a relationship between the trade balance on the one hand, and on the other hand, the propensities to save and to invest in the countries concerned, which means that the balance of the trade balance is in fact determined by intertemporal choices. It is therefore questionable to assume that this trade balance may also be determined by changes in exchange rates. But it is true that the trade balance is, as we know, the counterpart not only of the account of financial transactions, but also of the account of monetary flows. Therefore, we will see later how the trade balance can be influenced, indirectly, by exchange rate fluctuations and/or by changes in monetary and real growth rates, at least on a transitory basis.

# 15. The monetary approach to the balance of payments (under fixed exchange rates)

Part II of this book focused on the complementarity between the trade account and the capital account in the balance of payments (quite often assuming implicitly that the balance of the monetary balance was zero, that is assuming that, overall, individuals in each of the countries concerned did not want either to decrease or to increase the amount of their cash balances[1]). The focus now is on the relationship between the monetary balance and the trade balance and, in order to properly isolate each problem, we will make a similar assumption to this previous one, namely that (with possible exceptions) the balance of the capital balance is constant and even, more specifically, that it is zero. Under such an assumption, which does not alter the substance of the reasoning, the balance of the trade balance is exactly equal – with an opposite sign – to the balance of the monetary balance. Of course, in reality, the balance of the trade balance is equal – with an opposite sign – to the sum of the monetary balance and the capital balance.

The monetary approach to the balance of payments has been a significant contribution of Robert Mundell,[2] professor of economics at the University of Chicago. It can be seen as a logical consequence of the reasoning I have presented previously, and from this point of view it seems solidly established. But, to the extent that balance of payments problems are often inspired by an approach which is, more or less explicitly, Keynesian, I believe it is necessary to start by quickly recalling the essential characteristics of a Keynesian approach of the balance of payments. This chapter will make a study from the point of view of a small country which is under a fixed exchange rate system in relation to the rest of the

---

[1]  Of course, it could also have been assumed that each economic agent wished to transfer a given amount of cash from one country to another at each period, so that possible changes in the trade balance could not have been attributed to changes in the money balance. Possible variations of the latter would then depend only on the variations of the balance of the capital balance.

[2]  See, for example, Mundell (1971) and Frenkel and Johnson (1976).

world (indicated by the index *w*) and will assume that the variables related to the rest of the world (for example real income, real growth rate, interest rate) are given data for this small country.

## 15.1   THE KEYNESIAN APPROACH

According to this approach, the balance of the trade balance is determined independently from the capital balance and the monetary balance; in addition, the amount of imports and the amount of exports are also independent one from the other. This approach can be synthesized as follows:

$$b = b\,(y, E/P) \tag{15.1}$$

In this equation, *b* represents the balance of the trade balance (in real terms), *y* is the real income of the small country, *E* is the exchange rate (an increase of *E* representing a depreciation or devaluation of the national currency), and *P* is the general level of prices in the country.

According to the Keynesian approach, $db/dy < 0$, that is, an increase of the real national income of the small country translates into a negative change in the trade balance (what is usually called a 'deterioration of the trade balance'). This approach assumes that exports are determined by the level of income in the rest of the world (which is assumed constant for simplicity) and that imports are a positive function of the income of the small country (there would be a 'propensity to import' similar to the 'propensity to consume'). Given that the balance of the trade balance is equal to the difference between the amount of exports and the amount of imports, an increase of *y* thus translates into a decrease in *b*.

Now, the Keynesian approach also assumes that $db/d(E/P) > 0$, that is, there is a positive change in the trade balance if the exchange rate, *E*, increases (which means a depreciation or devaluation of the national currency), or if the general level of prices, *P*, decreases (in which case it is often said that there is an improvement of the country's 'competitiveness', according to a questionable expression[3]). One may recognize here what is known in the traditional theory of international economics as the

---

[3]   The concept of competitiveness ought to be considered only as a relative concept: the producers of a country are relatively 'competitive' for certain goods because they are relatively less 'competitive' for other goods, as is very well explained by the theory of international specialization. The concept of a 'global competitiveness' of a country is therefore meaningless.

'elasticity approach', which aims at studying the effects of a change in exchange rates on the balance of trade.

The Keynesian model, therefore, considers that the balance of the trade balance is determined independently of the other items of the balance of payments, by the variables which have been indicated. We can also write the balance of the capital balance in the following way:

$$T = T(r, r_w) \tag{15.2}$$

where $T$ represents the value in national currency of the balance of the capital balance, $r$ is the national interest rate, and $r_w$ the world interest rate. It is assumed here that the capital account contains only loanable funds (it is implicitly considered that flows of securities and flows of direct investment are given, or at least that they are not influenced by the variables which are contained in the model). Assuming also that $r_w$ is an exogenous variable, $T$ is a growing function of $r$, that is, an increase in the national interest rate leads to an increase in exports of national assets and a decrease in imports of foreign assets.

In this model, the balance of the monetary account in the balance of payments – what is sometimes called the 'balance of the balance of payments' – is determined by the other two items (trade balance and capital balance). In other words, the analysis of the balance of payments starts from the 'top' of the balance of payments and it considers that the monetary item – at the bottom of the balance of payments – only has a role of 'closing' the accounts (which means that this analysis does not incorporate the behaviour of economic agents as regards their desired money cash balances: the monetary account is purely compensatory). We can therefore write:

$$\Delta R_b = Pb + T \tag{15.3}$$

where $\Delta R_b$ represents the variations of 'official reserves' (which takes into account in the monetary balance only the monetary flows which affect the central bank's foreign reserves, but not private monetary flows); $P$ represents the general price level, so that $Pb$ represents the balance of the trade balance in monetary value. Thus, this expression can be written, by taking into account the previous equations:

$$\Delta R_b = Pb(y, E/P) + T(r, r_w) \tag{15.4}$$

Thus, the level of official foreign exchange reserves in a regime of fixed exchange rates (what is sometimes called the official balance of the balance of payments) is a decreasing function of $y$, an increasing function of $E$, a decreasing function of $P$, an increasing function of $r$, given the assumptions mentioned above.

We will later see how the monetary approach to the balance of payments is, among other things, a refutation of this Keynesian model. But several important shortcomings of this approach can already be pointed out:

- It does not consider explicitly the supply and demand for money in spite of the fact that a variation in the exchange rate is a monetary phenomenon, since it is the variation of the relative price between two currencies. As a non-monetary approach of a monetary phenomenon it is therefore a priori incoherent.
- This approach assumes that the monetary behaviours of individuals have no impact on the balance of payments, as it is solely determined by the phenomena concerning the trade balance and the capital balance, which do not incorporate monetary variables.
- It implicitly assumes that there is no relationship between foreign prices, domestic prices and the exchange rate, meaning that all of these variables can vary independently of each other. This implicit assumption is not compatible with the assumption of price arbitration which has previously been mentioned. Yet this latter assumption is the logical consequence of the fundamental assumption of the rationality of human choices, which is based on the correct idea that individuals are able to compare prices and to make their choices of supply and demand on the basis of these prices. As it is not compatible with what constitutes the very foundation of economic theory, the Keynesian approach of the trade balance cannot be considered as justified.[4]
- In a similar way the Keynesian approach implies that the national interest rate is determined regardless of the 'world interest rate', that is, that there is no interest rate arbitration.
- As we have seen, an increase in real income leads, in this model, to a 'deterioration' in the trade balance. This is due to the assumption that there is a positive 'propensity to import', that is, a positive relationship between the real value of imports and the real value of income. But this assumption does not correspond to a justified

[4] This approach is, however, more or less implicitly, what underlies many arguments and many economic policy measures. This results, in my opinion, from the fact that economic phenomena are complex because of the many interdependencies between variables, and people are quite often satisfied by artificially isolating certain phenomena or some variables and forgetting that they are determined by a network of interdependencies with other phenomena and variables.

assumption concerning the rational behaviour of individuals. If their income increases, individuals certainly wish to buy more goods, but there is no reason to assume that they want to maintain a constant ratio between imported goods and goods produced in their country. It is an ad hoc macroeconomic-type assumption, but it has no possible microeconomic basis and therefore it should not be accepted. We will see that the monetary approach to the balance of payments – which is based on justified assumptions of behaviour – leads to the opposite conclusion. These two approaches cannot logically be compatible, so that it is necessary to retain only the approach which is consistent with what is known of the rational behaviour of individuals.

Before analysing the monetary approach to the balance of payments, we can, however, recall that there is traditionally a further different approach to the balance of payments, the so-called 'absorption approach'. It introduces a monetary variable in the explanatory model of the balance of payments since imports are expected to be an increasing function not only of income, but also of real cash balances. But the fundamental assumptions of the Keynesian model are retained.

## 15.2   THE MONETARY APPROACH TO THE BALANCE OF PAYMENTS

This approach rightly clings to the idea that the balance of payments is a monetary phenomenon. While in the Keynesian approach, as we have just seen, the 'balance of the balance of payments' – that is, the monetary item of the balance of payments – is residual (determined by the other two items of the balance of payments), for the monetary approach to the balance of payments – hereinafter referred to by the acronym MABP – the monetary balance is rightly determined by the monetary behaviour of money-holders and the behaviour of money producers, especially of the central bank. In other words, the analysis of the balance of payments starts from the 'bottom' of the balance of payments (that is, the monetary item) and not from the 'top'. It incorporates knowledge of the rational behaviour of economic agents, whether as users of money or as money producers. Therefore, it is a logical consequence of the demand for money, the creation of money, as previously stated.

The demand for money function can be written in the following form:

$$M^d = L(P, y, r) \tag{15.5}$$

where $M^d$ is the demand for nominal cash balances (in the small country studied). It is an increasing function of the level of prices $(P)$ and of real income $(y)$, a decreasing function of the national interest rate $(r)$.[5]

To describe the money supply, we will first refer to the central bank's balance sheet. Previously, we had only registered as assets in the balance sheet the amount of claims held by the central bank. But we now distinguish domestic claims $(CD)$ and external claims $(R_b)$. The latter are sometimes referred to as official reserves or as exchange reserves of the central bank. Commercial banks hold reserves $(R)$ which are claims on the central bank, and the central bank holds reserves which are claims on foreign banks $(R_b)$. The central bank's balance sheet can then be written as follows:

The central bank's balance sheet

| Assets | | Liabilities | |
|---|---|---|---|
| CD | domestic claims | C | banknotes |
| $R_b$ | reserves (external claims) | R | reserves of commercial banks |

The balance sheet of the central bank – called the monetary base – can obviously be measured from the asset side or from the liability side. We can therefore write:

$$B = CD + R_b \qquad (15.6)$$

where $B$ is the monetary base.

As seen previously, the money supply is equal to a multiple of the monetary base, which can be written as follows:

$$M^S = mB = m(CD + R_b) \qquad (15.7)$$

where $M^S$ is the supply of money and m the 'money multiplier'.

By writing the equality (in nominal terms) between the demand for money and the money supply from equations (15.5) and (15.7), we obtain:

$$L(P, y, r) = mCD + mR_b \qquad (15.8)$$

from which we can draw the following equation:

---

[5]  To simplify the presentation, it is assumed implicitly here that the inflationary expectations are stable and that they therefore do not influence the demand for money.

$$\Delta R_b = \Delta \frac{1}{m} L\ (P, y, r) - \Delta\ CD \qquad (15.9)$$

This equation, which expresses the essence of the MABP, leads to a number of important statements.

First, there is a swing between *CD* and $R_b$: under a regime of fixed exchange rates, if the central bank undertakes an expansionary monetary policy, meaning that it accumulates domestic claims, this translates into a decrease of the same amount in its foreign currency reserves (or reserves of external claims).[6] In other words, the size of the central bank's balance sheet is determined by the outside world, which illustrates the idea already stressed that a country's monetary policy cannot be independent in a fixed exchange rate regime. It would be even more correct to say that monetary policy is impossible. If a central bank wishes, for example, to make an expansionary monetary policy (increase of *CD*), it cannot increase the monetary base, and therefore the money supply. The only consequence of its action is a modification in the structure of its balance sheet: domestic claims substitute for foreign exchange reserves. But it is clear that this pretence to an independent monetary policy at some point necessarily faces a limit, which appears when the level of official reserves is equal to zero. Later, we will see how the central bank can react in this case.

We can see from equation (15.9) that the change in foreign exchange reserves – what is usually called the balance of the balance of payments – is determined by three variables, *P*, *y* and *r* (assuming that the money multiplier, *m*, is constant). The variation of reserves is an increasing function of *P* and *y*, a decreasing function of *r*, as is the demand for money. Let us look at these three relationships.

Firstly, an increase in domestic prices increases the demand for nominal cash balances. Under a regime of fixed exchange rates, this additional quantity of money is obtained from an import of foreign currency (obtained at a fixed price), which is exchanged at the central bank against the national currency, since the fixity of exchange rates between two countries with different currencies comes from the fact that the central bank[7] is committed to exchange its currency against the foreign currency at a fixed price. If prices are increasing in the country, money-holders want more nominal

---

6   Of course, this equivalence between two variations does not exist in practice immediately, but with some delay. We will later see how the flow of currencies (or the variations of official reserves) specifically respond to changes in the stock of domestic claims of the central bank.
7   We assume, in this case, that it is the central bank of the small country studied which gives this price guarantee. Later on, I will explore how the choice of the central banks which give an exchange guarantee is determined.

cash balances and they buy money against commodities or financial assets (that is, present or future goods). Insofar as there is no domestic creation of money, they cannot, as a whole, get these additional cash balances except by buying them abroad, and therefore selling goods and financial assets as a counterpart. Thus, to use the usual accounting terminology, there is a positive change in the trade balance and/or in the capital balance, and a negative change in the corresponding monetary account. Economic agents who thus obtain foreign currency cannot use it in their country and they exchange it against the national currency from their commercial banks which, in turn, exchange it against the national currency with the central bank (given its convertibility guarantee at fixed price between the two currencies). However, it is very likely that the increase of prices in the country has been caused by an increase in prices abroad because there is a process of price arbitration in a fixed exchange rate regime (this is the so-called imported inflation). This increase in prices abroad comes itself, most likely, from a monetary creation. Thus the increase in the money supply in the rest of the world translates into increased prices in the whole area of fixed exchange rates and money flows from the country where it has been created (the 'rest of the world') to the other country. Of course, if there was a drop in prices in the country under review, there would be exactly symmetrical phenomena to those just analysed.

Secondly, an increase in real income in the small country, all things being equal, translates into an increase in the reserves of the central bank. In fact, the demand for nominal cash balances increases (since prices are constant, but the real income increases) and, as above, it can be met only by purchasing currency from the rest of the world. It is therefore here that the MABP leads to a statement which is exactly opposite to what we have met in the Keynesian model, since in the latter an increase in real income causes a 'deterioration' in the trade balance (because of the assumption of a positive relationship between imports and real income). Thus, the capital account being assumed constant, there would be a decrease in the exchange reserves of the central bank according to the Keynesian model. The two approaches are therefore incompatible. It is legitimate to retain the MABP and to reject the Keynesian approach, since the first is based on the justified assumption according to which there is a positive relationship between the demand for money and real income, while the Keynesian approach is based on the perfectly arbitrary assumption according to which there is a positive relationship between imports and real income.[8]

---

[8]   The MABP reduces to zero the value of the traditional argument that a recovery policy – consisting, according to the Keynesian tradition, in increasing aggregate demand, for example by increasing the public deficit – hits an 'external constraint', that is, the risk of a

Finally, an increase in the rate of interest in the country reduces foreign exchange reserves because it induces a decrease in the demand for money (substitution of financial assets for cash balances). The Keynesian approach leads to the opposite result because it considers the variation of reserves as a result of what happens in the trade balance and the capital balance. However, if the interest rate increases in the country there is a positive change of the balance of the capital balance (more claims are sold to the rest of the world; what is called an inflow of capital, as noted above). But the MABP implicitly assumes that there is arbitration of interest rates, that is, the increase in interest rates in the small country is the result of a phenomenon of contagion by the interest rates which have increased in the rest of the world, so that there is no reason for the capital balance to change. The only effect of an increase of the interest rate is therefore one that operates through the demand for money. This effect is normally only transitional. Indeed, while it can be realistic to assume that the real income increases constantly, it is not possible to imagine a continuous increase (or a continuous decrease) in the rate of interest. Therefore, it is more realistic to imagine a once and for all variation of the interest rate. During the adjustment period, there will be exports of money against present or future goods in the event of an increase in the interest rate, since people want less cash balances (or vice versa, there are purchases of money in the case of a decrease in the rate of interest). But once the economic agents reach the desired level of their cash balances (what is called 'full equilibrium'), there is no longer any excess supply (or excess demand) of money and this therefore leads back to the previous structure of the balance of payments. Of course, if the variation in the rate of interest in the small country is due to the same variation of the rate of interest in the rest of the world, due to a phenomenon of arbitration, the change in the structure of the balance of payments depends on the variations in the demand for money and the supply of money associated with this variation of the interest rate in each of the two countries.

---

deterioration in the trade balance, becoming unbearable by the shortage of foreign exchange reserves. However, even without taking account of the fact that it is wrong to believe that an economic recovery can be achieved by increasing aggregate demand, it is clear that this 'external constraint' does not in fact exist.

# 16. The processes of transmission between monetary systems under fixed exchange rates

Chapter 15 has studied the compatibility relationships which exist between some variables (or their rates of change) and, it made clear in which direction the causality was working. I will now begin to clarify the concrete ways by which these causal relationships take place. For this it will be assumed, for simplicity, that the balance of the trade balance is zero initially and that the small country studied is initially in equilibrium (which implies in particular that each individual owns the amount of real cash balances which he desires). I will then consider the consequences of an economic 'shock'. A 'shock' is an exogenous and large-scale variation of a variable. A useful distinction can be made between a real shock and a monetary shock. During the greatest part of the history of mankind the shocks were almost always real shocks (bad harvests, wars, epidemics, and so on) and monetary shocks were rare because there were very few monetary manipulations; thus, in a gold standard system the quantity of money increases very slowly and it cannot cause a large-scale 'shock'.[1] Nowadays the shocks are generally of a monetary nature as discretionary monetary policies allow monetary authorities to change the quantity of money quickly and deeply. Real shocks are rarer (wars, violent change in political regimes, and so on). It is sometimes assumed that there can be productivity shocks caused by a brutal variation of the productivity of factors of production due to variations in the rate of technical progress. But such an assumption is unrealistic because, while it is true that one can find many examples of large and fast changes in productivity in a specific sector, it is quite inconceivable that it would happen in all sectors of activity at the same time, in which case there would actually be a real shock.

---

[1] A notable exception was the arrival in Europe of large quantities of gold stolen from the inhabitants of the American continent after its discovery. This resulted in significant inflation; however, incommensurate with what has occured more recently.

## 16.1   INTERNATIONAL TRANSMISSION ACCORDING TO DIFFERENT ECONOMIC MODELS

I have already distinguished between the Keynesian model and the model of the monetary approach to the balance of payments (MABP). But I will now add another model, which can be called the 'Hume model' because it was designed by the Scottish philosopher David Hume who is generally considered to be the inventor of the quantity theory of money.

### 16.1.1   The Hume Model

Let us assume that we are in a fixed exchange rate regime (for example, a gold standard) and that the quantity of money increases suddenly in the small country (monetary shock). This will cause an increase in the demand for certain goods – those which are desired by the recipients of these new cash balances – and the prices of these goods will increase. Little by little, the additional cash balances will circulate and the prices of all goods will increase. During this first phase, therefore, prices have risen in the country where the increase in the quantity of money has occurred, but not yet in the rest of the world. But, obviously, the arbitration process will play its role as individuals realize – because there is a regime of fixed exchange rates – that the prices of goods are lower in the rest of the world. They will therefore import goods and sell money (such as gold). Thus, little by little, the new money will move from the country where it had first increased, towards the rest of the world, and prices will rise in the same way throughout the world. Therefore, the increase in the quantity of money has caused a trade deficit (with outflows of money as a counterpart), itself caused by a change in relative prices (between the domestic prices in the small country, $P_i$, and the prices in the rest of the world, $P_w$). This last variation can be called a change in the terms of trade, that is, in the relative price between the import prices (determined by prices in the rest of the world) and export prices (determined by prices in the small country). When all individuals around the world have the amount of real cash balances which they desire, we are back to the original relative prices and the trade balance deficit disappears.

### 16.1.2   The Traditional Keynesian Model

Unlike the model of Hume and the monetary approach to the balance of payments (MABP) model, the traditional Keynesian model can be considered as a non-monetary approach to the transmission processes. It does not incorporate, in particular, any assumption concerning the demand for real cash balances of economic agents, and therefore it implicitly assumes that individuals are indifferent to the level of their cash balances.[2]

Let us take the case of a monetary shock in a fixed exchange rate regime, for example an increase in the quantity of money. In the Keynesian theory, this translates into an increase in real income in 'normal' situations (that is, outside of the specific assumptions of this theory, especially the assumption of a 'money trap' in which monetary policy has no more real effects). The result is a trade deficit, because it is assumed that there is a 'propensity to import', that is, a positive relationship between imports and real income. There are therefore (assuming that the capital account does not change) sales of currency in return for this deficit. But these sales do not cause reactions on the part of money-holders, in spite of the fact that their money cash balances do change. The only reactions which are introduced in the model are the possible reactions of the central bank if it loses reserves. Now, in order to pay for the excess of imports over exports, individuals need foreign currency, which they get from the central bank against the national currency, since they are in a fixed exchange rate regime. The central bank therefore faces what is sometimes called an 'external constraint', meaning that its policy of monetary expansion – which leads to demand for foreign currency – finds a limit in the amount of its foreign exchange reserves.

In the Keynesian theory there is a similar process in the case of a real shock. Thus, a policy of public budget deficit is expected to increase aggregate demand and thus real income. But the increase in real income, resulting in an increase in imports, involves a trade deficit and thus losses of external reserves for the central bank. The recovery policy based on the so-called increased aggregate demand would therefore meet the 'external constraint' in a fixed exchange rate regime.

### 16.1.3   The Model of the Monetary Approach to the Balance of Payments

In this model, there is a symmetry between a monetary shock and a real shock, and the behaviour of individuals concerning their money cash balances plays a central role. In fact, a shock is always relative: thus an

---

[2]   This assumption in fact becomes explicit when the Keynesian theory evokes the 'liquidity trap', that is, the situation where individuals accumulate cash balances indefinitely rather than using them either for consumption or for savings. This is sometimes referred to as 'idle cash balances'. This assumption assumes that individuals can be 'irrational' – contrary to the founding assumption of any economic science – since they use their resources in an useless way. However, this assumption plays an important role in the Keynesian theory to explain an alleged situation of underemployment equilibrium.

increase in the quantity of money affects the relative scarcity of money against other goods – and therefore it affects the demand for money – and likewise for a real shock. Without going into the details of the adjustment process – which I will do later – for the time being a distinction can be made between two versions of the MABP.

In the first version, it is assumed that there is an immediate contagion of the prices of all goods between the small country and the rest of the world. Therefore, there is no change in relative prices (for example, the relative prices between tradable and non-tradable goods, or between the prices of imports and the prices of exports).

In the second version, it is assumed that the formation of prices is different for tradable goods and non-tradable goods. Thus, an increase in the quantity of money in the small country will result in an increase of the prices of non-tradables, but not of the prices of tradable goods, which are determined by external prices. There is a transitory change in their relative prices. But in the longer term, different processes of adjustment, due to modifications of demand and supply, will contribute to a return to the original relative prices (if nothing else has changed meanwhile).

The main characteristics of the three models just mentioned can be presented in the following table:

| Model | Monetary adjustment | Changes in relative prices | |
| --- | --- | --- | --- |
| | | $P_{ex}/P_{im}$ | $P_T/P_{NT}$ |
| Hume | yes | yes | no |
| Traditional Keynesian | no | yes | no |
| Monetary approach, 1st version | yes | no | no |
| Monetary approach, 2nd version | yes | no | yes |

Where $P_{ex}$ represents the index of the prices of exports, $P_{im}$ the index of the prices of imports, $P_T$ the index of the prices of tradables and $P_{NT}$ the index of the prices of non-tradables

## 16.2 THE INTERNATIONAL TRANSMISSION PROCESS ACCORDING TO MONETARY SYSTEMS

Assume, for simplicity, a world composed of two countries, country $i$ and country $j$, seen from the point of view of country $i$. I will consider, in a very general and simplified way, four types of monetary systems and there will be the opportunity later to clarify the processes involved in these different systems (and possibly other systems). Currently, only the fourth of these systems actually exists (with a few very rare cases corresponding to the third system). But all have existed in history and it is, in any case, important to consider all of them in order to better understand the working of monetary systems.

### 16.2.1 System 1: A Non-Hierarchical System, with 100 Per Cent Reserves

Let us assume that there is a currency $j$ in country $j$ and a currency $i$ in country $i$. The inhabitants of country $j$ use only the currency $j$ for their domestic transactions, and the inhabitants of the country $i$ use the currency $i$. We assume also that there is a firm in country $i$ which exchanges at a fixed price the currency $j$ against the currency $i$ which it produces. This firm can be public or private. One might be tempted to call it a 'bank', but it is better to call it an 'exchange office' or, as is usual, a 'currency board', and to reserve the term 'bank' for firms which transfer and transform savings. The system is non-hierarchical because the currency board is not linked to any other firm and it performs its operations independently. Its balance sheet is very simple and can be written as follows:

Balance sheet of the currency board

| Assets | | Liabilities | |
|---|---|---|---|
| units of currency $j$ (reserves) | 50 | units of currency $i$ | 50 |

The role of the currency board is to transform the units of currency $j$ into units of currency $i$ (which are monetary claims against it). To do this it promises to exchange one currency against the other at a fixed price without limits (it is a fixed exchange rate regime). If, for example, the inhabitants of the country need additional cash balances at any given time, they can obtain them by increasing their exports or decreasing their imports, that is, by causing a positive change in the balance of the trade balance (or possibly of the balance of the capital account). They obtain units of currency $j$ which they convert into units of currency $i$ via the currency board. Of course, the number of units of currency $i$ obtained against a given number of units of currency $j$ depends on the relative price between these two currencies (which can be called the exchange rate). Later, we will see how this exchange rate is determined (either by the market or by fixed-rate convertibility guarantees). In the previous balance sheet, the amount of money in currency $i$ and in currency $j$ has obviously been expressed in terms of the same numéraire (probably currency $i$, because it would be usual for the firm issuing currency $i$ to establish its accounts in terms of this currency).

It is usual to give the name of 'reserves' to the cash balances held in the 'assets' side of the balance sheet of an organization such as this currency board (or of the banks, which will be considered later). In the system which we are studying at the moment, one speaks of '100 per cent reserves' because all the cash balances denominated in currency $i$ correspond exactly to the amount of cash balances in currency $j$ held as assets by the currency board, that is, the amount of its 'reserves'. Moreover, this gives to the holders of currency $i$ the certainty that they can, if they wish, exchange currency $i$ against currency $j$, since the currency board holds a quantity of currency $j$ equivalent to the existing amount of currency $i$. As we shall see, reserves may consist of gold, instead of monetary cash balances composed of monetary units created by external organizations.

In this system, monetary policy is simply impossible, because the currency board cannot decide to increase or to decrease the amount of money $i$ at will. It has a purely passive role, which is to accept the conversion of currency $j$ against currency $i$ without limits (and vice versa). However, there is a small difficulty in the working of the system, namely that the issuer of currency $i$ must incur costs (for example, the printing of banknotes or the management of accounting for its customers) and receives no remuneration for the services it thus supplies. This difficulty can be overcome in two ways: either the currency board is financed otherwise (for instance by exercising other activities and thus establishing the loyalty of its customers thanks to its monetary activities), or else the state supports the operating costs of the currency board. But one can also question whether it would not be simpler for the inhabitants of the country $i$ to use the currency $j$ without any need to convert it into currency $i$.

### 16.2.2   System 2: A Non-Hierarchical System with Fractional Reserves

Let us now assume that the exchange office[3] of country $i$ decides that it is not essential to retain reserves (gold or foreign currencies) exactly equal to the amount of currency it is issuing. It considers, based on the experience which it has, that only a part of the holders of its currency desire to exchange their units of currency $i$ against its reserves (in currency $j$) during a given period. Its reserves therefore represent a fraction of its liabilities (banknotes or deposits) lower than 100 per cent. Since a balance sheet must necessarily be in accounting equilibrium, there is necessarily a counterpart to the excess of liabilities over reserves, and this counterpart consists of credits granted by the exchange office (credits of monetary origin). In other words, through simple accounting entries, the firm undertaking foreign exchange transactions increases its liabilities (that is, it issues banknotes and/or deposits) and it buys claims on borrowers of country $i$. Its balance sheet is then as follows:

Balance sheet of the firm producing currency $i$

| Assets | | Liabilities | |
|---|---|---|---|
| units of currency $j$ (reserves) | 50 | units of currency $i$ | 100 |
| domestic claims | 50 | | |

In this example, reserves represent 50 per cent of the total balance sheet, which means that the units of currency $i$ issued by this firm benefit from an actual exchange guarantee (in terms of currency $j$) representing 50 per cent of their value. If, for example, reserves are made up of gold and the firm holds 50 ounces of gold, it has issued monetary units the value of which is equal to 100 ounces of gold, since each unit of currency is supposed to benefit from a gold exchange guarantee equal to 1 ounce of gold. In this case, we can say that the firm has a reserve coefficient equal to 50 per cent (or 0.5), the reserve coefficient being defined as the ratio of the amount of reserves to the amount of units of the currency which is supposed to benefit from an exchange guarantee in terms of these reserves. Of course, this guarantee would not be honoured if all the holders of monetary units were to request the conversion of their monetary units into gold at the same time.

The exchange office is induced to adopt fractional reserves – for instance,

---

[3]   I now use the term 'exchange office' and not 'currency board', because it is usual to use the term 'currency board' only in the case of 100 per cent reserves.

a reserve coefficient equal to 0.5 in our example – because that allows it to make credits, meaning that it buys debts which provide interest; while, most likely, it pays a lower interest rate – and possibly even zero – to the holders of its units of currency. Therefore, the lower the reserve coefficient, the higher is its rate of profit. But the risk of not being able to fulfil its convertibility commitment of exchanging units of its currency $i$ against reserves in currency $j$ increases with the decrease in the reserve coefficient. The firm must therefore choose the reserve coefficient which seems optimal for it, by taking into account these two factors which play in an opposite direction. The choice of the optimal coefficient obviously depends on the level of the interest rate on claims held by the exchange office (and, possibly, on its liabilities), on the estimated probability of the demands for conversion of currency $i$ into currency $j$, on its propensity to take risks, and so on.

A bank can be defined as a firm which is specialized in financial transformation, that is, it uses either its own funds or borrowed funds to invest in the equity capital of other firms or to make loans. It can therefore be considered a priori as likely – and experience shows that this is the case – that a firm which is thus specialized in credit activities also embarks upon an activity of creation of currency, since in a fractional reserve system this activity has a counterpart of credit operations. This is why we can now give the name 'bank' to the firm which creates monetary units. Its balance sheet is then as follows:

Balance sheet of bank $i$

| Assets | | Liabilities | |
|---|---|---|---|
| units of currency $j$ (reserves) | 50 | equity capital and borrowed funds | 100 |
| domestic claims | 150 | units of currency $i$ | 100 |

Thus, the domestic claims contained in the balance sheet of bank $i$ have as their counterpart equity capital (own funds) and borrowed funds (for a value equal to 100) and monetary claims (for a value equal to 50, since otherwise an amount of currency units equal to 50 is the counterpart of the holding of reserves). It is extremely important to note that there are two very different counterparts of the loans granted by bank $i$, and we will see later that this difference has considerable macroeconomic consequences. Equity capital and borrowed funds are the outcome of voluntary and preliminary savings: economic agents have decided to refrain from consuming a part of their resources in order to save. The corresponding savings allowed them either to buy shares of bank $i$ – that is, property rights which constitute the equity capital of the bank – or to lend to bank $i$ (these are borrowed funds). Now, the loans granted in return for the creation of monetary units have absolutely different natures. They do not correspond to prior and voluntary savings but to simple accounting entries: one is acting as if corresponding savings were to exist, but it is purely fictional. Insofar as the holding of monetary units represents the holding of property rights over real resources, this process is necessarily at the origin of inconsistencies in the economic system. That is what we will see later.

This system nevertheless has a regulatory mechanism. Indeed, let us suppose that the currency-issuing bank $i$ decreases its coefficient of reserves, which means that it increases the amount of currency in relation to the amount of its reserves. All things being equal, the users of currency $i$ will find themselves with an excess of cash balances (assuming a constant amount of real transactions and stability of prices, prices being determined by the outside world since country $i$ is small compared to the rest of the world). They will therefore try to get rid of their excess cash balances by selling them against real goods (or, possibly, financial assets). But to the extent that this is a global phenomenon – which concerns all the inhabitants of the country $i$ – they cannot sell these surplus cash balances in country $i$, but only outside it. Country $i$ therefore records an increase in its sales of currency and an increase in its purchases of real goods (and financial assets). Actually this means that bank $i$ will redeem a portion of the cash balances issued in excess, and in return sell part of its reserves in currency $j$, which will enable the inhabitants of country $i$ to acquire real goods in the rest of the world. The decline in its reserve ratio is a signal for bank $i$ indicating that it has made an excessive monetary expansion. How will it react? It can – which would be wise – go back to a less expansionary monetary policy in order to be closer to its optimal coefficient of reserves. But if, instead of choosing this usual reaction, it persists in its expansionary policy, it takes the risk that too great a decrease of its reserve coefficient would not allow it to honour the demands from its customers for a conversion of currency $i$ into currency $j$. It may therefore lose the trust of its customers and see its profits decline. It may even, at the limit, go bankrupt, insofar as it would be required to sell quickly and at loss much of its assets in order to obtain the amount of currency $j$ which woud be needed to honour its convertibility commitment. The adjustment process which requires the bank $i$ to pursue a monetary policy in harmony with what is happening in the rest of the world is certainly not automatic, but it is not less efficient. As there will be the opportunity to emphasize specifically later, this process works better when the decisions relating to the management of bank $i$ are taken by responsible persons, which implies that they are owners of the bank's capital, because they will wish to avoid bankruptcy or, at least, a sharp deterioration of profits.

### 16.2.3    System 3: A Hierarchical System with External 100 Per Cent Reserves

We now come back to a pattern of organization which we have already met, in which there exists a monetary system of commercial banks which hold deposits – also called reserves – with another bank located above them. We can call this latter bank a 'central bank', although central banks nowadays are playing several roles, while we will focus for the moment on just one of these roles: that which establishes a relationship between money creation in country $i$ and the monetary situation in the rest of the world (country $j$). Under the assumption which we are now considering, commercial banks can create money in relation to their reserves with the central bank, but also in relation to credits granted to economic agents, while the central bank in fact only plays the role of an exchange office (as with the firm of our first system), since it holds 100 per cent external reserves. But inside country $i$ (or the currency area, made up of several countries, in which the currency $i$ is created), there is a process of money multiplier, as previously studied in Chapter 11. It can be given in the following form, already met in Chapter 11:

$$M = B / \{c + r (1 - c)\} \tag{11.7}$$

or, more simply:

$$M = kB$$

where $M$ is the quantity of money (total amount of the monetary liabilities of banks) and B the monetary base (the value of the central bank's balance sheet).

The balance sheets of banks have the following characteristics:

Balance sheets of commercial banks producing currency $i$

| Assets | | Liabilities | |
|---|---|---|---|
| reserves with the central bank | 50 | equity capital and borrowed funds | 100 |
| domestic claims | 150 | units of currency $i$ | 100 |

Balance sheet of the central bank (exchange office)

| Assets | Liabilities |
|---|---|
| external reserves in   50 | reserves of commercial banks  50 |
| currency $j$ | in currency $i$ |

Thus, commercial banks hold reserves with the central bank equal to the external reserves in currency $j$ of the latter. As in any monetary system, the reserve ratio – in this case that which exists between the monetary liabilities of banks and their reserves with the central bank – plays a central role in the working of the monetary system. As seen previously, this reserve coefficient of commercial banks may be a desired or required coefficient.

Let us now assume that, for some reason, the exports of the inhabitants of country $i$ increase, *ceteris paribus*. They will obtain units of currency $j$ which they will exchange against units of currency $i$ at their commercial banks. In turn, the banks will exchange with the central bank the units of currency $j$ which they have acquired against reserves in currency $i$. The increase in their reserves will allow them to increase the amount of currency $i$, while maintaining their reserve coefficients at the desired (or required) levels.

Suppose now that commercial banks decide to reduce their reserve coefficients, thus making a monetary expansion. All things remaining equal – in particular the world prices of goods and the level of transactions in real terms – there is an excess of nominal balances in country $i$. This will cause, as in the previous situation, sales of currency abroad against imports of goods and financial assets. Importers buy units of currency $j$ against units of currency $i$ from commercial banks which, in turn, will obtain the necessary units of currency $j$ from the central bank. Thus the central bank loses external reserves, and the reserves of the commercial banks decrease. The central bank being under the present assumption a purely passive exchange office (it merely buys and sells without limits one currency against the other at the fixed price which has been promised), it has no way to react to such a situation.[4] The monetary policy of the central bank is non-existent. Only commercial banks can react, if they feel that they have decided an excessive monetary expansion which might put them in a difficult situation.

---

[4] Except, of course, if it has the right to impose a compulsory reserve coefficient upon commercial banks.

### 16.2.4    System 4: A Hierarchical System with Fractional Reserves

In this case we again find the features of the monetary systems which exist nowadays. There is a dual system of fractional reserves since commercial banks have a reserve coefficient lower than 100 per cent in terms of reserves with the central bank (hence the money multiplier mechanism), and the central bank has a reserve coefficient lower than 100 per cent in terms of reserves in the foreign currency $j$. This translates as follows in their balance sheets:[5]

Balance sheet of the central bank

| Assets | | Liabilities | |
|---|---|---|---|
| external reserves in currency $j$ | 50 | reserves of commercial banks | 100 |
| domestic claims | 50 | | |

Balance sheets of the commercial banks producing currency $i$

| Assets | | Liabilities | |
|---|---|---|---|
| reserves with the central bank | 100 | equity capital and borrowed funds | 100 |
| domestic claims | 200 | units of currency $i$ | 200 |

In this case the central bank can undertake an active monetary policy by varying its coefficient of external reserves, that is, by purchasing more or less domestic claims (against reserves of commercial banks) for a given level of external reserves. Let us then assume that the central bank increases its assets in domestic claims and correspondingly increases the reserves of commercial banks. They will have the ability to create new money balances, maintaining the same reserve coefficient. Excess money balances – all things being equal – will, as previously, translate into purchases of goods and financial assets abroad, and therefore into a decrease of the foreign reserves of the central bank. This decline is a signal that it undertook a too-expansionary monetary policy. As we have seen previously, it can react in various ways:

● It can go back to a less expansionary monetary policy, which is the normal adjustment process in any system of fixed exchange rates.

---

[5]  For the sake of simplicity no account is taken here of the fact that the central bank more often produces banknotes which constitute a part of the quantity of money.

- It may persist in its wrong policy, with the risk of not being able to fulfil its convertibility guarantee at a fixed price between the currency *i* and the currency *j*.
- It can, under some institutional assumptions which will be considered later, proceed to what is called a devaluation, that is, a change in the price at which it exchanges currency *i* against currency *j*.[6]

We can write the equations of this system in the following way:

$$M = kB = k\,(R_{ext} + Cr_{int}) \qquad (16.1)$$

where $M$ is the money supply, $B$ the monetary base, $k$ the money multiplier, $R_{ext}$ the external reserves of the central bank and $Cr_{int}$ the amount of internal claims held by the central bank.

Given that there is a reserve coefficient between the external reserves of the central bank and the amount of its assets, we can represent this relationship in the following way, which means that the domestic claims in its balance sheet are proportional to its external reserves:

$$Cr_{int} = sR_{ext} \qquad (16.2)$$

from which we can obtain the following equation:

$$M = k\,(1 + s)\,R_{ext} \qquad (16.3)$$

which indicates that the money supply is a multiple of the foreign reserves of the central bank. There is indeed a double multiplier process: between the external reserves and the overall balance sheet of the central bank, and between the reserves of the commercial banks and the money supply. Of course, the coefficients $k$ and $s$ can vary, especially in the short term, but when operating in a long-term perspective – as I generally do in this book, to focus on the logics of the working of monetary systems – it is legitimate to assume constant coefficients.

Finally, it should be noted that, in the three systems in which the central bank has only the role of exchange office, it is probably not remunerated for the exchange services which it provides. In the fourth system it gets a return, since it receives interest on its domestic claims, allowing it to offset the possible free character of its exchange services.

---

[6] The possible outcome of such an expansionary monetary policy is studied in Chapter 19.

# 17. International monetary equilibrium under fixed exchange rates

So far, the point of view of a country assumed to be small in relation to the rest of the world has been considered, and the processes by which this country adjusts to the external situation. We will now retain the simplifying assumption of a world composed of two countries (now called country A and country B) linked by a system of fixed exchange rates, but will consider this set of countries and study how the different variables adjust simultaneously in both countries. This is all the more justified in that a fixed exchange rate regime implies that all monetary units are perfectly substitutable, irrespective of the organization issuing them (for instance, a bank located in country A or a bank located in country B) or whatever their names (for instance Ecu for the currency issued in country A and thaler for the currency issued in country B). Of course, the lessons which will be drawn from this analysis can easily be transposed to other situations, for example in studying the working of a currency area comprising several countries, the currencies of which are linked by fixed exchange rates, but being in a situation of flexible exchange rates with the rest of the world.

The instruments used for this analysis are inspired by those which have been devised by Robert Mundell (1971) because they seem to me to be both clear and consistent with the principles of monetary theory which I have previously developed. But before developing the analysis of the adjustment processes within the fixed exchange area (or the world), I will explain the analytical instruments to be used and their justifications, by taking temporarily the case of a single country which is assumed to be isolated from the rest of the world (either because there are no flows of goods and capital between this country and the rest of the world or, more probably, because this country is under a system of flexible exchange rates with the rest of the world, allowing it to have an independent monetary policy).

## 17.1 INSTRUMENTS OF ANALYSIS IN A CLOSED ECONOMY

These instruments are represented in Figure 17.1 where on the horizontal axis is the level of real cash balances per unit of product (which is written $m/y$, where $m$ is the amount of real cash balances in the country under review and $y$ is the real national income, which is actually an approximation of the amount of real transactions). On the vertical axis are different rates (the real interest rate, the nominal interest rate, the inflation rate and the real growth rate). The $rr$ and $ii$ curves represent, respectively, the equilibrium between supply and demand in the commodity market and in the money market.[1]

The $rr$ curve represents all combinations of values of the variables $m/y$ (real cash balances per unit of product) and $r$ (real interest rate) such that there is equality between savings and investment. To determine the form of this curve, let us assume that one initially lies in point $A$ and there is equilibrium between savings and investment at this point. If the unit real cash balance $(m/y)$ increases,[2] this causes a decrease in savings because there is a substitution effect between the real cash balances held and other forms of savings: holding a greater amount of real cash balances allows one to better address the risks of life, which is one of the roles of savings. For equilibrium to be be maintained on the commodity market (equality between savings and investment), it requires an increase in the real interest rate, which reduces investment and which also increases savings. If the real cash balances shift from point $A$ to point $B$, the increase in the real interest rate leads to point $C$, located on the $rr$ curve. Thus, to any level of the $m/y$ variable can be associated a value of the real interest rate such as there is equilibrium between savings and investment. The following remark may also be added: an increase in real cash balances, facilitating transactions and risk-taking, increases the marginal productivity of capital. In other words, one could consider that real cash balances are a factor of production (the economy is the more efficient,

---

[1]   These curves may be considered to replace the famous *IS* and *LM* curves of the macro-economics textbooks which correspond to very specific assumptions, which are inspired by the Keynesian theory. In addition, to simplify the presentation, straight lines are represented here, but these curves would most likely have a different form in reality, taking into account the specificities of the human behaviours that determine them. But, for the reasoning that follows, it is not necessary to know the exact shape of these curves, but only their ascending or descending form.

[2]   It is very likely that this increase in the unit real cash balances is the result of a decline in inflationary expectations, which encourages individuals to hold more money because it better maintains its purchasing power. Illustrations of this process will be provided later.

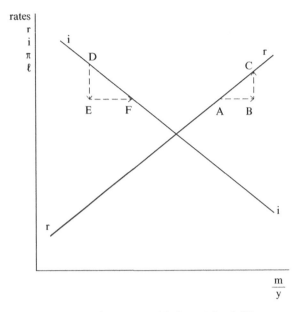

*Figure 17.1    Drawing ii and rr curves (Robert Mundell)*

the more real cash balances individuals hold) and we do know, according to economic theory, that the increase in the quantity of a factor of
production increases the marginal productivity of other factors of production. It is therefore logical to associate an increase of unit real cash
balances to an increase in the real interest rate due to the increase in the
return of capital.

Thus, it can be said that an increase in the real interest rate causes an
excess of savings over investment, which must be compensated by an
increase of *m/y* which reduces savings and increases investment (the efficiency of which is thereby increased). Such is the rationale for the upward
characteristic of the *rr* curve in the space (*m/y*, *r*).

As regards the *ii* curve, it represents the equilibrium in the currency
market (against financial assets). As we have seen in Chapter 4, the interest
rate represents the opportunity cost of the holding of money: the demand
for money is a decreasing function of the interest rate (because of the substitution effect between financial claims and money). Let us assume that
one is initially in point *D* at which there is equality between the supply
and the demand for money (in real terms as well as in nominal terms). If
the interest rate decreases (there is a shift from *D* to *E*), the demand for
money increases. How will this demand be met? As we know, it is not
necessary, in order to meet an additional demand for money, to change

the (nominal) quantity of money: the real cash balance effect is the way by which adjustments take place. Thus, the increase in the demand for cash balances, all things being equal (in particular, the prices of goods and the quantity of money), translates into an excess demand of money against other goods, so that there is an increase in the price of money in terms of goods, that is, a decrease in the prices of goods in terms of money (so-called deflation). For a given nominal quantity of money, there is an increase in the level of real cash balances (there is a shift from $E$ to $F$). It can be said that the real cash balance effect makes it possible to always be on the equilibrium curve of the money market *ii* (recognizing, however, that this effect may not be instantaneous).

The determination of the *rr* and *ii* curves having thus been made, they can be used to analyse different phenomena. It will be assumed, for simplicity, that inflation expectations are correct, which allows us to assume, in a regime with a constant inflation rate, that the expected inflation rate is equal to the observed rate. Of course, this assumption is not consistent with what is actually happening in reality, but it does not alter the substance of the reasoning insofar as we are only looking at the consistency of the long-term developments in monetary systems.

To analyse the relationship between monetary and real variables, two equations already met in Chapter 4 will be used, namely:

$$\mu = \pi + \rho \tag{4.15}$$

that is, the rate of monetary growth ($\mu$) is equal to the sum of the inflation rate ($\pi$) and the real growth rate ($\rho$):

$$i = r + \pi \tag{4.10}$$

that is, the nominal interest rate ($i$) is equal to the sum of the real interest rate ($r$) and the inflation rate ($\pi$). Two different situations can now be considered, as follows.

### 17.1.1 First Situation: A Zero Real Growth Rate and a Positive Monetary Growth Rate

Thus we have $\rho = 0$ and $\mu > 0$ and it follows that the inflation rate is equal to the rate of monetary growth from equation (4.15) above. This situation is represented in Figure 17.2. In the absence of money creation, the equilibrium would be at $P_0$ which is the point of intersection between the *rr* and *ii* curves. In fact the rate of inflation is zero if there is no monetary growth and no real growth, according to equation (4.15). At this point the

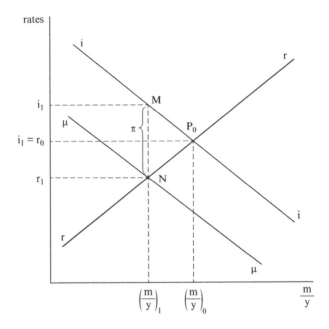

*Figure 17.2    Money creation and inflation*

nominal interest rate would be equal to the real interest rate, in accordance with equation (4.10).

But let assume now that monetary growth is positive ($\mu > 0$). In the absence of real growth, the inflation rate is equal to the rate of monetary growth. As a result, the nominal interest rate is higher than the real rate of interest by the amount of the rate of inflation. This can be represented in Figure 17.2. The *ii* curve reflects the fact that the demand for real balances is a function of the nominal interest rate (which represents the opportunity cost of the holding of currency). From this *ii* curve can be represented a $\mu\mu$ curve, such that all its points are located at a vertical distance from the *ii* curve equal to the rate of monetary growth. In the present example, the real growth rate being zero, the gap between the two curves also represents the inflation rate which is equal, in this case, to the rate of monetary growth. Equilibrium is then performed at points *M* and *N*. Point *N* – which is at the intersection of the curves *rr* and $\mu\mu$ – corresponds to a real interest rate $r_1$. Point *M*, located above, corresponds to the nominal interest rate $i_1$. It is interesting to note that the consequences of money creation at a rate higher than the real growth rate are not only to produce inflation, but also to reduce the real interest rate (and therefore the rate of return on capital) because this reduces the demand for real cash balances. Traditionally it is assumed (usually in an implicit manner) that the real interest rate is constant regardless of the rate of inflation. The approach of Robert Mundell rightly incorporates a real effect of monetary expansion: the decline in the real interest rate. There is also in Figure 17.2 an illustration of the statement – presented previously – according to which the creation of nominal cash balances decreases the amount of real balances held. Later, some other very significant effects of monetary expansion will be seen, namely distortions in the productive structures and price structures (Chapter 22).

### 17.1.2   Second Situation: A Positive Real Growth Rate and a Zero Monetary Growth Rate

This situation is shown in Figure 17.3. A $\rho\rho$ curve is derived from the $rr$ curve as a result of a vertical gap from curve $rr$ equal to the real growth rate $\rho$. Equilibrium is achieved at the intersection of this curve with the $ii$ curve, namely point $S$. In this case, as monetary growth is zero, there is a negative inflation rate – that is, a rate of deflation – equal to the rate of real growth: $\pi = -\rho$. The nominal interest rate $i$ is therefore lower than the real interest rate, the difference between the two being equal to the rate of deflation. One can see in Figure 17.3 that the nominal interest rate is equal

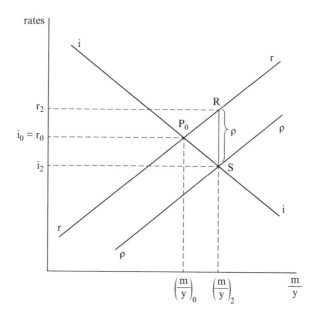

*Figure 17.3    Real growth and deflation*

to $i_2$ and the real interest rate is equal to $r_2$. It is also interesting to note that, in this case, individuals hold a level of unit real cash balances $(m/y)_2$ higher than is the case in the absence of deflation (the level of unit cash balances is, for instance, equal to $(m/y)_0$ when there is neither inflation nor deflation). In fact, deflation increases the purchasing power of money cash balances from one period to the next, which induces individuals to hold more real cash balances, as we have seen previously.

### 17.1.3    Third Situation: Real Growth and Positive Monetary Growth

This situation is shown in Figure 17.4, in which it has been assumed that the monetary growth rate is higher than the real growth rate. As the monetary growth rate is equal to the sum of the real growth rate and the inflation rate (equation 4.15), there is a positive inflation rate. Therefore equilibrium prevails at points $T$, $U$ and $V$. The monetary growth rate is equal to the difference between the curves $ii$ and $\mu\mu$, that is, $VT$, the real growth rate is equal to $UV$ (gap between the curves $rr$ and $\rho\rho$) and the inflation rate is equal to $TU$ (difference between the real interest rate and the nominal interest rate). Given that the rate of inflation is positive, the nominal interest rate is greater than the real interest rate and the level of unit cash balances is lower than it would be in the absence of inflation.

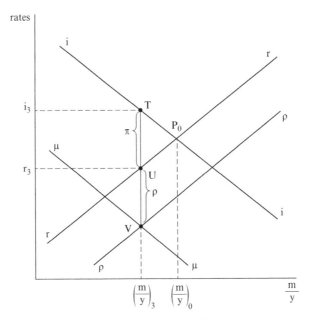

*Figure 17.4    Monetary growth and real growth*

We thus now have the instruments which will enable us to study how the key variables fit together internationally; that is, we will abandon the assumption that the country under review is in the situation of a closed economy. As previously, to simplify the presentation, a world (or a monetary area) consisting of two countries, A and B, will be assumed.

## 17.2 INTERNATIONAL EQUILIBRIUM

To study the relationships between the various variables of countries A and B, the analytical instruments just seen will be used, considering several different assumptions in turn.

### 17.2.1 First Assumption: Real Growth in One Country

Let us suppose, first, that there is positive real growth in country B, zero real growth in country A, and no monetary growth either in country A or country B. This assumption is shown in Figure 17.5, where data relating to country A are on the right and those of country B on the left. As there is real growth in country B, a curve $\rho_b\rho_b$ can be drawn. If country B was in isolation, the equilibrium would be at point $S$, as shown in Figure 17.3. What happens if country B is under fixed exchange rates with country A? There is deflation, since there is a positive real growth in country B, but no money creation, either in country B or in country A. The drop in prices of

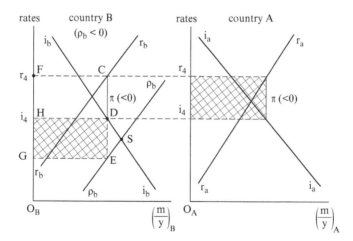

*Figure 17.5    Real growth in country B, deflation and balance of payments*

goods in country B is transmitted to country A, given that international exchanges exist. Therefore this increases the real value of the cash balances held by the residents of country A, and these inhabitants have excess cash balances which they will try to redeem against goods. The balance of payments of the country is thus characterized by a trade deficit and exports of money (if we neglect, to simplify, the possibility of selling the excess cash balances against financial assets).

Obviously, there is an inverse balance of payments for country B, since its residents are importing the currency exported by the residents of country A. For the world as a whole, there is deflation because the real growth in the world is positive and there is no monetary growth. This is reflected in the fact that the nominal interest rate is lower than the real interest rate, the difference between the two corresponding to the rate of deflation. In Figure 17.5 the rate of deflation is represented by the *CD* segment, and the *DE* segment represents the rate at which country B increases its cash balances (from country A). In other words, this segment is the representation of the expression $\rho = \mu - \pi$ (derived from equation 4.15). The hatched rectangle *DEGH* represents the value (in real terms) of the imports of money (the number of units of real cash balances multiplied by the rate of accumulation of currency from country A). The area of this rectangle is obviously equal to that of the hatched rectangle of country A (on the right side of the figure) which represents the exports of real cash balances by country A. We see therefore that the rate of deflation in country B is less important than it would be in isolation, and that money moves from the country where it is relatively abundant to the country where it is less abundant (taking into account monetary and real growth rates). Furthermore the nominal and real interest rates are the same in both countries. It can also be stressed that the increase in the demand for money due to the real growth in country B is met on the one hand by imports of money from country A (hatched rectangle of country B) and, on the other hand, by the fall in prices (deflation) which increases the real value of cash balances (which corresponds to the rectangle *CDHF*).

### 17.2.2  Second Assumption: Money Growth in a Country

Let us now assume that there is positive monetary growth in country A, no monetary growth in country B, and no real growth in country A and country B. For the world as a whole, consisting of these two countries, there is positive monetary growth and no real growth, so that there is a positive inflation rate and the nominal interest rate is higher than the real interest rate. This assumption is shown in Figure 17.6. The rate of inflation – which is the same in both countries – is lower than the rate of

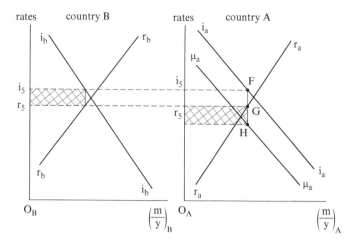

*Figure 17.6   Monetary growth in country A, inflation and balance of payments*

monetary growth of country A. In fact, for these new prices resulting from the confrontation between the two countries' money supply and their real transactions, the inhabitants of country A have excess cash balances and the inhabitants of country B a lack of cash balances. Part of the money produced in country A is therefore exported to country B, at a rate represented by the segment *GH*. The hatched rectangle of country A is the amount of its exports of money and it is equal to the hatched rectangle of country B which imports inflation from country A and part of its money supply. The segment *FG* represents the inflation rate (equal to the difference between the nominal interest rate and the real interest rate), *FH* is, by construction, the rate of monetary expansion, and *GH* is the rate at which country A exports its currency. As can be seen, country A gains an advantage from its status as an issuer of money. In fact, the creation of money costs almost nothing, because it is simply obtained by the writing of accounts. But, as a counterpart for the money cash balances thus produced, the inhabitants of country A – or, at least, the producers of money – receive real goods, which correspond to a trade deficit (they receive more goods that they export). There is therefore a risk in a regime of fixed exchange rates in that producers of money in each country may be tempted to take advantage of this easy way to gain, and there may therefore be an escalation of money creation, which is necessarily harmful.

### 17.2.3    Third Assumption: Real Growth and Monetary Growth

We can now look at a slightly more complex case, for example one in which there is real growth in both countries and monetary growth in country A only. This case is shown in Figure 17.7. Under fixed exchange rates, everything works as if there was a single monetary system and a single country; which implies, for instance, that the rate of inflation for the whole world (or the area of fixed exchange rates) is determined by the difference between the rate of monetary growth throughout the world and the rate of real growth in the whole world. In the case under consideration now, we will assume that the monetary growth, although it has its origin only in country A, is higher than the real growth of both countries, so that there is positive inflation. As this case combines situations which have been examined above, it is not necessary to explain Figure 17.7 in detail. We see that, in country A, the rate of monetary growth (*KN*) is equal to the sum of the rate of inflation (*KL*), the rate of real growth (*LM*) and the rate at which country A sells currency to country B (*MN*). The exports of money by country A are represented by the hatched rectangle, which is equal to the sum of the two hatched rectangles of country B. In fact, the inhabitants of country B need additional cash balances, firstly because there is inflation (difference between the nominal interest rate and the real interest rate), and secondly because there is real growth. As in the previous case, the balance of payments of country A records a trade deficit (and/or

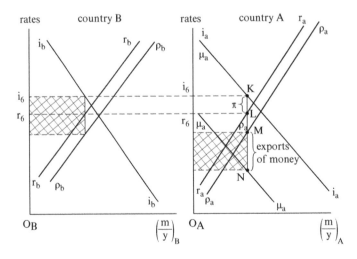

*Figure 17.7    Real growth in country A and country B, monetary growth in country A, inflation and balance of payments*

a deficit in the capital balance) as a counterpart of the 'monetary account' surplus. We thus see that the structure of the balance of payments of a country under fixed exchange rates is determined by the real growth rates and the money growth rates of the different countries which are members of the area of fixed exchange rates.

In the three cases which we have seen, the structure of monetary systems has not been specified and, in particular, it has not been made clear, for instance, whether these systems are hierarchical or not. The monetary units are in any case issued by separate currency producers, but the existence of fixed exchange rates implies that they are perfectly substitutable with one other, even if, for instance, they have different names (Ecu in country A and thaler in country B). As we know, exchange rates are fixed, although the monetary units are produced by separate firms, because somewhere in the world, one or more organizations give credible convertibility guarantees at fixed price. The possible consequences of the location of these organizations will be considered later, since, as we have just seen, there is an incentive to produce currency. Note, for the time being, that if it is assumed that there is a public central bank in country A and that it determines its monetary policy in a discretionary way, it may be justified to say that country B pays an inflation tax to country A (in the second and third assumptions) in the form of a trade surplus: because they suffer from the inflation created by the central bank of country A, the inhabitants of country B are obliged to buy cash balances from country A. This is a very special case in which a public authority can levy a tax on 'taxpayers' who do not live in the country where this authority has, in principle, decision-making powers. As will be seen later, the determination of organizations which give the convertibility guarantee at fixed rate is essential for this process to be possible.[3] But as we have already seen, if the convertibility guarantee is given by the central bank of country A, its excess of money creation translates into losses of reserves made up of units of the currency of country B, which does not allow it to continue this expansionary monetary policy indefinitely. But other institutional assumptions are possible. Furthermore, freely flexible exchange would in any case release the inhabitants of country B from the payment of this inflation tax.

We have not, of course, examined all possible assumptions. But, whatever the case under study, we always find the same principle: under fixed exchange rates money flows from the country or area where it is relatively abundant (compared to real transactions), to the country or the area

---

[3]   I will later address the problem of the determination of the organizations which give convertibility guarantees at a fixed price (see, in particular, Chapter 21).

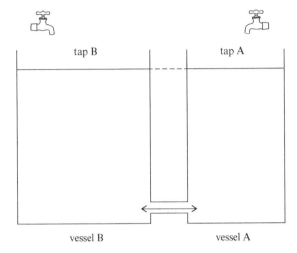

*Figure 17.8   Communicating vessels*

where it is relatively scarce. The scarcity and relative abundance are obviously determined by a comparison between real and monetary growth rates. A pictorial representation of these phenomena can be given by comparing the well-known problem of communicating vessels. Figure 17.8 represents two vessels, A and B (obviously, countries A and B). The size of these vessels is symbolic of the real income of each country. There is a hose of communication at the bottom of the two vessels and they are full of 'liquidity' (quantity of money). As is well known, the level of liquidity is the same in the two vessels, regardless of their relative size. Now, for a given volume of liquidity, if there is expansion of the vessel A, the liquidity moves from vessel B to vessel A until the level of liquidity (that is, the level of prices) is the same in the two vessels. On the other hand, if the dimension of the two vessels is constant and one opens a tap over one of them, for example tap A, the volume of liquidity increases and will be divided between the two vessels until the level is the same in both. Depending on whether the additional liquidity (money creation) takes place in A or B, the flows of liquidity go in one direction or the other (the trade balance is in deficit or surplus).

In other words, the inflation rate depends on the gap between the world real growth rate and the world monetary growth rate, and it is the same in both countries (if the same price index is used, and if there are no changes in the relative prices between tradable and non-tradable goods). It does not matter, from this point of view, that the monetary growth or the real growth take place in one country or the other. Under fixed exchange rate regimes there is an undifferentiated quantity of money for the whole area of fixed exchange rates, regardless of precisely who the issuers of monetary units are, and the names given to these units. But this quantity of money is distributed according to needs. As greater or lesser rates of monetary growth and real growth take place in different countries, so, as a consequence, flows of goods and money (possibly also of financial assets) take place in one direction or the other, which means that the balances of payments is affected by these different rates in different countries. But, of course, possible changes in the balance of payments are transitory if the differences in growth rates are transitory.

# 18. The monetary approach to exchange rate variations

Let us now assume that there is a regime of flexible exchange rates between country A and country B, which means that the exchange rate is determined on the foreign exchange market. Given that the exchange rate is the relative price between two currencies, its evolution is obviously determined by the relative changes in the supply and demand for one of the currencies against the other. We previously studied the determinants of the supply and the demand for money, which allows us to easily and quickly analyse changes in the exchange rate.

In order to simplify the presentation let us first assume that there is a perfect equalization of prices internationally, that is, all goods are perfectly mobile and there are no transaction and transportation costs. It is assumed also that price indices have exactly the same composition in both countries.

If we define the exchange rate $E$ as the number of units of the currency of country A obtained against one unit of the currency of country B, we can write:

$$P_a = EP_b \qquad (18.1)$$

which implies that the exchange rate is equal to the ratio of the two price indices:

$$E = \frac{P_a}{P_b} \qquad (18.2)$$

We know furthermore (according to Chapters 4 and 15) that for each country the equality between supply and demand for money can be given in the following form:

$$M = PL\,(i, y) \qquad (18.3)$$

where $M$ is the money supply (the existing quantity of money), $P$ the price index, $L$ the demand for real cash balances, which is a function of the nominal interest rate, $i$, and of the real income, $y$. There is equality between the nominal quantity of money supplied and the nominal quantity demanded $(PL)$. It is not necessary to explain here the explanatory factors of the money supply; it can be assumed to be constant without any loss of useful information.

Equation (18.3) can obviously be written in the form $P = M/L$, which allows equation (18.2) to be rewritten in the following form:

$$E = \frac{M_a}{M_b} \cdot \frac{L_b}{L_a} \tag{18.4}$$

from which can be drawn the following equation which gives the relationship between the different rates of change of the considered variables:

$$dE = \frac{(dM_a}{M_a} - \frac{dM_b)}{M_b} + \frac{(dL_b}{L_b} - \frac{dL_a)}{L_a} \tag{18.5}$$

This equation expresses the fact that variation in the exchange rate is determined by variations in the supply and demand of both currencies. Thus $E$ increases – which means that the currency of country A depreciates because more units of the currency of country A are required to obtain one unit of the currency of country B – if the money supply increases in country A (relative abundance of currency A); $E$ decreases (appreciation of currency A, that is, depreciation of currency B) if the money supply of country B increases.

Which are the effects of changes in the demand for money in one or the other country? As we know, the demand for money is a decreasing function of the nominal interest rate and an increasing function of real income. Therefore, if the nominal interest rate increases, the demand for currency A decreases and the exchange rate increases (the decrease in the demand for money creates a relative abundance of currency A – all things being equal – and therefore the currency depreciates). If the real income increases in country A, the demand for money increases and $E$ decreases, that is, there is an appreciation of the exchange rate (the demand for money increases compared to the money supply, which is constant).

From this point of view, what is happening in flexible exchange rates and in fixed exchange rates can be compared. If, for example, the demand for money increases as a result of an increase in real income, the exchange rate appreciates in a flexible exchange rate regime; the prices of goods fall in terms of currency A (the quantity of money being constant), and they remain constant in country B where no variable has changed. Thus the additional demand for cash balances is satisfied by the real cash balance effect. In a fixed exchange rate regime the increase in real income also causes an increase in the demand for real cash balances and this additional demand is satisfied not only by the real cash balance effect – which occurs across both countries – but also by flows of currency from the other country (which thus creates a change in the structure of the balance of payments).

Of course, the reality does not fit perfectly to what is described above, in particular because we assumed identical price indices in both countries and a perfect and immediate international contagion of price changes. Therefore, the results above must not be interpreted as perfect representations of reality, but as a more or less qualitative information about the direction of the variations of the variables. Thus, we know that an increase in real income in a country leads to an appreciation of its currency, but we cannot specify the rate of change in a perfectly accurate way.

Changes in price structures resulting from an increase in the quantity of money will subsequently be considered (Chapter 22), in particular as regards the relative prices between capital goods and consumer goods. But, for the moment, we will only consider changes in relative prices which can exist between two classes of goods, tradable and non-tradable goods, a distinction which has already been made in Chapter 13.

Let us now consider that the exchange rate is not equal to the ratio of the indices of overall prices in both countries (which was the case in equation 18.2), but only to the ratio of the price indices of tradable goods:

$$E = \frac{P_{Ta}}{P_{Tb}} \tag{18.6}$$

where $P_T$ is the price index of tradable goods

We can write in addition that the general price index $P$ is itself a composite index which includes two components, the price index of tradable goods ($P_T$) and the price index of non-tradable goods ($P_N$), which can be written:

$$P = \alpha P_T + (1 - \alpha)P_N \tag{18.7}$$

If we write $\beta$ as the ratio $P_N/P_T$, we can write the equation above in the following form:

$$P = \{\alpha + (1 - \alpha)\beta\} \, P_T \tag{18.8}$$

or

$$P = \gamma \, P_T \text{ or } P_T = P/\gamma \qquad (18.9)$$

where: $\gamma = \alpha + (1 - \alpha)\beta$

By replacing $P_T$ by its value $P/\gamma$ in equation (18.6), we get:

$$E = \frac{Pa}{Pb} \cdot \frac{\gamma_b}{\gamma a} \qquad (18.10)$$

which leads to rewriting equation (18.5) in the following form, by proceeding as before:

$$\frac{dE}{E} = \left(\frac{dM_a}{M_a} - \frac{dM_b}{M_b}\right) + \left(\frac{dL_b}{L_b} - \frac{dL_a}{L_a}\right) + \left(\frac{d\gamma_b}{\gamma_b} - \frac{d\gamma_a}{\gamma a}\right) \qquad (18.11)$$

Therefore, the variations of the exchange rate are determined not only by the variations in the supply and demand for money, but also by the changes in the relative prices between tradable and non-tradable goods (influence of the coefficient $\beta$ above), or by the changes in the structure of the index of prices between tradable and non-tradable goods. Moreover, short-term exchange rates are also influenced by changes in interest rates and the capital flows which result.

The gap which exists between the observed exchange rate and the exchange rate which would correspond to the purchasing power parity, that is, which would exist if the simplified assumptions we made at the beginning of this chapter were actually verified, is sometimes called the 'change in the real exchange rate'. Of course, it is virtually impossible to measure precisely – let alone to predict – the differences in question. This is why no one should claim to know the equilibrium exchange rate and therefore claim that an observed exchange rate is overvalued or undervalued, so that it would possibly be necessary to 'correct' it.

But, to repeat, what is of interest in the study of the working of monetary systems is not their day-to-day changes, but their internal consistency and their long-term working. From this point of view, the simplifying assumptions which have been made are justified. What matters is essentially knowledge of a qualitative nature which focuses, for instance, on the (increasing or decreasing) direction of the variations of the variables and the interrelations which necessarily exist between them.

# 19. The devaluation

A question of vocabulary must first be raised. We have just seen how an international monetary equilibrium occurs when there is a flexible exchange rate system, that is, a regime in which the exchange rate – the relative price of two currencies – is determined freely on the foreign exchange market on the basis of the evolution of supply and demand. One speaks in this case of the appreciation or depreciation of a currency. But the devaluation – or the revaluation – of a currency refers to a totally different situation, in which there are in principle fixed exchange rates between two (or more) currencies and in which, despite this, the monetary authorities decide in a discretionary way to change the exchange rate they were supposed to maintain. We know that fixed exchange rates exist between two different currencies (that is, currencies issued by different monetary systems) only because there is a convertibility guarantee at fixed price given for the exchange of one currency against the other. In hierarchical and national systems nowadays this guarantee is given by the central bank which promises to exchange without limits its own currency against another currency. A devaluation may therefore be seen as the breach of an earlier commitment. As such, it has an ambiguous character since it consists in modifying a price which the central bank had promised to keep constant. And one can even say that it is close to a despoilment, since the organization which had promised to exchange its own currency (Ecu for instance) against another one (thaler) at a fixed price (for instance, 1 Ecu = 1 thaler) unilaterally decides to deliver a smaller quantity of foreign currency against its own currency (for instance, 0.5 thaler against 1 Ecu) to those who ask the exchange in question.[1]

These remarks being made, let us analyse the effects of a devaluation. There is, from this point of view, a traditional approach, usually called 'elasticity approach'. It consists in considering that the main consequence of a devaluation is essentially to increase the prices of imports (in terms of the national currency of the devaluing country) and to reduce the price

---

[1]  A very long time ago the convertibility guarantee at a fixed price was printed on the banknotes, which made explicit the existence of a contract between the issuer of money and money-holders.

of exports (in terms of foreign currencies). One therefore infers that the normal effect of a devaluation is to cause a positive change in the trade balance, because imports are discouraged and exports encouraged. For the proponents of a Keynesian approach to macroeconomics, this means therefore that there is an increase in aggregate demand, which is supposed to stimulate economic activity.[2] However, fundamental criticisms can be applied to this approach, which justify not presenting it in detail here. It is based on the idea that a devaluation leads to a change in the relative prices between imports and exports. Even if this can happen in the very short term, this variation may not be sustainable, as the prices of tradable goods – whether they are imported or exported – are determined in external markets, and the devaluation of the currency of a country which is of small economic size in relation to the rest of its area of fixed exchange rates cannot cause a lasting change in relative prices. On the other hand, we know (from Part II of this book) that the trade balance cannot be determined regardless of the desired balances in the other items of the balance of payments, that is, 'capital movements' and 'monetary flows'. Finally, it can be stressed that it is illusory to think that an increase in aggregate demand – if ever a devaluation could cause this, which is more than debatable – could stimulate growth and employment. In fact, the study of the actual effects of a devaluation – to which we shall now proceed – is the best possible criticism of the elasticity approach.

If we must reject the idea that a devaluation can permanently alter relative prices between imports and exports, we can, however, consider as significant another variation of relative prices due to a devaluation: that which can exist between tradable and non-tradable goods. In fact, the process of international contagion of prices exists necessarily for tradable goods, but not for non-tradable goods which are not subject to competition from foreign goods. Thanks to the devaluation, the prices of tradable goods (imports or exports) increase 'mechanically' in terms of the currency of the country which devalues, which is not the case for non-tradable goods. But even from this point of view it is not at all certain that the variation in relative prices between tradables and non-tradables is lasting. In fact, the demand expressed by the inhabitants of the country which has devalued will partly shift away from tradables to non-tradables, the prices

---

[2] Detailed analysis of this approach can be found in any textbook on international economics. It shows, for instance, that according to the respective values of supply and demand elasticities in the country and outside, there is a 'normal effect', that is, an 'improvement' of the trade balance, or a perverse effect, namely a 'deterioration' of this balance. Analysis of the so-called absorption approach can also be found. I do not consider it necessary to review these analyses in detail, because I believe that they are questionable, for reasons that I will specify.

of which have temporarily increased less. Meanwhile, some factors of production will move from the sectors of non-tradable goods to the sectors of tradable goods. Thus, little by little, the prices of non-tradable goods will increase until the original relative prices are restored (all things being equal). This is why it is justified to introduce temporary changes in relative prices between tradables and non-tradables in the analysis which follows, and in which various assumptions will be considered successively.

## 19.1    INITIAL MONETARY EQUILIBRIUM

We will assume at the outset that there is monetary equilibrium, that is, that all individuals in country A – which we are studying – and in the rest of the world, have exactly the amount of nominal and real cash balances they desire (taking into account the existing values of the variables which determine the demand for money, in particular real income, the level of prices and inflationary expectations). Furthermore we will assume at the outset that there are no non-tradable goods, and we will reintroduce them later on in the analysis.

### 19.1.1    Scenario 1: Absence of Non-Tradable Goods

A devaluation implies an increase of the prices of all goods in terms of currency A. To maintain the amount of real cash balances which they desire, the inhabitants of the country should therefore increase their nominal cash balances. It may be the case, however, that their demand for real cash balances decreases if individuals, anticipating the inflation caused by the devaluation, consider that the currency of country A is of lower quality and therefore they wish to hold a smaller amount of real cash balances. In this case, the demand for nominal cash balances does not increase in proportion to the rise in prices. Whatever the case, how can the need for nominal cash balances be met?

First of all, it can be supposed that the monetary authorities will increase the quantity of money to exactly the desired amount. This obviously implies that the monetary system increases the distribution of credits of monetary origin for an equivalent amount. This translates into an increase in the profits made by the banks (the commercial banks and the central bank), since money does not cost anything to produce, but banks receive interest on the credits they have thus granted. But this process probably also causes distortions in the productive structures and price structures, as will be seen later (Chapter 22). It can also be supposed that the banking system – in particular, the central bank – for this purpose buys a certain amount of treasury bills. The devaluation coupled with monetary creation therefore facilitates the financing of a state which has got into debt. In addition, the concomitant increase in prices reduces the real value of the public debt. But it must be understood that this decrease in real debt is akin to a hidden tax, and that it can be considered as a despoilment. The devaluation coupled with money creation therefore alters the distribution of resources between the state and the citizens, but it also modifies the distribution of resources between the citizens. In fact, the first to obtain the credits of monetary origin can use these resources at the very beginning of the inflationary process and buy more goods against their new cash balances than others will be able to later.

If the monetary authorities do not accompany the devaluation by corresponding monetary growth, there will be a net excess demand for cash balances expressed by the inhabitants of the country. This demand will be met by a positive variation of the trade balance (exports increase and/or imports decrease). People will then have the feeling that there is a 'normal effect' of the devaluation, corresponding to what is described by the elasticity approach. But this consequence of the devaluation is not due to a change in relative prices between imports and exports: it is due to the increase in the demand for cash balances, in the absence of a corresponding monetary creation. And, of course, it ends when the inhabitants of the country have received the amount of nominal and real cash balances they want, which means that the positive change of the trade balance is only transitory (contrary to what is implied by the elasticity approach). It can also be stressed that this positive variation of the trade balance is actually a levy on the real resources of the inhabitants of the country: to obtain money cash balances – which cost nothing to produce – they must deliver goods for export (or reduce their purchases of imported goods, which would otherwise give them additional satisfaction).

Thus, a devaluation causes a series of monetary or real effects which can all be considered as harmful: temporary inflation, a positive change in the trade balance, changes in the distribution of resources, the payment of an inflation tax to the state, distortions in the price structures and production structures, as well as in the rate of interest (as a result of the possible expansionary monetary policy), and an increase in uncertainties insofar as it is difficult to forecast the duration and rate of inflation and the duration and value of distortions.

Note, finally, that the devaluation approach proposed here is a monetary approach, which makes sense since the devaluation is a monetary phenomenon (it changes the relative price of two currencies). Conversely, the elasticity approach is a non-monetary approach, since it is based on elasticities of supply and demand for real goods. It can legitimately be viewed as contradictory to study a monetary phenomenon – the devaluation – and while excluding any monetary variable from the analysis.

### 19.1.2    Scenario 2: Existence of Non-Tradable Goods

In this case the process is basically the same as before, with the addition only of the fact that the changes in the relative prices between tradable goods and non-tradable goods lead, in the short term, to the real effects already underlined, namely changes in the structure of demands for goods and transfers of factors of production. But, insofar as there is a gradual return towards the initial relative prices, there is no real lasting change. It can simply be pointed out that the possible movements of factors of production across sectors are transitory, and they therefore represent a waste of resources, since such transfers can never be free. Therefore, this consequence must be added to the list of harmful effects of the devaluation.

## 19.2    NO INITIAL MONETARY EQUILIBRIUM

This assumption means, for instance, that the inhabitants of country A have excess money cash balances, taking into account existing prices and real incomes. This may result from the fact that country B has employed a very restrictive monetary policy which has caused a fall in prices for the whole of the area of fixed exchange rates, so that there is an excess of cash balances in country A. But let us analyse instead the case – which is the most likely assumption in reality – according to which this is the result of the fact that the central bank of country A has not complied with the discipline of a fixed exchange rate regime, and has employed a too-expansionary monetary policy. These excess cash balances created by the monetary system of country A can result initially in an increase in the prices of non-tradable goods compared to those of tradable goods. The normal adjustment processes which we have previously studied imply that the excess monetary cash balances move to the rest of the world (country B) until a monetary equilibrium is found in all countries of the area of fixed exchange rates. As we have also seen, this outflow of money implies that individuals exchange currency A against currency B, taking into account the convertibility guarantee at fixed prices promised by the central bank of country A. The latter thus loses reserves of foreign exchange, and this should normally be a signal that it should implement a more restrictive monetary policy. This is, as we know, the normal adjustment process. Unfortunately it is not necessarily respected, and the central bank of country A may then decide a devaluation, claiming for instance, as a justification, that there is a so-called 'balance of payments problem'. However, it is not a balance of payments problem, but a monetary policy problem, this policy being inconsistent with the exchange rate regime chosen by the monetary authorities. Instead of considering that the 'deterioration' of the trade balance is the result of an excess of money creation in A, it is wrongly assumed that, for some reason, the inhabitants of the country buy too much abroad or do not export enough, for instance because of a so-called 'lack of competitiveness', from which 'losses of foreign exchange reserves' would follow. In other words, the causality is incorrectly reversed by assuming that the trade balance determines the money outflows.

The central bank, unable to adjust its policy of money creation to what is implied by the existence of a system of fixed exchange rates, instead of adjusting the quantity of money then adjusts the price of money, thanks to the devaluation. If it has been correctly calculated, this devaluation will help to restore the equilibrium between the money supply of countries A and B and the respective needs of money, or between the prices of tradable and non-tradable goods. But it would be necessary that it be correctly calculated, which is not obvious. And the possible return to a monetary equilibrium can be sustainable only if the central bank of country A now plays the normal game of a system of fixed exchange rates, meaning that it adjusts its monetary policy on the basis of the signals given by the changes in its foreign exchange reserves. If it maintains a too-expansionary monetary policy, it may be induced to decide periodic devaluations, which is a source of great uncertainty for the inhabitants of country A, as well as for those of country B.

To summarize, whatever the assumptions and situations under consideration, devaluation should never be considered as a legitimate instrument of economic policy. Either a fixed exchange rate regime has been chosen, and its rules should be accepted – that is, adjusting monetary policy according to the changes in foreign exchange reserves; or, if it is not possible to abide by the rules of the game of a fixed exchange rate regime, flexible exchange rates should simply be adopted. Devaluation – which can be termed 'flexibility in the fixity' – should therefore be avoided.

# PART IV

# Monetary problems

The previous chapters have supplied all the necessary instruments to understand and evaluate the working of monetary systems and their inter-relationships. Thus, they can now be used to analyse specific problems, for instance the monetary integration of several countries or the role of money in financial and economic crises.[1] It is obviously not possible to explore all conceivable problems and I have therefore chosen those which seem to me to be the most important, or the closest to current concerns. However, I begin with a very general approach of the evolution of monetary systems, which will relativize the contemporary systems which are generally considered the norm.

---

[1]  Some specific applications of my previous analyses can be found in my book, Salin (2015).

# 20. The very long-term evolution of monetary systems

The aim of this chapter is not to provide precise information on the historical evolution of monetary systems such as this can be known – even if the 'real' evolution is referred to here – and for more detail it would be better to refer to the specialized textbooks on monetary history. The aim of this chapter is, rather, to build logically a somewhat imaginary history of the steps in the course of which monetary systems have been modified, taking into account what we know about the behaviour of individuals and the ways in which politicians behave. But it will, however, be apparent on several occasions that this imaginary story is not fundamentally distinct from actual history.

## 20.1    FIRST STEP: A BARTER ECONOMY

It seems logical to assume that money was not invented at the very origin of mankind, and for a long time human beings resorted to barter, as soon as they discovered that making exchanges allowed them to specialize and therefore to increase their well-being. But barter obviously implies that an individual who wishes to exchange one good against another has to find another individual who wishes to make an exactly symmetrical exchange, and that they are able to agree on a price between the two goods which they want to exchange. From a formal point of view we can say that there is a numéraire – that is, a standard of value – on the occasion of each transaction. Thus, if two individuals agree to exchange one tomato against two apples, we may consider that the apple is the numéraire for this transaction and that the price of a tomato is equal to two apples. But, as not all transactions are made up of the same goods, this numéraire cannot be considered as a 'generalized numéraire', that is, a numéraire which can be used as a standard of value in all transactions.

Savings very likely exist in this barter economy. Let us take the case of Robinson, alone on his island. He feeds himself on fruits which he finds growing around the island. However, suppose that he decides to devote a few hours not in looking for his food or resting, but in digging a small trench in order to bring water from a source to plantations which he wishes to develop. The sacrifice which he accepts in the use of his time represents savings, and the work which he carries out is the investment correspond-ing to his savings. Of course, Robinson accepts the initial sacrifice because he believes that the return will more than offset, from the point of view of his satisfactions over time, the sacrifice. When another person, Friday, joins Robinson, exchange becomes possible between them, including the exchange of savings: Friday provides fruits to Robinson in order to allow him to survive while he digs his trench, and Robinson promises to deliver to Friday a certain amount of fruits – higher than the initial transfer – at a future date. Friday saves and Robinson invests. They exchange fruits against a verbal promise of reimbursement (and possibly an interest payment). This promise is what might be called a claim. But Robinson and Friday can also pool their resources of savings – in the form of food and hours worked – and agree on the distribution between them of property rights on the yields of these common savings and investments. Thus it can be said that finance – that is, transactions on claims or property rights – comes before money. It is even possible to suppose that, in a more complex society, there are financial intermediaries, while money still does not exist.

## 20.2    SECOND STEP: THE INVENTION OF MONEY

As already noted, the use of barter involves the bearing of transaction costs, since each potential trader must find another who is ready to make the symmetrical exchange at a price which suits both of them. This is why it is easy to imagine that, individuals being rational, they progressively and spontaneously discovered that they could reduce or even remove these transaction costs. To achieve this aim, an individual may decide to buy a good which he does not need against one which he sells; but he considers that the purchased good is sufficiently desirable to other people that it can be sold to them against the goods which he wishes to buy. This good carries out a monetary function, namely being a 'generalized purchasing power' (as seen in Chapter 4).

Under the assumptions which we are making for the time being, pre-sumably every individual chooses a different commodity to fulfil this monetary function. But the members of a human society will probably find it more useful for all of them to use the same monetary good, or at least a limited number of monetary goods. They therefore select a good particularly suitable to perform this monetary function. It is preferable, from this point of view, to choose a durable good, clearly defined, easily measurable, and so on. Let us decide to call this monetary good 'gold', even though, historically, many other goods have played this role: for instance, silver and copper, but also cattle, pieces of cloth and blocks of salt. It might also be interesting to study the relationship between different monetary goods – as done previously, regarding the exchange rate in modern monetary systems – but for the sake of simplification for the upcoming reasoning, let us assume for the moment that there is a single currency in the world, namely gold.

As we know, it is its ability to constitute a 'generalized purchasing power' which gives a good its monetary character, and not the fact that it may be used as a numéraire, that is, a standard of value. To be sure, a monetary good most often also plays a role of numéraire. But, from the point of view of the origin of money, two assumptions can be made (as already suggested in Chapter 4). Firstly, it can be assumed that individuals found it convenient to measure relative prices in terms of a specific good, which therefore played the role of numéraire without initially playing a monetary role (a role which it may play subsequently). We can also assume, conversely, that they found it convenient to express relative prices in terms of a good which they already used as a currency. But it is probably more realistic to assume that the role of numéraire and the role of 'generalized purchasing power' emerged gradually and more or less simultaneously. It seems that historians do not have the means to give an answer to this question, or even to specify how money appeared. This is certainly because its appearance was progressive, so that it cannot be dated, but also because it certainly appeared even before writing, so that there is no evidence on this subject. In any event, it was born from practice, spontaneously, as the result of trial and error, and not as the result of a political decision imposing the use of a currency, invented *ex nihilo*.

In this assumed universe, where gold is the only currency, the quantity of money is obviously equal to the amount of gold, so that we can write:

$$M = G \qquad (20.1)$$

where $M$ is, as previously, the quantity of money and $G$ is the global monetary gold stock.

From this equation one can obviously draw the following equation:

$$\mu = \gamma \qquad (20.2)$$

where $\mu$ is the growth rate of the quantity of money and $\gamma$ the growth rate of the stock of monetary gold.

We have already analysed the factors which determine the growth of the stock of gold (Chapter 5). It is clear that the evolution of the relative price of gold compared to other goods depends on the evolution of the relative scarcity of gold compared to these goods, and therefore on the evolution of supply and demand for gold compared with other goods. If, for instance, the growth rate of the stock of monetary gold is lower than the growth rate of real transactions, and if the demand for money function remains stable, there will be deflation, that is to say a decrease in the prices of goods compared to gold (or an increase in the price of gold in terms of goods; that is, an increase in the purchasing power of gold).

In this system, in which there is an actual circulation of gold, in the form of coins or ingots, the prices of goods are directly expressed in terms of a quantity of gold; for instance, 1 pound of wheat = 1 ounce of gold. It is not necessary to give a name to the currency and, for instance, the weight of gold it contains is engraved on a gold coin. Moreover, the quality of the currency is the greater, the higher is the confidence of the users of the currency in the information given to them. Thus, the quality of a gold coin will be the greater, the more it benefits from credible guarantees about its actual weight and its title, that is, the percentage of pure gold it contains (since alloys are usually used, pure gold being too soft).

These guarantees may obviously be provided by those who strike the coins, and this has often been the case in monetary history. One can also imagine that each producer of coins thus provides a kind of label, but that the credibility of the various labels varies, so that the relative price of different gold coins may not exactly match their alleged gold content: a coin of 1 ounce produced by producer A will not be exchanged against a coin of the same weight and the same title of producer B if there is a suspicion that the guarantees provided by producer A are not as credible as those given by producer B. From this point of view there is competition between the various producers of coins and, normally, the poor-quality coins disappear from the market in favour of good-quality coins.

There is also, in this monetary system, a problem to overcome. Indeed, minting gold coins has a cost, and the producer must find a way to be paid for his work and his production equipment (and even, possibly, to obtain a small profit from possible innovations). Insofar as, specifically, people do not exchange the ounces of gold in raw form, but they use gold coins to obtain a guarantee of quality, the remuneration of the producer can come, for instance, from the fact that he sells a gold coin against 1 ounce of gold, although his coin contains less than 1 ounce of gold.

As is confirmed by history, political authorities have always been interested in the production of money, and such was the case with the production of metallic money in the form of coins. Money-holders may be ready to admit – wrongly or rightly – that the guarantee concerning the weight or the title of coins is more credible if it emanates from a public authority, which also avoids users having to inquire about the greater or lesser credibility of guarantees given by different producers. So it is not surprising that, since earliest antiquity, most coins (in gold or other metals) have borne the mark of the sovereign. But political authorities, because they have the monopoly of legal coercion, tend to grant monopoly positions, that is, to prohibit others from engaging in activities which they wish to take part in. Thus, they will award themselves the monopoly of providing guarantees about the quality of coins, and more specifically, the monopoly of striking them in each of the regions over which they exercise their powers. But they also understand that they can make significant gains through monetary manipulations. Monetary history offers proof of this: many princes and sovereigns have clipped coins – so that the actual weight was lower than the advertised weight – or have constantly decreased the title of currencies so that coins contained a continuously decreasing percentage of gold. This was, obviously, a despoilment of money-holders by the political power, made possible by the state monopoly, and which announced practices of the same order in the most recent periods.

Thus, by practising a deterioration in the quality of a currency, a public monetary authority artificially increases the quantity of money (expressed in terms of ounces of gold). It is as if there was more monetary gold than there is in reality. If the monetary authority is constantly deteriorating the quality of a currency, the result is a more important positive variation of the prices of goods in terms of gold than would have been the case in the absence of these practices. We can find in modern times an echo of these ancient practices in the continual creation of nominal cash balances by monetary authorities, which is – as we know – the cause of inflation. But it remains no less true that it is much more difficult to continuously deteriorate the quality of gold coins than to indefinitely create monetary units by simple accounting entries, as is the case in modern monetary systems. Thus it is not surprising that the rate of inflation was zero or low (sometimes negative) from the beginning of the Christian era to the nineteenth century (with the exception of higher inflation due to the plundering of gold from Latin America after the discovery of the continent), while it has often reached considerable rates subsequently.

Finally, it is clear that we can no longer speak of a world money supply if there are different monetary authorities, each of them benefiting from a monopoly position for the issuance of coins in a given territory (a country). But even in this case, it is difficult to prevent the use in a country of coins issued in other countries, so that a certain degree of competition remains and makes harder for monetary authorities to continuously deteriorate the value of their coins. Thus the Maria Theresa thaler – a silver coin originally issued in Austria-Hungary from 1741 – circulated beyond the borders of this country, particularly in the Middle East, Africa, India and the United States. It was even produced in many overseas workshops, in Bombay as well as in Milan.

## 20.3    THIRD STEP: PAPER CURRENCY AND 100 PER CENT RESERVES

Thus, metallic coins play their role as monetary goods in a satisfactory manner insofar as they are not subject to a rapid deterioration of their quality, and insofar as the growth rate of the stock of coins is not much higher than real growth (that is, the growth of production and income). However, the assumption of a relatively high growth rate of the stock of coins is unlikely since it would require a very rapid improvement in the techniques of discovery of precious metals for mining or in the techniques of extraction of this metal. The growth of the world gold stock has been very slow, and this is one of the reasons why gold has been praised as a monetary good. From this point of view, therefore, a monetary system based on gold (or any other precious metal) is satisfactory.

However, there is a difficulty arising from the fact that the use of metallic coins is not without cost. Indeed, the coins are heavy, somewhat cumbersome, and likely to be stolen. But above all, each of them has a relatively great value and therefore it is hard to pay with gold coins, for instance, for a purchase of very low value or a purchase the value of which is not a precise multiple of the value of a coin. Obviously, it is for this reason that monetary units of smaller value were invented and produced. Made of copper, iron or various alloys, they had a much lower value than gold coins. But another innovation helped to overcome all difficulties related to the circulation of coins, namely not to circulate the metallic coins themselves, but property rights on coins (or ingots). For convenience, I will call these property titles on coins 'gold certificates'.

How are these gold certificates created? The owner of a certain number of gold coins entrusts them to an intermediary's care, playing the role of a safe in a storehouse. The intermediary, in return, delivers papers – which we will later call banknotes – on which it is written, for instance: 'I promise to deliver to the holder of this title, at any time, 1 ounce of gold.' The individual who gives to the intermediary 1 ounce of gold receives in return a title to 1 ounce of gold held by the intermediary. The gold certificate has a convertibility guarantee at a fixed price, meaning that it can be exchanged at any time, by anyone, for the same amount of precious metal; for instance, 1 ounce of gold. These certificates are easy to carry and they are easily divisible: thus, instead of receiving a gold certificate for 1 ounce of gold, an individual may prefer to receive ten gold certificates for 0.1 ounces of gold.

Convertibility guarantees at a fixed price are an essential element of the working of these monetary systems and these have already been encountered in the modern-day systems studied previously, for instance regarding the relationship between a central bank and commercial banks, or the working of a system of fixed exchange rates. Their origin lies in the 'gold certificates'. It is also interesting to note that the first gold certificates (or banknotes) were issued in England by the goldsmiths, and not by banks, the traditional role of which was not to produce money (in the form of coins or gold certificates), but to transfer and transform savings. Of course, the market value of gold certificates depends not only upon their face value – that is, the amount of gold against which they can be exchanged – but also upon the confidence in the ability of the issuers of the certificates to honour their promise of convertibility at fixed prices. If, for instance, it is considered that an issuer of certificates may go bankrupt, these certificates will have a lower value than their face value. And probably, in this case, the holders of certificates will rush to request from this issuer the exchange of their certificates for real gold (which can precipitate the bankruptcy of the issuer if he has been imprudent in not just sticking to the role of a storehouse, but instead, for instance, has lent a part of the gold which belongs to his customers).

Of course, the services rendered by the issuer of gold certificates have a cost, as was the case for minting gold coins. He must, for instance, implement security measures to prevent the gold deposited in his coffers from being stolen, he must print the gold certificates, keep accounts, take the time to make the exchange between coins and certificates, and so on. To do this, he may request compensation from those who buy gold certificates, but he can also be paid indirectly. Thus, it may be considered that the gold certificates issued by goldsmiths constituted a sort of 'loss leader' to attract customers, and that these goldsmiths gained enough profit from other activities to be able to supply the service of issuing gold certificates for free.

From a macroeconomic point of view, the production of gold certificates does not change anything compared to the second stage (circulation of gold coins). In fact, the quantity of gold certificates in circulation (expressed in terms of ounces of gold) is exactly equal to the amount of gold held as collateral by the monetary intermediaries which are producing the certificates. This system is called a system of 100 per cent reserves. The gold certificates simply attest that their holders are owners of a corresponding quantity of gold held by certificate issuers. Thus, the quantity of money consists, on the one hand, of coins in circulation and, on the other hand, of gold certificates corresponding to a stock of monetary gold 'in reserve'. From the existing monetary gold stock, individuals are therefore circulating either directly gold coins or property rights on gold. The growth rate of the money supply is therefore equal to the growth rate of the stock of monetary gold, so that the above equation (20.2) remains valid. The growth rate of the quantity of money being exactly equal to the growth rate of the stock of monetary gold, the rate of inflation is the result of the respective growth rates of this stock of gold and of real transactions (of which real income growth can give an approximation, as seen in Chapter 4). As regards the growth rate of the stock of gold, it is determined by a number of factors, for instance the possible discovery of new gold mines, the potential improvement in productivity in extraction techniques of gold, or even changes in the demand for non-monetary gold (for instance, for jewellery or industry). It thus depends on the decisions of a considerable number of people, so that it cannot be manipulated by any public authority, except to the extent that the gold coins, produced by monetary public monopolies, are subject to a deterioration in their quality. But in the latter case, issuers of gold certificates will be induced to accept not gold coins, but ounces of pure gold not processed into coins, which will dampen the tendency of monetary authorities to degrade the quality of their coins. As in all areas of activity, competition makes it possible to prevent producers from cheating their customers.

One can imagine that monetary prices may be directly expressed in terms, for instance, of ounces of gold and that, moreover, the certificates indicate only the weight of gold which they represent (that is, the weight of gold against which they can be exchanged). Thus, one may say, for instance, that 1 pound of wheat is worth 1 ounce of gold. But one can also imagine that producers of certificates give a name to their certificates. For instance, let us imagine that a producer called 'Gimmick' produces certificates called 'gimmicks', on which it is written '1 gimmick is convertible at any time by its holder against 1 ounce of gold from the producer Gimmick'. Thus, the following equalities will prevail: 1 pound of wheat = 1 ounce of gold = 1 gimmick. It may also be the case that all the producers of certificates have decided, for the convenience of their customers, to give the same name to all certificates, whoever the producer, for instance the Ecu. The value of the quantity of money can then be expressed in terms of ounces of gold or in terms of Ecus. If 1 Ecu is redeemable against 1 ounce of gold, and the stock of monetary gold is equal to 1000 ounces, the quantity of money is worth 1000 ounces of gold or 1000 Ecus, according to the good – gold or the Ecu[1] – which is used as the numéraire.

---

[1]   According to economists such as Ludwig von Mises, money is gold and banknotes are called 'monetary substitutes' (they are property rights on gold).

Even if all certificates are defined in terms of ounces of gold, they may be assessed differently. In fact, they are promises of convertibility into gold, but these promises may be regarded as more or less credible. If, for instance, it is anticipated that a producer of certificates may go bankrupt (as a result of the unprofitability of his other activities), customers will be induced to accept the gold certificates issued by this issuer at a price lower than their face value (that is, the amount of gold they are supposed to represent). In all monetary systems, the confidence in the guarantees offered to users of money plays an important role (for instance, the credibility of inscriptions concerning the minting of gold coins, or the credibility of convertibility guarantees in gold of gold certificates) and other examples will be given later on.

Let me re-emphasize, finally, that in the stage of monetary evolution just considered, there is no particular reason for gold certificates to be issued by banks. This is why I prefer to speak of 'gold certificates' instead of 'banknotes', the latter term becoming more justified subsequently. A bank is a firm which transfers and transforms savings, activities which have nothing in common with the role of the certificate issuers who exercise a monetary function consisting, in this case, of keeping gold and producing claims on the gold thus deposited.

## 20.4   FOURTH STEP: PAPER CURRENCY AND FRACTIONAL RESERVES

The monetary system just considered is satisfying because it is convenient for money-users and because it allows the avoidance of an excessive issuance of money, which, as we know, is necessarily harmful. There is, however, a small problem in this system, namely that the services provided by the producers of gold certificates have costs (costs of the custody of deposited gold, of printing and managing the gold certificates). As we have seen, the remuneration may be indirect, since gold certificates can be used as 'loss leaders' by producers – for instance the jewellers – who derive their profits from other activities. But if the use of gold certificates develops, as is normal, because of their usefulness, this substitute return is random and probably insufficient. Therefore another mode of remuneration must be found.

One can certainly imagine that the producer of gold certificates will ask that the services rendered be paid at their cost price (to which can be added a small profit margin). But this does not completely solve the problem. Indeed, the expense of keeping the gold depends on the duration of custody. However, the gold certificates are kept for various lengths of time before their refund in gold is requested. Therefore, rather than asking a fixed price at the time of the issuance of a gold certificate, the issuer of certificates should ask for a payment in proportion to the duration of the holding of this certificate. But this would imply dating certificates and calculating the amount of gold which should be given when a refund is required (which implies deducting from the initial value at the time of issuance the amount of the costs of custody, proportional to the term of holding). However, this practice would much reduce the usefulness of gold certificates. In fact, all certificates would have an actual value different from their face value (that is, the value written on certificates at the time of their issuance), which would make transactions difficult: for instance, a certificate issued against 10 ounces of gold would be exchangeable at one date against 9.90 ounces of gold, at another against 9.85 ounces, and so on. Gold certificates could not easily play their roles of reserve of value and means of transaction, and not even their potential role as numéraire.

Therefore, it is easy to understand that issuers of gold certificates had to imagine an indirect way to be paid for their services without reducing the liquidity of their certificates. The logical solution was to shift from a 100 per cent reserve system to a fractional reserve system. The issuer of gold certificates, having observed that there is on average a certain delay between the issuance of a certificate and the demand for a refund in gold of this certificate, does not feel obliged to hold at any time exactly the amount of gold corresponding to the certificates issued. It can be assumed that there is an infinitely low probability that all holders of gold certificates will ask for a conversion into gold of their certificates at the same time. The issuer of gold certificates will therefore lend a part of the gold held in reserves. The interest rate which he charges will bring him a remuneration which makes it possible to offset the costs of his monetary activity over time and, probably, to obtain a profit.

The balance sheet of an issuer of certificates (regardless of other possible activities) is therefore, for instance, shown as follows:

Balance sheet of an issuer of gold certificates

| assets | | liabilities | |
|---|---|---|---|
| gold reserves | 50 | gold certificates | 100 |
| claims | 50 | | |

In the example above, the issuer of gold certificates decided to maintain, on average, gold reserves representing 50 per cent of the amount of gold certificates he has issued. In this case, he has a reserve coefficient equal to 50 per cent, this being defined as the ratio of gold reserves to gold certificates. The gain obtained by the issuer is obviously the more important, the lower is this coefficient, since claims bring interest, but not the gold reserves. But the risk of being unable to honour the promise of convertibility into gold is the greater, the lower is the reserve coefficient. The issuer of certificates must arbitrate between performance and risk (as is the case for many human activities). On the basis of his own assessments, the nature of his loans, the characteristics of his clients, each issuer will probably choose a different reserve coefficient which he will consider as optimal for him.[2] Furthermore, it is obvious that this differentiation will have consequences on the assessment of the value of the certificates by their potential holders. They will, for instance, have an incentive to look at the risk which is involved in more or less important reserve coefficients. If the reserve coefficient of an issuer is viewed as too low, they will be induced to get rid of the certificates of this issuer and to use other certificates. This issuer may then lose his monetary function and perhaps even go bankrupt.

We can understand, at this point, how the monetary function (issuance of gold certificates) could be taken up, more or less quickly, by banks. As their role consists in transforming and transferring savings, they are, in particular, specialized in looking for borrowers and negotiating loan agreements. Thus, it is understandable that they used this specific knowledge to carry out credit operations which have become the counterpart of the issuance of gold certificates in monetary systems with fractional reserves. It is therefore also understandable that at this stage gold certificates took the name of 'banknotes'. But it remains true that the role of financial intermediary – which defines a bank – and the monetary role are different roles. Although they are generally performed by the same firms nowadays, they have not always been, and one can very well imagine that they may no longer do so in the future, in other types of monetary systems.

The transition from a 100 per cent reserve system to a fractional reserve system has two important consequences. First of all, during the period of transition between the two systems, there is an increase in the quantity of money compared to the stock of monetary gold held by the issuers of money certificates. Assuming that all the monetary gold serves as a reserve, and that gold coins are no longer used, we can write:

$$M = G/r \tag{20.3}$$

---

[2] As usual, the optimum cannot be defined by outside observers. It is by nature subjective and individual. For convenience, I will generally not take into account this diversity of reserve coefficients in the subsequent reasoning, and will use an average reserve coefficient for the whole set of certificate issuers.

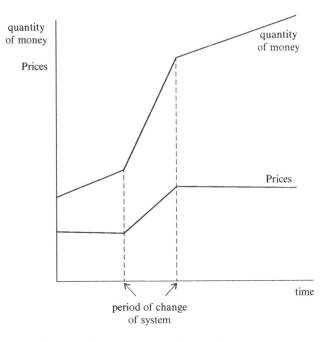

*Figure 20.1    Money and prices during changes in monetary systems*

where *M* represents the quantity of money (evaluated in terms of a numéraire which can be the gold ounce), *G* represents the stock of monetary gold (that is, the total gold reserves of the issuers of gold certificates, evaluated in the same numéraire) and where *r* is the average reserve coefficient for all issuers.

If, for instance, the issuers of money certificates keep on average a 50 per cent reserve coefficient, the quantity of money is worth twice the value of the stock of monetary gold. This increase in the money supply therefore causes a corresponding increase in prices during the period of transition from one system to another. But this increase takes place once and for all: once all certificate issuers have reached the reserve coefficient they desire, the growth rate of their certificates is equal to the growth rate of their gold reserves, that is, the above equation (20.2) remains valid. This situation is represented in Figure 20.1, where it is assumed that there is a constant growth rate of the stock of monetary gold, that the change of system involves a doubling of the quantity of money, and where in addition it is assumed, for simplicity, that the real growth rate is equal to the growth rate of the stock of gold, so that prices are constant if the quantity of money increases at the same rate as the stock of monetary gold, which is the case before and after the time period during which there is a change of system. We see in this figure that the doubling of the money supply, due to the change of system, causes a doubling of prices during the transitional period during which there is a change of system, but afterwards prices remain at the level they have reached, insofar as we assume an equality between monetary growth and real growth. To summarize, the change of system is inflationary during the transition period. But the fractional reserve system, once implemented, is not inflationary, at least insofar as the average reserve ratio remains constant. We will see later why this coefficient can, however, fall under certain conditions, which means that a fractional reserve system is potentially inflationary, in circumstances that need to be clarified. But, for the moment, there is no reason to suppose that certificate issuers decide to reduce their reserve coefficients indefinitely, below what they consider as optimal.

The second consequence is that if the change of system leads to a once and for all change in the growth rate of prices, it implies a permanent – and potentially harmful – change in the financial sector. In fact, in a system without fractional reserves, banks invest or lend the savings which are voluntarily desired by individuals who decide to make a sacrifice of consumption in order to save in the form of equity funds or loanable funds. They hope to get a future return, either in the form of profits (for equity funds), or in the form of interest (for loanable funds). Banks may serve as intermediaries for these financial transactions. However, when an issuer of money – which can be a bank – delivers a credit by using a portion of the gold reserves it had received from money-holders, it is lending resources which do not correspond to prior and voluntary savings. Those who benefit from these credits therefore receive gold certificates which they can use to purchase goods, in particular factors of production. They will therefore get resources which would otherwise have had another use. The entire economic system is thus modified. Later on, we will see that this phenomenon is at the origin of illusions with harmful consequences (Chapter 22). Because people are behaving as if there is more money (gold) than there is in reality, people are also behaving as if there are more savings than there are in reality. A fractional reserve system is therefore a source of potential macroeconomic risk. But we may perhaps consider that this consequence represents an inevitable, and perhaps even acceptable, cost in order to have a monetary system which works in a more satisfactory way than the previous one. It is only when there is an excessive use of the fractional reserve system, creating illusory savings in large quantities, that the consequences can be very harmful, as we will see later.

We have therefore assumed, in this stage of monetary developments, that a fractional reserve system was substituted for the 100 per cent reserve system. In reality – and as has been the case in history – there has been, over a relatively long period, a coexistence of issuers of monetary certificates faithful to 100 per cent reserves, and other issuers using fractional reserves. There was competition between these different types of issuers and, as this is always the case when there is competition, the best ones have won. The others are possibly excluded from the market because they do not produce goods and services as attractive for customers. This is what happened because of the competition between issuers of gold certificates with different gold guarantees: the fractional reserve systems were preferred to 100 per cent reserve systems because they seemed less expensive for users and/or producers of monetary certificates.[3]

One can also imagine that, during a certain period, there was competition in the field of the production of monetary certificates between banks and other businesses (jewellers, for instance). But history seems to show that the market freely selected banks as being more efficient to perform this activity (which corresponds to the fact that they are specialized in credit activities).

As already stressed, gold certificates representing promises given by different organizations can be evaluated differently by their holders, who attribute to them more or less confidence. If the issuers of monetary certificates give a name to their certificates, the differentiation takes on a formal appearance, but this obviously does not change the nature of a monetary system. Gold certificates are held because they are convertible at any time and by anyone against a fixed quantity of gold. For instance, suppose that a bank named 'Trick Bank' issues certificates which it calls 'tricks' and it promises to exchange without limits 1 trick against 1 ounce of gold. It would obviously be a temptation for it to obtain a considerable gain by deciding to give back, for instance, only 0.5 ounces of gold to anyone who asks for the exchange of their tricks for gold. This operation – which nowadays is called 'devaluation' – would obviously constitute a theft and it would be sanctioned as such: the firm, which would thus not have honoured its promise of convertibility, would be brought to the courts for having not respected its contract. It would also lose its customers and would therefore fail. That is why, in a system of this kind, based on convertibility guarantees given by firms in competition, a unilateral change in the value of certificates (or banknotes) is impossible: convertibility is a contractual obligation agreed between an issuer of currency units and its customers, and a contract must be respected in a civilized society.

---

[3]    But, admittedly, none of them is probably aware of this overall effect according to which fractional reserves create distortions in the financial system, by creating the illusion of savings being more abundant than they are in reality.

Note, finally, that the monetary units which we have called 'gold certificates' may take different forms without changing the nature of the monetary systems. Thus, after the invention of banknotes, monetary units of a new kind have emerged which are called 'deposits', that is, dematerialized monetary units which correspond to the written acknowledgement of property rights. The fact that people 'deposited' gold in the coffers of the gold certificate issuers probably gave rise to the term 'deposits', which is used to name what are in fact precisely the counterparts of these deposits of gold, at least when they do not take the form of 'banknotes'.[4] The distinction between notes and deposits has only formal importance, except in the case studied previously (Chapter 11) in which the production of banknotes is made by a compulsory public monopoly (the central bank).

## 20.5   FIFTH STEP: THE EMERGENCE OF MUTUAL CONVERTIBILITY GUARANTEES

As seen in Chapter 4, the quality of a currency depends essentially on two factors: its ability to maintain its purchasing power (or even to increase it, as is the case in deflation) and the economic dimension of its area of circulation. The existence of convertibility guarantees at fixed price of gold certificates in terms of gold (or, of course, any other good) makes it possible to avoid a deterioration in the purchasing power of a currency (except in the very specific cases in which the stock of monetary gold would increase in a significant and rapid manner, as was the case during the looting of gold from the indians of South America after the discovery of the continent). As the historical experience proves, the growth of the stock of monetary gold was slow enough over centuries (relative to the growth of the real economy) to allow great price stability and thus to avoid any inflationary adventure in gold standard systems[5] (at least the ones reviewed here so far). But what of the second factor determining the quality of a currency: the size of its area of circulation? In fact, it is obvious that a currency is the more useful insofar as it is accepted as a currency

---

[4]   The term 'deposits' is ambiguous because, although it is true that one is 'depositing' gold at a monetary intermediary, one does not deposit the corresponding claims. Deposits are registered in the accounting books of the issuers of monetary units, but there is not a 'deposit' made by money-holders. A claim is not 'deposited': it belongs to the creditor and it is recognized by the debtor.

[5]   The term 'gold standard' is used to name the monetary systems in which gold plays a monetary role. But this term is questionable since what is important in so-called 'gold standard systems' is not that gold has a role of standard of value, but that it has the monetary role of being an available purchasing power.

by a larger number of people. Moreover, from this point of view, there is a virtuous circle: the more a currency is circulating, the more useful it is, and therefore the more it is demanded and the more it circulates. If I hold a currency which preserves its purchasing power efficiently, but which is accepted only by one other person, its liquidity is low and it is not very useful to me. For a currency to be useful it must match its definition, that is, being redeemable at any time, against anything and with anyone (as we saw in Chapter 4). But this does not necessarily imply that the best solution would be to have a single currency in the world. In fact, if one makes the assumption of a currency which benefits initially from a limited area of circulation, and if this area is increasing gradually, its usefulness will also increase gradually. But it may be that, from a certain size of the area of circulation, the marginal gain which can be obtained by further increasing the size of the area of circulation is negligible so that it is not justified to have a single currency in the world (taking into account the fact that the usefulness of a currency also depends on other factors).

In the previous step, we have seen the appearance of gold certificates produced in fractional reserve systems, but with a convertibility guarantee into gold. But we also assumed that there is a large number of producers of gold certificates (or banknotes). Each producer has its own currency and there is therefore a large number of different currencies (which are claims on different issuers). From this point of view none of these currencies provides the best services expected from a currency, namely to be redeemable against anything with anyone. Thus, individual A will use the currency called 'gimmick' because he has confidence in this currency and the ability of its issuer to honour its promise of convertibility, while individual B will prefer to use a currency called 'trick' (for instance because it is issued by a producer of certificates located in his neighbourhood, whom he knows well and with whom he is used to undertake banking activities). We can easily imagine that producers of certificates realize that it would be possible to increase the liquidity of their currencies, and thus their desirability, by expanding their circulation area. The best way to do this is to make these currencies perfectly substitutable one to the other in such a way that it becomes indifferent to hold a currency issued by one or another issuer. By holding 'gimmicks', an individual knows he can redeem them at any time and at a fixed price, for instance against 'tricks' (or any other existing currency). If, for instance, each of these monetary units benefits from a convertibility guarantee into 1 ounce of gold, we will have 1 trick = 1 gimmick = 1 ounce of gold.

For all the monetary units produced by different issuers in a given area (which is not necessarily a country or a specific territory, but the circulation area of a currency) to be considered as perfectly substitutable – so that they constitute a single and same currency – different methods are possible.

First, it can be assumed that all issuers give to the holders of their gold certificates a double convertibility guarantee at fixed price: a convertibility into gold, but also a convertibility into other currencies. Thus, the issuer of the 'gimmick' currency promises to buy and sell without limits and at a fixed price the currencies of other issuers against its own currency, which is convertible into gold at a fixed price. These commitments of convertibility may be taken independently by each of the issuers or as the result of an agreement signed between them. Thus, if a certificate issuer A gave a convertibility guarantee at a fixed price between its currency and the currencies of issuers B, C, D, E and F, and if these last five do the same relative to all the others, the currencies of all of these issuers are perfectly substitutable (at least, if currency-holders have confidence in these commitments). But one can imagine that these producers meet and decide together to take the commitments in question. Regardless of the practical arrangements for their decisions, these issuers constitute what might be called a 'cartel'. Traditionally a cartel is defined as an organization by which various producers agree to eliminate competition between them, in order to constitute a monopoly power and therefore to plunder consumers by taking a 'monopoly super-profit' on them. Here, we see that this is not the case, quite the contrary. This is why it is better to define a cartel as a system of coordination between different firms. Thus, different issuers of money constitute a cartel specifically to improve the quality of their currencies, and thus to provide better services to their customers who thereby hold currencies which have a larger circulation area.[6] Even if the currency units issued by the various members of the monetary cartel have different names (gimmick, trick, and so on), they are the same monetary units, since they are perfectly substitutable one with another. But, of course, this perfect substitutability is subjective; that is, it exists only insofar as it is perceived as such by the users of money. If the holder of a currency fears, for instance, the bankruptcy of an issuer of currency, he does not consider this currency as perfectly substitutable for other currencies produced in the monetary cartel (even if all of them benefit formally from a convertibility guarantee at a fixed price).

How does this monetary cartel work? Let us imagine that a large number of people ask bank A to sell to them units of its currency against units produced by other issuers of the cartel. The bank issues additional monetary units and therefore its reserve coefficient decreases (its stock of gold being

---

[6]  For an analysis of competition and cartels, see Salin (2015).

constant, while there is an increase of the banknotes or deposits it has issued). It will therefore ask the other members of the cartel to redeem their units of currency against gold (since all currency units benefit from a convertibility guarantee into gold). These gold movements allow each issuer to keep the reserve ratio which he wishes. One can also imagine – and this is what actually happened – that an organization centralizes all monetary units received by the various banks of the cartel, that it calculates the debit and credit balances, and that these balances are settled in gold by the banks. This is what is called a clearing house. It can be created by different banks of the monetary cartel and be a common subsidiary of all these banks; but it can also be an independent body asking for payment from the banks of the cartel for the services it provides to them.

When giving a convertibility guarantee to its own currency against other currencies, a bank takes risks. In fact, if it holds currency units issued by another bank which goes bankrupt, it will no longer be able to convert them into gold and it must bear a net loss. This is why one can imagine that the members of the monetary cartel implement mutual monitoring procedures, consisting for instance of looking at the reserve coefficients of the members of the cartel, and of suspending or removing the convertibility guarantees with a currency produced by an issuing bank which has a reserve coefficient regarded as too low. In this case, the cartel is based not only on a system of coordination (resulting from the decentralized commitments of all members), but also on an explicit system of cooperation.

A cartel like that just presented can be called a 'non-hierarchical cartel' or a 'symmetric cartel'. All members of the cartel are on an equal footing, without any link of dependency, and each decides its own convertibility commitments. The existence of a clearing house does not change this feature, since the clearing house is not placed 'above' the banks of the cartel (and it may even be a subsidiary of these banks).

The monetary cartel may be asymmetric or even hierarchical if one of the banks of the cartel has a role different from the others. This may be the case if a number of banks decide to give a convertibility guarantee at a fixed price for their own currencies in terms of one of them (which we will call the 'reference currency'), issued by a 'reference bank'. The reference bank is probably large and well known, and/or people have particular confidence in it (while in the cartel above, each bank gives commitments of convertibility into the currencies of all the other banks). Insofar as each bank makes this same commitment, all monetary units, produced by all banks, can be considered as substitutable with one another. But one can also imagine that a bank decides to buy and sell without limits the currencies of other banks (which thereby constitute a cartel), without these other banks giving a convertibility commitment other than the commitment to convertibility into gold. In these two cases the currencies are perfectly substitutable with one another. The system is asymmetric since not all the banks of the cartel play the same role. But it is not necessarily hierarchical, which would imply that the 'reference bank' would have the ability to give orders to the others. This cartel could become hierarchical if, for instance, the 'reference bank' granted a convertibility guarantee into the currency of another bank under the condition that the latter accepts some degree of monitoring from the reference bank. The latter could, for instance, threaten to suspend or permanently remove its convertibility guarantee if it considered that the other bank had issued too many monetary units (that is, that its reserve coefficient had become too low). In this case, the reference bank would consider it risky to hold monetary units of another bank which could go bankrupt, so that the monetary units produced by this latter bank would no longer be convertible into gold.

When an asymmetric cartel is the result of an unilateral commitment by a bank to exchange its currency against another currency at a fixed price, this necessarily implies that this bank plays the role of a clearing house. In fact, all exchanges between the currencies issued by the various members of the cartel necessarily use the 'reference currency' as an intermediary. The reference bank sells and buys the other currencies of the cartel, and if it feels that it holds too many currency units from one of the issuers, it requests the conversion of these currency units into gold, since each bank gives a convertibility guarantee for its currency into gold. It can thus maintain its reserve coefficient at the level which it considers optimal. In the case where the asymmetric cartel results from the decision taken by all banks (except the reference bank) to give a convertibility guarantee in terms of the reference currency, a clearing house is useful, but it has no reason to operate within the reference bank since it has not given any convertibility guarantee in terms of the other currencies of the cartel; that is, it has not promised to buy and to sell the other currencies of the cartel without limits at a fixed price.

The creation of monetary cartels have been viewed here as a logical consequence of the evolution of monetary systems. Therefore it is not surprising that the structures described above are not purely imaginary, but that they correspond to the historical reality.[7] Precisely because it is rational for the issuers of money to organize into cartels, they have created structures of this type. It can be said that a monetary system necessarily implies convertibility guarantees and cartel structures. Thus a monetary

---

[7] One of the historical cases which has been best studied is that of Scotland in the eighteenth century.

system can even be defined as a monetary cartel (when there is more than one issuer of currency).

At this stage of evolution, one can easily imagine that there are a number of monetary cartels in the world. One can also imagine that, in one of them, banks give a convertibility guarantee into gold, that in another the guarantee is given in terms of silver, in another in terms of copper, and so on. Furthermore, some of these cartels may be symmetrical and others asymmetrical. Within any one given cartel all monetary units are perfectly substitutable, so that it can be said that the cartel issues a currency, while another cartel issues another currency. As these different currencies produced by these different cartels have different characteristics and do not enjoy any convertibility guarantee at a fixed price between them, their relative prices – that is, their exchange rates – are normally variable according to the evolution of supply and demand. But it must also be pointed out that the area of circulation of each of these currencies has no reason to coincide with a specific geographical area or political area (such as a country). Thus individuals scattered throughout the world can participate in the same area of circulation of a currency (the same monetary area) without a border creating geographical limits between the different areas. This also implies, of course, that the same individual may hold currencies issued by different cartels. Thus, monetary areas are overlapping and the holders and/or the issuers of one given currency may be scattered all over the world (or a part of it).

From a macroeconomic point of view, there are no great changes in comparison with the previous situation, discussed in the fourth stage, the inflation rate being determined by the relative growth rates of the quantity of money and of real transactions. But if there are several monetary cartels, and therefore several differently defined currencies (for instance in gold, silver, copper, and so on), there is a different rate of inflation in each area of monetary circulation. On the other hand, the price level and the creation of fictitious savings – resulting from the loans made as counterparts of money creation in fractional reserve systems – depend of course on the reserve coefficient maintained on average in each of these cartels. Differences in inflation rates determine changes in exchange rates between the currencies produced by different cartels. But it is nevertheless true that, in all cases, inflation is limited insofar as the rules of convertibility of currency units (banknotes or deposits) in terms of a 'base currency' (gold, silver, and so on) are respected.

## 20.6   SIXTH STEP: APPEARANCE OF PUBLIC PRIVILEGES GIVEN TO A BANK

So far we have assumed that monetary systems developed spontaneously and the successive innovations essentially had the role of better meeting the needs of money-holders (explained in Chapter 4). But we have seen, however, that there could be some state interference, because the holders of a state power have always understood that they could collect resources by getting involved in the management of monetary systems. The possibility was mentioned of the situation where a political power assigns itself a monopoly in the minting of coins, and where it decreases in a discretionary way the weight and the title of the coins. We have not, so far, considered any state intervention in monetary systems characterized by the existence of gold certificates or the development of fractional reserves. In order to come closer to the historical reality, state interventions will now be introduced. First of all, the state may implement banking regulations under various pretexts. Thus, it may require that the banks issuing currency units participate in an asymmetric cartel or even a hierarchical cartel. It can impose a ratio of equity capital to banks or a minimum reserve coefficient, as mentioned previously (Chapter 11). But one of the essential features of this intervention consists in a state granting a privilege to a bank in the territory of the country where it has powers of national sovereignty. Most often the state has granted to a particular bank a monopoly on the issuance of banknotes, the other banks operating in the same territory having the right to issue only deposits. One can thus see the emergence of a characteristic of modern monetary systems, analysed previously when referring to what is called the 'money multiplier', that is, the fact that the money supply is a multiple of the monetary base (Chapter 11). This practice has become widespread little by little and there are now only a very limited number of systems in which the issuance of banknotes is not monopolized by a specific bank under the coercitive power of the state. Thus, in Hong Kong several private banks issue banknotes of different designs, even if they are all denominated in the same way and are redeemable against each other at a fixed price.

As an example, in France in 1803, Napoleon gave the Banque de France the privilege of issuing banknotes for an area corresponding roughly to Paris and its environs (which was later extended to the whole of France). This privilege meant that it became prohibited for all other banks to issue banknotes. The Banque de France was not particularly important or famous, but Napoleon had simply understood that a monopoly of public origin could provide significant gains. He cared about that because he and his family were shareholders of the Banque de France. Even if this privilege of issue was given to specific banks for various reasons, there was a generalization of this situation, especially in the nineteenth century. However, this monopoly brings an advantage to the users of banknotes, because they have a single kind of banknotes, at least in the area where there is a monopoly of issue, which facilitates the use of these banknotes. But if this monopoly had not existed, we can imagine that the various banks of the monetary cartel (which constitutes a monetary system) may have agreed to issue banknotes with about similar characteristics regardless of the issuer (but bearing the name of the issuing bank). This is why it must be recognized that there are not really solid justifications for the establishment of these public privileges.

At this stage of the evolution of monetary systems, this change in their structure – namely the creation of privileges of issuance – does not fundamentally alter the working of monetary systems. The privileged bank guarantees the convertibility in gold of banknotes, other banks give a convertibility guarantee into gold for deposits. If the reserve coefficients are the same in both cases, this is a situation similar to that of the previous step from the point of view of the creation of monetary units. The money supply in a given monetary system is composed of notes and deposits, but it is a multiple of the stock of monetary gold, determined by the average reserve coefficient, as was the case in the previous step.

With this compulsory differentiation of roles across the banks issuing currency units, one can, however, see the emergence of different monetary systems, namely hierarchical systems such as those studied previously (Chapter 11). In these hierarchical systems, in order to meet the demands for conversion of deposits into banknotes, the banks – except the privileged bank – need to hold reserves with the privileged bank, which is at the origin of a process of 'money multiplier', as seen previously.

But we must not anticipate: for the time being there is no hierarchy among banks, there is only a differentiation of roles. All banks provide convertibility guarantees into gold, and convertibility guarantees between the different monetary units issued by the banks participating into a given monetary cartel. This implies, in particular, convertibility at a fixed price between banknotes and deposits. But to implement these exchanges banks must simply provide the banknotes requested by their customers by giving gold to the privileged bank. To evaluate the optimal value of their reserve coefficient, they must take into account, among other things, the need to deliver gold – against banknotes – to the privileged bank. Thus, if the customer of a bank asks to convert into banknotes a sum equal to 10 ounces of gold (held under the form of deposits worth 10 ounces of gold), this bank must reduce the amount of its deposits for an amount equal to 20 ounces of gold, if it has a reserve coefficient of 50 per cent. In its balance sheet, gold reserves are reduced by an amount of 10 ounces of gold and claims are reduced by the same amount. The privileged bank, holding 10 additional ounces of gold, may increase its issuance of money by an amount equal to 20 ounces of gold, if it has the same reserve coefficient of 50 per cent. It therefore issues banknotes for a value of 10 ounces of gold and the rest – worth 10 ounces of gold – can be in the form of banknotes or deposits, and it is issued in return for an increase in its assets in claims. All in all, the quantity of money has remained constant, but its structure has changed (banknotes have been substituted for deposits) and the total amount of bank assets also remains constant (but the privileged bank has increased the amount of its assets in claims and gold at the expense of the bank which had to cope with a demand for banknotes).

## 20.7 SEVENTH STEP: NATIONALIZATION OF THE PRIVILEGED BANK AND STATE CONTROL OF THE MONETARY SYSTEM

As we know, political powers have always tried to interfere with the working of monetary systems because of the opportunity to make profits. This temptation is particularly important at this stage of development, and the imaginary story which we have presented coincides particularly well with the historical facts at the point we have now arrived at. A public authority has an apparently strong argument to nationalize the privileged bank. It relies on the fact that the bank enjoys a monopoly position and therefore could despoil its customers, as seems to be well proved by the traditional theory of monopoly. But the political power forgets to say that this monopoly position has been created by itself, since it gave a privilege to a specific bank. Institutional aspects are so important in the analysis of monetary systems that it is not possible to have a correct view of the working of these systems without referring explicitly to the general theory, especially the theory of competition, monopoly and cartel.[8] Now, it can be shown that there cannot be any true sustainable monopoly except in cases where, specifically, a public power gives to a specific firm production authorizations which it denies to all other firms. Observing monetary systems allows this idea to be illustrated perfectly. As we will see, it also provides a striking illustration of the idea that a monopoly can 'despoil' its customers.

During the nineteenth and twentieth centuries, most governments nationalized privileged banks and they also gave them an increasing number of privileges denied to other banks. Privileged banks became central banks, placed at the top of the hierarchy of monetary systems, which had become pyramidal.

---

[8] For this, refer to my book, previously mentioned, Salin (2015).

In the previous step, each bank gave a convertibility guarantee into gold at a fixed price for its own currency, and convertibility guarantees at a fixed price for its currency against the currencies of other banks (at least those that belonged to the same monetary cartel). Now, these guarantees are removed and replaced by others: only the central bank gives a convertibility guarantee into gold to its currency and the currencies of other banks (now called the commercial banks) benefit from convertibility guarantees at a fixed price against the currency issued by the central bank. These guarantees may be given by the commercial banks themselves, or only by the central bank. Thus, the currencies (deposits) issued by commercial banks are indirectly convertible into gold because they are convertible into the currency of the central bank, which also implies that they are convertible between them at a fixed price. All of these monetary units, whether they are issued by the central bank or by commercial banks, usually have the same name (dollar, pound, franc, euro, and so on). Moreover, a currency system in which the same money is issued by several producers implies the possibility to exchange the currency units issued by one of them in monetary units produced by others. We have seen that the existence of a clearing house facilitates these exchanges. In the system where we are now, trade between currency units ultimately uses the currency issued by the central bank as an intermediary. As a result, most often, the central bank adds to its various roles the role of a manager of the clearing house. But one could very well imagine, however, that the clearing house is independent from the central bank.

We have thus arrived at monetary systems the structure of which we examined previously in Chapter 11. The balance sheets of the central bank and commercial banks have the following form (if we take into account only their monetary activities and not their financial activities, that is, the transfer and transformation of savings, which are normally performed by commercial banks):

The balance sheet of the central bank

| assets | | liabilities | |
|---|---|---|---|
| claims | A | C | banknotes |
| gold stock | G | R | reserves of commercial banks |

Balance sheet of commercial banks

| assets | | liabilities | |
|---|---|---|---|
| claims | A | D | deposits |
| reserves at the central bank | R | | |

The central bank does not usually issue deposits held by the public (individuals and businesses), but only by commercial banks (the so-called reserves of commercial banks with the central bank). The money supply consists of the deposits of banks and the banknotes of the central bank ($M = C + D$).

The value of the money supply is a multiple of the gold stock. For a given level of the gold stock, it depends on the reserve coefficient of commercial banks ($R/D$) and the reserve coefficient in gold of the central bank, which is the ratio between gold reserves and the monetary base ($G /(C + R)$, the monetary base being the total of the liabilities of the central bank.

When shifting from the monetary system of the previous step to the monetary system of the step which we are considering, the quantity of money becomes a higher multiple of a given gold stock. There is therefore a situation exactly similar to the one which we met in the shift from the third step to the fourth step (shift from 100 per cent reserves to fractional reserves): during the phase of transition between the two successive steps, the money supply increases faster than the stock of monetary gold, and commodity prices rise more than in the previous step. But when the long-term values of the various reserve coefficients of the system (reserve coefficients of commercial banks and of the central bank) have been reached, the growth rate of the quantity of money again becomes equal to the growth rate of the stock of monetary gold and the rate of inflation regains its long-term value.

The evolution of monetary systems in the previous steps could be deduced from pure logic: any change in the nature and the working of the monetary system corresponded to a need of producers or users of money, and each time a logical answer could be given. But we are now at a very different step, since the evolution of monetary systems is now due to state decisions. Now, what characterizes the state decisions is that they can be taken in a discretionary way: to the extent that the state has a monopoly of legal coercion, it can impose reforms without the possibility for the real needs of citizens to be expressed, unlike what is happening in a competitive private economy where any decision of a producer is subject to the ratification of the market, that is, of those who are concerned. This is why, from now on, we can no longer imagine a logical progression in the evolution of monetary systems. To describe the evolution we instead need to gather the most important features of this evolution, such as have usually been imposed by the states in reality. This evolution is therefore discretionary, although states generally seek to give acceptable justifications for their decisions.

We have just seen that, little by little, central banks gained the monopoly of the commitments of convertibility into gold. But this monopoly has been most often reinforced by other elements, for instance – as already mentioned – because the central bank also plays the role of a clearing house. However, one of the most important elements of this monopolization has been the legal tender laws. This means that the residents of a country are obliged to use the 'national' currency for domestic transactions, that is, the banknotes issued by the central bank and the currency units which are convertible at a fixed price against the currency of the central bank. Whereas previously monetary cartels did not necessarily have a territorial base, there is now a coincidence between a monetary area and a political area (already noted in Part I of this book). Thus, monetary systems have acquired the characteristics which we know nowadays: they are national, public and hierarchical. However, as we have seen, these three characteristics are absolutely not necessary for the proper functioning of monetary systems, since the systems which we have previously studied had none of these features and they worked perfectly, which means that they were providing to money-users the services they expected from them in a fully satisfactory way.

Obviously, the public and national character of modern monetary systems has led states to enact different kinds of regulations relating to the operation of commercial banks and the assignment of various roles to the central bank. This latter, among other roles, is expected to play a role of 'lender of last resort', meaning that it may guarantee the liquidity of a bank which would have difficulties in meeting the demands for the conversion of its currency into the currency of the central bank, or more generally, to help a bank to avoid bankruptcy. Later, we will see that this function of the central bank, far from being a guarantee for the proper functioning of a monetary system, may instead encourage irresponsible behaviours and therefore contribute to monetary instability.

But there is one aspect of these monetary systems that is particularly important and particularly regrettable. As we know, the convertibility guarantees of a currency into gold are now given by the central bank and no longer by the issuers of money (commercial banks) for the monetary units produced by each of them. In the monetary systems of the previous steps, the convertibility guarantee had a contractual basis and it was, from this point of view, credible and useful. Let us imagine that a private bank in these earlier systems had issued a currency called the dollar with a convertibility guarantee of 1 dollar against 1 ounce of gold. And let us imagine that, one day, one of its clients comes and asks the exchange of 1 dollar against 1 ounce of gold, in accordance with his contract, and that the bank answers: 'I will give you only half an ounce of gold against your dollar.' This would clearly be a theft and the bank would probably be brought to the courts for breach of contract. Furthermore it would probably lose customers, who would prefer to use the monetary units issued by other banks with which it competes. Therefore, it would probably go bankrupt. However, it is obviously not in the interest of the owners of this bank to go bankrupt and this is why the banks in the monetary systems of the previous steps avoided practising such plunder. The competition between producers, and the contract, are the best guarantees for clients in all activities. This is the case for monetary activities.

However, when the system became public and national, rather than operating according to the usual standards of life – involving respect for contracts – it was conceded that it could work in accordance with the customary state practices. In this latter case, one admits, oddly enough, that the state may at any time change its commitments in a discretionary manner, that is in fact, that it does not undertake any contractual commitment. If the central bank had sold a banknote of 1 dollar against 1 ounce of gold, it allows to itself the possibility to decide at some date in a discretionary way that, henceforth, it would only give 0.5 ounce of gold against a banknote of 1 dollar. This is called a devaluation. Thus it is obvious that a devaluation represents a theft which, although it is legal, is nevertheless a theft.

Furthermore this possibility greatly modifies the macroeconomic effects of the working of monetary systems. As we have seen, until this step of development, fluctuations of the gold stocks were the means by which the issuance of money was monitored and this avoided an excessive growth of the money supply. If a bank issued too much money, its reserve coefficient in gold decreased and it had to react by stopping, and even reversing, its money creation in order to effectively maintain the convertibility of its currency into gold. But if a bank can resort to a devaluation, as is the case for a public central bank, this discipline no longer exists. If a central bank is employing a too-expansionary monetary policy – which implies that commercial banks and the central bank provide too many credits, taking into account the existing gold stock – the result is inflation and the creation of fictitious savings, thanks to the distribution of credits which do not correspond to voluntary savings. But, by devaluing the currency, the central bank can indefinitely continue its expansionary monetary policy. Let us thus suppose that initially the stock of monetary gold is equal to 100 ounces in a country, and that 1 dollar = 1 ounce of gold (so that the stock of gold is worth 100 dollars in terms of dollars) and that the money supply is equal to 400 dollars, so that there is a money multiplier equal to four, that is, a reserve coefficient in gold of 25 per cent. If monetary authorities practise an expansionary monetary policy leading to a quantity of money equal to 800 dollars, by devaluing the dollar by half in terms of gold, 1 dollar will be worth 0.5 ounce of gold, and 100 ounces of gold held as reserves by the central bank will be worth 200 dollars, so that there will be a multiplier equal to four (in terms of dollars). Formally, the reserve coefficients of the commercial banks and of the central bank remain constant, but the exchange rate between gold and the national currency has been modified arbitrarily. As a result there is obviously both a creation of inflation and a creation of fictitious savings, since monetary policy was made possible by the proliferation of claims held by the banking system (that is, credits provided without corresponding voluntary and preliminary savings). Simultaneously, to get this growth in credits, the central bank has to cause a decline in the rate of interest (which induces investors to borrow). In such a case inflation does not result from the exceptional circumstances in which there is a shift from one step of development to another, as was the case previously. Inflation can be continuous and accompanied by frequent devaluations, and we can find innumerable examples in real economic history. Thus the fiction of a convertibility into gold at a fixed price is maintained, but this price (supposed to be fixed) is changed regularly. It is the very significance of the monetary regime which is thus disrupted.

If such a situation can exist, it is obviously because there are fractional reserves, but mainly because there is a (public) monopoly and because this can determine the price of a currency (in terms of gold) at will. But legal tender laws also play an important role in this regard. In fact, if there were no such laws, money-holders would divert from the most inflationary currencies to use other better-managed currencies. In this case one could say that 'the good currency is chasing out the bad currency', as this is normally the case in any competitive situation where individuals are obviously encouraged to choose goods that give them the best satisfaction, at the expense of others. However, this may seem contrary to a well-known precept, the so-called 'Gresham's law'. According to this (alleged) principle, 'the bad currency is chasing out the good one'. But Gresham's law plays only in special circumstances: when monetary authorities arbitrarily keep a fixed price between two currencies, while one of them is the subject of a money creation at rates much higher than the other, individuals obviously forecast that the less expansionary currency will necessarily be re-evaluated one day compared with the other. They are therefore not circulating the 'good currency' because they keep it in this perspective, and thus only the 'bad currency' can be seen in exchanges. But in reality the 'good currency' does not disappear, quite the contrary, since people want to hold it and they try to get rid of the 'bad currency' (so that only the 'bad currency' may be observed on markets, although it circulates because people want it to disappear).

During the previous phases of evolution, money creation was passive.

It was the result, in particular, of the confrontation between the growth in the production of gold, the evolution of the demand for non-monetary gold, and real growth. It is in the present phase of evolution that we see the appearance of the concept of 'monetary policy', that is, the ability of monetary authorities to manipulate monetary growth. Monetary policy is regarded nowadays as inevitable and even desirable. Yet it did not exist during most of human history, and this did not prevent the proper working of monetary systems; quite the contrary, as we have seen.[9]

The term 'gold standard' is generally used to refer to this system in which the central bank gives convertibility guarantees into gold at a fixed price (but in reality, modifiable). But it is necessary to distinguish carefully between different types of gold standards. In fact, the systems studied previously (except the case of barter) could all be entitled gold systems, since gold circulated as currency or constituted the basis from which the fiduciary currencies – that is, currencies based on confidence in the value in gold of monetary units – were created. But we can clearly see that there are different kinds of gold standards and must also be aware that the most important is not knowing whether currencies are formally convertible into gold, but knowing who gives the convertibility guarantee into gold: is it a private firm, the owners of which are responsible and therefore have interest in maintaining confidence in convertibility into gold at fixed price, or is it a public authority – the central bank – which makes no irrevocable commitment of convertibility into gold and thus can at any time change its alleged commitment to convertibility? This is why, when discussing the possibility of returning to the gold standard to solve the current monetary problems, one should clarify which gold standard is considered. History has clearly shown that it is not enough to have a gold standard system if the convertibility guarantee at a fixed price is not credible, which is the case in a public system.

## 20.8 EIGHTH STEP: THE DISAPPEARANCE OF CONVERTIBILITY INTO GOLD

This last step of the evolution corresponds to what has been the case in reality for several decades. The central bank stops giving a convertibility guarantee into gold. It eventually sells its gold reserves, or if it keeps them, does not give them a role of adjustment and thus it does not accept the

---

[9] As Friedrich Hayek once told me, he heard the term 'monetary policy' mentioned for the first time when he went to the United States in 1923. This concept was pretty much ignored until then, that is, up to a period that is not extremely distant from the present time.

conversion of its currency (banknotes or reserves of the commercial banks) against gold. Now, it is the growth of the claims held by the central bank which determines the growth of the quantity of money (as we saw earlier, in Chapter 11). The growth of the quantity of money therefore depends only on the discretionary decisions of the central bank, and money-holders have no certainty as regards the real value of their cash balances in the future. Now, money creation and inflation are limitless.

During the previous step, a continuous monetary expansion was possible only by using periodic devaluations of a national currency in terms of gold, and the fiction of a system called a gold standard was maintained. It is now possible without limits and without conditions. This is why we can say that the modern world entered into an era of inflation in the twentieth century. In fact, it is in relatively recent times that any reference to the gold convertibility of currencies has been abandoned. The Bretton Woods agreements, signed in 1944 between the main countries of the free world, had intended to return explicitly to a gold standard system (with central banks). It was intended that each country should announce a parity of its currency in terms of gold, but it could be expected to fulfil its obligations in this regard by maintaining a convertibility at fixed price between its currency and any other currency, itself convertible into gold at fixed prices. However, only the United States announced, in 1948, its desire to maintain a fixed parity between the dollar and gold. Other countries then announced that they would maintain a fixed parity between their currencies and the dollar, creating the so-called 'gold exchange standard'. The pyramidal scheme of which we have seen the development at the national level has become an international pyramidal scheme. The stock of gold of the US central bank allowed the creation of a certain amount of dollars (on the basis of a certain money multiplier) and the dollar reserves of the other central banks allowed the creation of a national money supply in each country (according to the money multipliers implicitly existing in each country). There was, therefore, a system of fixed exchange rates between national currencies. At the limit, all the world stock of monetary gold could have been held as reserves of the US central bank (the Federal Reserve, or Fed), but most central banks still kept some reserves of gold as a safety asset, even if they no longer exchanged their own currencies against gold.

This system of gold exchange standard mainly helped to maintain the fiction of an international monetary system based on gold. But it was in fact a fiction, because in reality the Fed declined to sell gold for dollars to holders of dollars, contrary to what is normally implied by a system of convertibility guarantee into gold, and it simply agreed to transfer gold to some central banks in certain circumstances and for a certain period of time. But with the mechanism of adjustment brought about by the convertibility of a currency into gold largely missing in this system, a monetary expansion virtually without limits was possible. This is what happened, and ultimately the Fed closed what was called the 'gold window' in 1968. It has officially maintained a price of the dollar in terms of gold ($35 per ounce), but this price was fictitious since the Fed declined virtually any transaction between the dollar and gold. In 1971 it was argued that it had devalued the dollar against gold, but this decision was purely formal since the US monetary authorities changed a price – the price of the dollar in gold – at which no more transactions could take place. Therefore, from then on, for the first time in history, there was a situation in which money had no more definition in real terms (in gold or silver, or in terms of any other good). The dollar had no other definition than being a dollar, a pound a pound, a franc a franc, and so on. It became clear that monetary expansion had no more limits and that monetary policy would evolve in accordance with the discretionary decisions of monetary authorities. As each country finally wanted to decide its own monetary policy independently of the others, there was only one solution: adopting a floating exchange rate regime under which – as we have seen – monetary policies are independent from one another. This is what has been done, with the exception, in particular, of the subsequent efforts to maintain fixed exchange rates between European currencies (the European Monetary System, EMS) before the creation of the euro.

At the end of this long evolution, public authorities now have the ability to decide an unlimited money creation. Some countries do take this opportunity, in particular to finance their public deficits, and it is not surprising that in the twentieth century extraordinarily high rates of inflation occurred, never before seen in the history of mankind. At the limit, in the case of hyperinflation, people stop using a currency the quality of which has become too bad and go back to barter – which corresponds to a very damaging regression – or find bad substitutes by using various kinds of real goods to play the role of intermediary in exchange. Thus, a little surprisingly, cigarettes played this role during the German hyperinflation of 1923 (and a restaurant waiter had to climb on a table every 30 minutes to announce the new prices of the dishes). We will see later how, in modern monetary systems, monetary policy can be used and how it is possible to limit the propensity of public authorities to practise inflation.

# 21. The working of fixed rate systems without an international currency

For a long time the working of monetary systems has been determined by convertibility guarantees between various money units (created, for example, by commercial banks or central banks), on the one hand, and on the other hand, an international currency, for example gold. Thus, in the case of a gold standard in which the convertibility guarantee into gold at a fixed price is given by central banks, commercial banks of a country issue deposits based on the reserves they hold at the national central bank, the latter guaranteeing the convertibility of its currency in gold. Thus all the monetary units issued in different countries are indirectly exchangeable at fixed price because they enjoy guarantees of convertibility into gold at a fixed price. However, the fixity of exchange rates is not absolutely perfect for two reasons:

First of all, there are so-called 'gold points' which determine a margin – normally limited – within which the exchange rate between currencies may vary around the parity. The latter is determined by the price in gold for each currency. Thus, if 1 Ecu is worth 1 ounce of gold, and 1 ducat is worth 1 ounce of gold, the parity between the Ecu and the ducat is equal to 1/1 (1 ducat is exchanged against 1 Ecu). For convenience international transactions are settled in national currencies and not in gold, but the use of gold is always possible in a system of this type. In accordance with the possible changes in supply and demand for two currencies, the exchange rate between these two currencies changes on the market. But if, for instance, an individual who holds ducats must obtain Ecus to pay for an import, and if the Ecu has a price in terms of ducats higher than the corresponding parity, he may have an interest in buying gold, in paying the costs of transport and insurance to export this gold to the country where he uses the Ecu, and in buying Ecus against gold. The amount of the costs of transport and insurance determines what can be called the 'exit gold point', that is, the exchange rate between the two currencies beyond which it is preferable to use gold to pay for an international transaction. Likewise, there is an 'entry gold point' when the price of the foreign currency is low compared to what corresponds to parity. Of course, the size of the margin of fluctuation in the exchange rate between the gold points is variable since, for example, transportation of gold may depend on the distances between the concerned countries.

Secondly, as we have seen, when the guarantee of convertibility into gold is given by a public central bank it may, in a discretionary way, change the 'guaranteed' price – that is, decide a devaluation or a re-evaluation – so that the exchange rate between currencies can be changed.

But at the end of the evolution of the monetary systems which we have previously studied, there is no longer an international currency – such as gold – determining the exchange rates between national currencies thanks to the convertibility guarantees at a fixed price. As we have seen, the only remaining guarantees now are the convertibility guarantees between the currency of the central bank and the currencies of the commercial banks within a national monetary system. Currencies have no more definition in real terms. Under these conditions the currencies issued in different national monetary systems have no a priori reason to be exchanged at a fixed price, since there is no longer a common system of convertibility guarantees for all these systems. The monetary units issued by these systems are different and, most importantly, are perceived as different, inasmuch as in each country monetary authorities can implement different monetary policies. Therefore, it is natural, under these conditions, that exchange rates be flexible. Just as the relative price between two goods changes according to the changes in the supply and demand for each of these goods, so the relative price between two different currencies will be variable according to the evolution of supply and demand for these currencies.

However, it is often the case that, in spite of these differences, the monetary authorities of a country wish to maintain a fixed exchange rate between their currency and one or several other foreign currencies. How are they to get this result? Generally, in order to obtain a given price for a good, a government acts through compulsion, through a law or a decree which imposes the price which is desired by the government for this good (or, possibly, a maximum or a minimum price). This is not possible for an exchange rate because public authorities do not have any power of coercion over the activities of non-residents, and they cannot prevent foreigners from using an exchange rate different from the one they would like to prescribe. The only option, then, is to give a convertibility guarantee at a fixed price between a national currency and one or more other national currencies. This convertibility guarantee at a fixed price can be given unilaterally, or it may result from an agreement of cooperation between several monetary authorities.

## 21.1    THE FIXITY OF THE EXCHANGE RATE BETWEEN TWO CURRENCIES

Let us suppose that there are two currencies in the world, controlled by two central banks. If one of them wants to establish a regime of fixed exchange rates between the two currencies, it must buy and sell its own currency against the foreign currency at fixed price to achieve this goal. But this can be done in two ways.

The central bank can, first of all, refrain from announcing its intention to maintain a fixed exchange rate, but it sells and buys the foreign currency on the exchange market depending on the day-to-day fluctuations of the exchange rate so that it constantly stays very close to the objective it has decided. Thus, if its currency appreciates against the foreign currency, the central bank will buy a certain amount of foreign currency. On its balance sheet, there is an increase of its assets in foreign currency and a correlating increase of its liabilities, that is, there is a money creation (and, of course, there would be a decrease in the quantity of its currency if it wanted to prevent the depreciation of its currency). This simply illustrates the fact already stressed that monetary policy cannot be independent in fixed exchange rate regimes. In other words, for a central bank, choosing the fixity of the exchange rate of its currency is choosing to import the monetary policy of the other central bank, for better or worse. This means also that, inflation being necessarily harmful, it would be desirable that a central bank chooses to set its exchange rate with a foreign currency which would be the least inflationary as possible (or even deflationary). But there is also a difficulty for the operation of such a system. Let us imagine that there are two central banks, A and B, and that each wishes to maintain a fixed exchange rate between their two currencies, but that they are aiming at different values for the exchange rate. It is obvious that there is an inconsistency. This may result in disordered fluctuations of the exchange rate on the basis of the reactions of each central bank until, eventually, at least one of them abandons its exchange rate goal.

Secondly, the central bank may announce that it is ready to buy and sell without limits its own currency against the foreign currency at a fixed price. As we have seen previously, the monetary policy of the central bank which makes this decision is dependent on the monetary policy of the other central bank. If, despite everything, it claims to implement an independent monetary policy – for example, an excessive issuance of money – it loses foreign exchange reserves. It cannot indefinitely carry on this policy because its foreign exchange reserves are necessarily limited. The logic of the operation of a system of fixed exchange rates implies that the central bank adjusts its monetary policy on the basis of changes in its foreign exchange reserves. These variations are an indication of the too-expansionary or too-restrictive character of its monetary policy, compared to the monetary policy of the foreign central bank with which it had decided to be linked. But it can also be the case that, since it does not accept the rules of the game of a fixed exchange rate system, the central bank decides to abandon its stated aim of exchange rate fixity – at least temporarily – and it devalues (or it re-evaluates) its currency.

## 21.2  THE *N* − *1* PROBLEM

Now suppose that there are not only two currencies, but a number, *n*, of currencies. There is in this case *n* − *1* exchange rates of these currencies in relation to one of them taken as the standard of value. Therefore, in order to obtain fixed exchange rates between these *n* currencies it is necessary and sufficient that *n* − *1* central banks act so that exchange rates – which otherwise would be flexible – are made fixed. As we have just seen, each central bank can reach this target either by modulating its monetary policy according to the short-term variations of the exchange rate of its currency (in terms of the *n*th one) in such a way that its exchange rate remains close to the pursued objective, or by announcing its intention to buy and sell without limits its own currency against at least one other currency. In the first case, there is a risk of incoherence insofar as all central banks will choose exchange rate targets, although there are *n* − *1* exchange rates and not *n*. If the central banks make commitments of convertibility at a fixed rate this risk of inconsistency disappears, insofar as, at least, their statements are not divergent (which is likely). However, one can imagine various organizational arrangements for a system of fixed exchange rates.

It is possible that *n* − *1* central banks announce a commitment to convertibility at fixed rate of their currencies in relation to the currency of the *n*th central bank – the reference bank – whereas this *n*th central bank does not make any commitment of convertibility. The fixed exchange rate system is asymmetric, which is implied by the fact that there are *n* central banks, *n* currencies, but only *n* − *1* exchange rates. But the fact that the system is asymmetrical does not necessarily mean that it is hierarchical. This means only that all monetary policies are dependent on the monetary policy of the reference central bank, for better or worse. This latter, alone, can implement an independent monetary policy. Such was the case, for example, of what has been called the dollar standard, that is, a situation where, after the abandonment of the gold convertibility of the dollar, a large number of central banks have nevertheless chosen to fix the exchange rate of their currencies against the dollar, so that all monetary policies have been determined by the monetary policy of the United States. The system would become hierarchical if, for example, the reference central bank could exercise control or a power of decision over the other central banks. This is what happened inside the 'franc zone' when the representatives of the French Treasury (and not from the Banque de France, strangely enough) were members of the governing boards of the central banks of the other countries of the franc zone (mainly in French-speaking African countries).

There would be a somewhat similar situation if only some of the $n-1$ central banks undertook commitments of convertibility at a fixed price with the currency of the reference central bank, with other central banks undertaking convertibility commitments at a fixed rate with the currency of one central bank other than the reference central bank. There would then be a pyramidal scheme in which, for instance, central bank A would give a convertibility guarantee at a fixed price with the currency of central bank B, which, as far as it is concerned, would give a convertibility guarantee at a fixed price with the currency of the reference central bank (other central banks undertaking commitments either with the currency of the reference central bank, or with the currency of other central banks, for instance with the currency of the central banks A or B). An example of a pyramidal scheme is found in the case of the franc zone: the central banks of the 'peripheral' countries (especially the African central banks, BCEAO and BEAC) maintained a fixed rate with the French franc which, itself, had for some time a fixed rate with the dollar.[1] Whatever the structure of the convertibility guarantees is, the monetary policies of central banks are dependent on the monetary policy of the reference central bank which, as far as it is concerned, can implement an independent monetary policy. For the coherence of a monetary system of fixed exchange rates, the only requirement is to be respectful of the '$n-1$ principle', that is, the principle according to which only one central bank may implement an independent monetary policy.

We can, however, imagine that the structure of a monetary system of fixed exchange rates is somewhat different and that it is based on a system of cooperation between central banks, and not on a set of decentralized convertibility commitments. More precisely, all central banks could agree together on the rate of growth of the money supply of the entire system (since, in a fixed exchange rate system, all national currencies – although with different names, and issued by different banks – are perfectly

---

[1]    Now, as is well known, the CFA franc (in Africa), the Comorian franc and the Pacific franc have, in principle, a fixed rate with the euro.

substitutable with one another and can therefore be considered as part of the overall money supply). A rule would then be set to decide the amount of money creation by each central bank in a given period. The simplest method would consist in authorizing each central bank to increase the money supply of its currency at the same rate for all, and obviously equal to the rate agreed in common. But we know that, in a system of fixed exchange rates, there are flows of money from countries where the currency is relatively abundant to countries where it is relatively rare, which depends on the relative growth rates of the various supply and demand for money. However, insofar as the real growth rates and money demand functions are different in each country, the same rate of monetary growth in all countries would necessarily result in flows of money between countries. As a result, some central banks would accumulate indefinitely the currency of other central banks, while others would gradually lose their foreign exchange reserves. This situation might not be sustainable and therefore an additional rule can be envisaged to avoid these growing imbalances. The most logical rule would consist in asking the central banks that lose reserves to reduce the growth of their quantity of money and, vice versa, to allow other central banks to increase their rates of growth of the quantity of money (trying – which is not easy – to maintain the desired rate of monetary growth of the whole set of countries). But it would still be preferable to simply ask the central banks which lose reserves to moderate their monetary creation, since, as we know, a currency is better, the less money creation there is; that is, the less inflation.

It is therefore clear that a system of monetary cooperation would imply more uncertainty and may work in a less efficient way than a decentralized system like those we met above. But we must also recognize that the decentralized systems analysed above are necessarily asymmetrical. In fact, as we have seen, $n - 1$ central banks depend on the monetary policy of the reference central bank, which creates two problems.

Firstly, 'peripheral' central banks may disagree with the monetary policy of the reference central bank and find it too expansionary, or not enough. Certainly, they could, in this case, become independent, simply by abandoning their convertibility guarantee at a fixed rate, that is, by adopting flexible exchange rates. They could also become dependent of another central bank, belonging or not to their 'cartel of central banks'. As we know, a national monetary system can be analysed as a cartel of banks (possibly consisting of a central bank and commercial banks) within which there are fixed prices between different monetary units thanks to the convertibility commitments at a fixed price. An international monetary system of fixed exchange rates can be considered as a cartel of cartels, that is, an international cartel of national cartels. A national cartel may therefore enter into an existing international cartel, or create one with one or more other national cartels.[2]

In addition, the reference central bank and, possibly, the commercial banks in its monetary system receive a 'seigniorage' since they sell money cash balances – which cost nothing to produce – and receive in return claims which bring them interest and which are possibly exchanged for real goods. In the balance of payments of the country producing the reference currency one finds exports of money and, as a counterpart, a 'deficit' of the trade balance or of the capital balance; that is, the country receives present or future real goods so that it has more goods at its disposal than it produces. If this reference country is implementing an inflationary monetary policy, there is an 'inflation tax', a portion of which is paid by residents of other countries in the area of fixed exchange rates.

## 21.3  IMPERFECT FIXITY

The logic of a system of fixed exchange rates is clear: when they adopt a system of fixed exchange rates, currency producers – that is, the central banks in the present monetary systems – accept a limit to their power of money creation. If a money producer makes an excessive money creation, it loses reserves, which is the signal that it must reduce the rate of money creation. Reserves are reserves in gold in a gold standard system, reserves in foreign currency in a foreign exchange standard system, and reserves of commercial banks with the central bank within a national and hierarchical system (as are the monetary systems nowadays). But, as we know, the discipline of fixity is not always accepted since in some institutional contexts – those in which the producers of money can act in a discretionary way – the convertibility commitment at a fixed rate is not always respected, and devaluations or re-evaluations are decided upon. In such cases there is an inconsistency, as it is argued that the exchange rate must remain fixed, but it is admitted that it can change. This situation has even been formalized by advocating – especially at the time of the gold dollar standard or the dollar standard[3] – 'fixed but adjustable exchange rates' (also called 'crawling pegs'), which is a contradiction in terms.

---

2   Of course, there is no reason in principle for a monetary cartel – that is, a monetary system – to have a national basis. Yet, this is what currently exists.

3   These traditional names – for instance 'gold dollar standard' or 'dollar standard' – are questionable because they focus on the role of the currency as a standard of value, while this role is secondary. It would be preferable – but less concise – to talk, for instance, of the 'system of convertibility into gold via a foreign currency at fixed prices' or 'system of convertibility into a foreign currency at fixed price'.

But another exchange system must also be mentioned, that in which monetary authorities announce a reference price of their currency in terms of another – the so-called parity – but accept fluctuations in the value of the exchange rate around parity within certain margins (for example, 1 per cent or 2 per cent around the parity). The exchange rate is therefore determined on the foreign exchange market, but it cannot go beyond the announced limits, because operators on the market know that it is possible to buy or sell one currency against another at the central bank once the exchange rate reaches the price ceiling or price floor. Arbitrage operations prevent the exchange rate from going beyond the limits of the margin of fluctuation around the parity.

It is difficult to justify the choice of an exchange system of this kind. In fact, just as it is necessary that a door be open or closed, so an exchange rate must be fixed or flexible. The fixity of the exchange rate has the merit of imposing a constraint on monetary policy and of giving correct information for currency users concerned with international trade. The limited flexibility of the exchange rate reduces the scope of these two features. But it also may be the case that a central bank decides both a margin of flexibility around parity and a variable parity ('crawling peg'). In this case, the variations of the exchange rate within the margin of fluctuation are an indicator for monetary authorities: if, for intance, the national currency reaches its floor price against the foreign reference currency, the monetary authorities can be encouraged to ratify this indication of the foreign exchange market by formally devaluing the parity (which obviously changes the value of the price ceiling and price floor). At the limit, if the change in parity is practised very frequently, everything works – or almost – as if this was a flexible exchange rate regime. In other words, formally the existence of a parity indicates that monetary policy is dependent on the outside, but changes in parity according to the signals of the market mean that in reality an independent monetary policy is adopted. Instead of modulating the monetary policy on the basis of changes in foreign exchange reserves, a central bank is implementing an independent monetary policy, but the variations of the exchange rate which would normally occur are managed, more or less efficiently. This system may be justified by saying that it allows exchange rate fluctuations to be limited, without preventing the long-run evolution of the exchange rate on the basis of relative monetary policies. But it may also be surmised that it merely aims at 'hiding' the real exchange rate variations which would correspond to changes in monetary policy and in the economic circumstances of the countries concerned. It can also result in large uncertainties insofar as the decisions of parity changes are made in a discretionary way. It is not possible to know in advance precisely what will be the amount of the change in parity, nor on which date it will be decided. In these circumstances one may wonder whether it would not be better, quite simply, to adopt a system of flexible exchange rates, without any intervention by the central banks.

There are many recent examples of the different types of monetary organization just mentioned. Thus, what has been called the 'European monetary snake' (1972–78) was a system of fixed exchange rates between European currencies, with a margin of fluctuation of 2.25 per cent around the parity. One may also quote the case of the Chinese currency, the yuan, the pivot rate of which – that is, the parity – is defined by reference to a basket of currencies (including the dollar and the euro). There is a margin of fluctuation of 0.3 per cent around this pivot rate and this rate is set daily by the monetary authorities, who usually decide as a pivot rate the exchange rate actually recorded the previous day within the limits of the margin of fluctuation. Even if the Chinese monetary authorities keep the possibility to modify the pivot rate according to their discretion, it can be said that China is in fact in a system of flexible (but managed) exchange rate.[4]

---

[4]  Numerous examples could be cited of the exchange rate regimes studied in this book. But, as already stressed, my goal is not to present monetary history, but to be concerned with the coherence and the scope of the different monetary systems and their interrelationships. But it would no doubt be of interest to refer to the numerous existing books on monetary history, and to undertake personal reading through the instruments of analysis proposed in this book.

# 22. Monetary policy and monetary crises

Monetary policy is a specific modality of state interventionism. State interventionism consists generally either in the determination by the state of the quantity of a certain good (from which results an equilibrium price determined by the relative supply and demand for this good), or the determination by the state of a certain price for a good (from which results a certain quantity of this good, supply and demand being modified by the state decision on the price). In the case of monetary policy this interventionism obviously consists mainly in determining the rate of change of the quantity of money, the result of which is a certain rate of inflation. Moreover, even if the state usually does not directly determine the price of money, for instance in terms of commodities (except in the case in which it imposes a comprehensive control of monetary prices for all commodities, therefore controlling the purchasing power of money), it can determine the cost of money creation (by manipulating the interest rate) or the price of a currency in terms of another currency (for instance by deciding fixed exchange rates, devaluations or re-evaluations, which, as we know, have consequences on the monetary prices of goods).

Monetary policy does not necessarily exist. Such was the case in the previously studied monetary systems in which the currency producers gave a guarantee of convertibility in terms of some real good, for example gold, and, in particular, if there are 100 per cent reserves. In the case of fractional reserves, there is a possibility to implement a monetary policy if the reserve coefficient is modified, but monetary policy still remains very limited and exceptional. We also know that monetary expansion is made easier when the convertibility guarantee is given by a public institution and when it can resort to devaluations. Finally, in modern monetary systems, where there is no convertibility guarantee, monetary policy is unrestricted. But it is, however, dependent on fixed exchange regimes, at least so long as the fixity is actually respected. Nowadays, only some rare examples of monetary systems without monetary policy remain. This is the case with the so-called 'currency boards'. A currency board is a kind of exchange office which merely exchanges monetary units denominated in a national currency against foreign currency units at a fixed price, that is, there are

100 per cent reserves. This system was used in the nineteenth century for English and French colonies. There are a few current examples, in particular that of Hong Kong, where the Hong Kong dollar is exchanged at a fixed price against the dollar (and where private banks issue banknotes).

## 22.1  WHICH ROLE FOR MONETARY POLICY?

Monetary policy is often proposed or used to solve macroeconomic problems. Thus, it is very generally accepted that an expansionary monetary policy is an instrument for economic recovery. But in order to justify this recommendation it is necessary to clarify how the creation of money can influence macroeconomic variables (for example, the growth rate of output and employment), which logically implies investigating the causes of the phenomena that it is wished to modify.

However, it is clear from what has been analysed previously that it is never necessary to create an additional quantity of money. Let us assume a situation in which economic agents hold the amount of real cash balances which they desire. If new cash balances are created, they will be considered as excessive by these economic agents, who will therefore try to exchange them for real goods (present or future). This will result in higher prices, as is well known, but there is no reason for it to translate into an increase in real output. Indeed, what determines the level of production is the set of productive incentives of producers (entrepreneurs and employees). Now, the incentives to make productive efforts (work efforts, innovation efforts, saving efforts, and so on) depend on the return anticipated from these efforts and of the degree of risk attached to them. Let us assume, for instance, that productive incentives have been partially destroyed by excessive regulations and compulsory levies which impair the yields of efforts (and possibly enhance the degree of risk insofar as the state can change its regulations and taxes in a discretionary way). It is obvious that money creation by itself – that is, the fact that there is a greater amount of money – cannot change these incentives and correct the root causes of the economic situation (for example, low growth and high unemployment). This is also the case if, contrary to our assumption above, economic agents do not initially have the amount of real cash balances they desire. In fact, in this case, their need of cash balances can easily be satisfied by the 'real cash balance effect', and money creation cannot in any way change the productive incentives the weakness of which is explained by real factors (regulations and taxes) which have nothing to do with monetary phenomena. It is therefore an illusion to believe that by providing more means of payment to individuals, stronger growth or lower unemployment may be achieved.

In reality those advocating an expansionary monetary policy may instead consider – more or less implicitly – that any monetary creation, nowadays, has a counterpart in a distribution of credit. For this distribution of credit to occur, it is obviously necessary that the interest rate decreases, which increases the incentives to invest of potential borrowers. This possible increase in investment can be regarded as a means of increasing production in the longer run or – in a Keynesian perspective – as a means of increasing total demand.

Thus the expansionary monetary policy is considered as desirable because it is actually a way to manipulate the interest rate. But what happens is the same as what happens whenever an interventionist policy on prices is practised. By comparison, when a government has a policy of blocking rents under the pretext of helping the tenants, the consequence is an additional scarcity of supply which ultimately is harmful for the tenants. Similarly, one gets what is sometimes called a perverse effect by manipulating the interest rate. Doing so increases the incentives to invest, but reduces the incentives to save, thus creating a disequilibrium between the demand and the supply of loanable funds. We must not forget that the interest rate is the price of time and it normally reflects the intertemporal choices of individuals. Manipulating the interest rate thus imposes a price of time different from the equilibrium price and therefore creates a particularly important disequilibrium. This policy consists in behaving as if the resources in savings are more important than they are in reality. But the illusions cannot last indefinitely. In fact, this policy diverts the factors of production from the sectors of consumer goods (while consumption has increased due to the decrease in voluntary savings) so that they can be used in the sectors of capital goods. In addition, investors decide investment projects which are less profitable or more risky than would have been the case if the equilibrium interest rate had been respected. The expansionary monetary policy therefore does not solve macroeconomic problems since it does not correct the causes of these problems. But it is creating illusions by imposing a price of time different from the price which would correspond to the intertemporal choices of individuals. As analysed by economists of the so-called 'Austrian school' (in particular, Ludwig von Mises and Friedrich Hayek), this policy is the source of business cycles in the modern era. It creates distortions in the production structures and price structures and it is at the origin of monetary and economic crises.

The expansionary monetary policy brings about other illusions. Thus, it increases the prices of goods, but it takes a while until nominal wages adjust to the new price level, so that, during a short period, real wages decrease. This encourages producers to increase employment and this creates the illusion that the unemployment rate changes in a direction opposite to that of the inflation rate, as it systematized by the Phillips curve. But this illusion cannot last and nominal wages adjust gradually to the level of prices, so that monetary authorities are tempted to accelerate money creation to create new illusions indefinitely, until they find themselves in a situation of hyperinflation in which money plays its role very poorly and where, consequently, the economy is disorganized. Milton Friedman demonstrated in a very convincing way[1] that the Phillips curve could exist in the short term, as a result of the illusions created by inflation, but that in the long run there is instead more unemployment, the higher is inflation.

From a general point of view, it can be said that it is illusory to want to use monetary instruments to solve real problems (for example, slow growth or a high rate of unemployment). This is true for monetary policy, but also for monetary manipulations consisting, for instance, in devaluing a currency or in intervening on the foreign exchange markets to influence exchange rates. We have also seen that there is a one-to-one relationship between the exchange rate and the money supply. Money creation decreases the price of a currency in terms of goods (inflation) or in terms of a different currency (depreciation or devaluation). Likewise, a devaluation translates into an increase in the money supply and it cannot have any more real positive effects than any policy of monetary expansion can have.[2]

## 22.2   MONETARY AND FINANCIAL CRISES[3]

It has been stressed above that the excesses of money creation were at the origin of the financial and monetary crises of modern times. But to understand the emergence of these crises, it can be helpful to keep in mind a reference model that may be defined by two characteristics.

Firstly, the existence of a 'stable' currency or, more specifically, the existence of a monetary system in which an arbitrary monetary creation is impossible. In a system of this kind, monetary policy cannot exist, that is, no public authority may change at will the quantity of money, creating phases of inflation or deflation. Such a situation is, for instance, what could be known within a gold standard system in which gold serves as a base currency, but it is impossible to indefinitely multiply the quantity of

---

[1]   Friedman (1968).
[2]   On all of these issues, refer to my study in Salin (2014).
[3]   This section is extracted from my text, 'La crise financière: causes, conséquences, solutions' (Salin, 2009).

money by arbitrarily creating banknotes or bank deposits with a decreasing ratio of gold to the quantity of money. In this case, prices are certainly not perfectly stable, because the amount of money may vary (in one direction or the other) in relation to the amount of commodities and financial assets, but they evolve slowly and in a relatively predictable way.

Secondly, there are abundant and voluntary savings, that is, these savings match the desire of individuals to give up present consumption in order to gain more abundant resources in the future. These savings are composed of equity capital – with a rate of return which is risky and therefore variable – and of loanable funds on which savers receive a fixed interest rate, decided in advance on a contractual basis between lenders and borrowers.

The interest rate is determined on the market for loanable funds between the lenders and borrowers. The behaviour of lenders is determined by their 'preference for time', meaning that they require compensation – the interest rate – to renounce their preference for the present. The behaviour of borrowers, in particular owners of capital, is determined by the rate of return that they hope to obtain by the use of borrowed resources. Normally, there is no reason for the interest rate, thus determined, to change abruptly and greatly. In fact, the determinants of this rate – the time preference and the rate of return of capital – evolve only slowly and within narrow limits.

The world just described for reference is a world of relative stability of prices and interest rates. It corresponds roughly to what was known until the nineteenth century. Unfortunately, the modern world is very different. First of all, capital accumulation is discouraged by excessive taxation and consequently there is a temptation to create savings artificially in order to meet the demand of investors. Furthermore, the interest rate is no longer determined only by the market for loanable funds, but has become an instrument of monetary policy. Money creation is in the hands of public authorities which determine the rate of interest, either directly or indirectly, by the purchases and sales of financial assets by the central bank. As a result, a more or less significant gap may exist between the interest rate resulting from monetary policy and the interest rate which would reflect the relative scarcity of loanable savings and which would therefore be determined by the wants of lenders and borrowers.

This 'political' determination of the rate of interest is at the heart of the 'Austrian theory of the business cycle'. In an effort to stimulate economic activity and investment, monetary authorities implement a 'cheap money policy', which means that monetary policy is expansionary and interest rates are low. Insofar as savings are insufficient to finance both private investment and public deficits, monetary authorities are tempted to open the floodgates of bank credit, with a creation of money as a counterpart. The corresponding decline in the rate of interest is totally artificial since it suggests that loanable savings are more abundant than they are in reality. In doing so, public authorities therefore give wrong information to markets. Thus, not only do public authorities not have better information than the markets, but in addition they create bad information and they change the behaviour of economic agents accordingly. As interest rates are low, borrowers are encouraged to borrow more in order to finance investments, to buy financial assets or to purchase housing (case of the United States or Spain at the beginning of the twenty-first century).

It is thus that 'financial bubbles' or 'real estate bubbles' are born. There is a tendency to regard them as the product of the irrational behaviour of investors who have a sheeplike attitude: thus an increase in the prices of shares would be interpreted as the indication of an indefinite increase of their prices, encouraging investors to increase their demand for assets, which makes prices increase again, and so on. It is basically what the former president of the Fed, Alan Greenspan, called 'irrational exuberance' in markets. But this should be analysed very differently: the expansionary monetary policy and credit policy suggest that savings are much more abundant than they are in reality. This is also wrong in that, in reality, the decline of the interest rate reduces the supply of loanable funds, thereby increasing the difference between the existing interest rate and that which would correspond to the equilibrium between supply and demand of voluntary loanable funds.

Of course, it could be wished that economic agents would better understand what is happening and realize the artificial and temporary character of the decline in interest rates. But this understanding is difficult to achieve, and that is why it would be justified to say not that economic agents are irrational, but that they are rational, given the – very wrong – information they have. And if information is incorrect it is because of the monetary policy of monetary authorities. It is therefore wrong to say that the free working of financial markets makes 'bubbles' appear because markets are 'short-termist' and because economic agents are irrational, which would justify a regulatory adjustment by public authorities which are both rational and well informed. What is happening is quite different: there is a destruction of information by public authorities, precisely because they are 'short-termist', that is, because of the existence of the short horizon prevailing in the political world (which is mainly the horizon of the next election). Governments are tempted to create appearances – the appearance of easy credit and the recovery of economic activity – at the price of future disorders. All people are rational: politicians choose to create illusions in the short term, economic agents act on the basis of the information which they possess, the quality of which has been deteriorated by state action. The solution to these disorders obviously does not consist in increasing state intervention under the guise of adjustment, but in the refusal of state interference in the functioning of markets and in money creation.

## 22.3 SYSTEMIC RISK AND ECONOMIC INSTABILITY

In general, it is argued that a central bank is necessary because there are systemic risks in the field of money, and it should therefore be necessary that the central bank avoids a series of bankruptcies by playing the role of lender of last resort. In reality, there is no reason for a systemic risk to exist in the production of money more than in any other productive activity. And it is, instead, the existence of the central bank and the fact that the monetary system is hierarchical, public and national which creates systemic risks.

In a decentralized system, if someone is implementing a wrong policy (overexpansion of money) he may possibly go bankrupt. And if the firm issuing money belongs to a private owner (or a small number of owners) who, as such, is responsible, this owner is encouraged to avoid an excessive creation of money, precisely to avoid bankruptcy. A systemic risk appears when the decision-making process is centralized and when decisions are made by people who do not directly bear the consequences of their decisions, which is the case with monetary authorities: if the central bank is implementing a too-expansionary monetary policy, it creates a systemic risk, since it is the whole monetary system which creates too much money. This risk would result in the bankruptcy of all the banks if the monetary system in question was in competition with other monetary systems, as all customers would move towards a producer from a monetary system issuing a better currency. By using devaluations, exchange controls and legal tender laws, the central bank tries to hide the proofs of systemic instability, but it can obviously not end its existence.

In other words, for a systemic risk to exist it would be necessary that all banks exhibit the same behaviour, for example that there is an overexpansion of money and that convertibility is no longer provided. Modern monetary systems operate as if this risk did not exist, not because the central bank plays the role of lender of last resort, but because it removes the appearance of risk and its consequences. This behaviour is exactly comparable to that of public companies for which the appearance of risk is removed by preventing bankruptcy. But the risk is not removed in reality;

it is simply transferred (for instance to taxpayers, who pay the deficits of these firms). In a centralized monetary system in which an overexpansion of money is not sanctioned, individuals try to preserve the purchasing power of their cash balances by resorting to convertibility guarantees. But if these guarantees no longer exist, because of the existence of central banks which have suppressed convertibility and imposed legal tender rules, the risk, rather than being borne by those who have created a bad currency, is borne by everyone in a diffuse way. The fact that there is no bank bankruptcy because the central bank plays a role of lender of last resort does not mean that the system is thus made more stable. In fact, bankruptcy should be considered as a mechanism of adjustment in a productive system. The fear of bankruptcy encourages the producers to sell good-quality products. And as historical experience has shown, in a system of free banking, bankruptcies are rare or non-existent, not because the producers of money are artificially saved by a central bank, but because the decisions about the production of money are taken by responsible persons.

In a system of free banking, a systemic risk therefore cannot appear. As Lawrence White (1992) has shown, there is self-adjustment in money creation. For each bank the risks from lending and creating money grow with the expansion of their activities, thereby limiting the propensity to create money. This is also the reason why there is no need to impose upon banks a legal obligation to maintain 100 per cent reserves.

In a free banking system, specific risks for any particular bank can certainly exist, but there is no systemic risk. The problem is absolutely not different from that of non-monetary activities. If a company goes bankrupt, it generally does not cause the failure of all other companies in its sector or other sectors. These other failures may happen only if some of these companies have a very high debt ratio and a very low yield rate, which makes them very fragile and dependent on the failure of a debtor. But obviously, the solution to this problem cannot be found in regulation which seeks to avoid these possible series of failures or in any prohibition of bankruptcies, as is the case for public companies. The real solution to the problem is simply that the equity capital of enterprises is important compared with their debts. In a free productive system, the owners of enterprises are able to understand by themselves the importance of equity capital, and there is no need for regulations or nationalizations. But modern tax systems, the predominance of pay-as-you go pension systems instead of capitalization systems, and the excess of regulations, have killed the propensity to develop equity capital. One of the tragedies of the twentieth century is that there has been a shift from a world of equity capital to a world of borrowed funds (which are also often of monetary origin). Thus, within the same monetary system, there was a contrast in the early nineteenth century between, for instance, the banks in the state of New York and, on the other hand, the banks of Massachusetts or Rhode Island.[4] The first group of banks, very regulated, had low equity capital and were very unstable (with variability of the production of money, and bankruptcies). The second group, unregulated, had substantial equity capital and bankruptcies were non-existent, which illustrates the fact that a non-regulated monetary system is a stable system.

Modern business cycles are not real cycles, but monetary cycles. It is because of the specific features of the modern monetary systems that systemic risks exist, which does not depend on the nature of monetary systems in general. But nowadays circular reasoning takes place: one can observe monetary cycles and 'global' monetary phenomena (changes in interest rates, bankruptcies of banks which provided too many credits, and so on). One concludes that the operation of any monetary system induces systemic risks and that a mechanism for stabilizing the system should therefore be incorporated. The central bank is expected to play this role. However, this mechanism, intended to 'stabilize', is the one which actually destabilizes.

## 22.4 LIMITS ON MONEY CREATION

As has been seen in the different parts of this book, there can be no justification for a policy of monetary expansion. In fact, such a policy necessarily causes inflation, and inflation is necessarily bad because it reduces the purchasing power of money. Moreover, this policy may create harmful instability. Monetary policy is also unable to solve real economic problems. It is therefore justified to seek ways to minimize the creation of money as much as possible, and even, if possible, to stop it completely (in which case there is deflation if there is also real growth). This is largely what could be obtained in monetary systems based on a guarantee of convertibility at a fixed price into some commodity (such as gold). Therefore, should we return to the gold standard, as is sometimes claimed? In fact, as we have seen, there are several gold standards and the main problem is not whether a currency is convertible in gold or in some other good, but knowing who gives the convertibility guarantee: is it given by firms or persons who are responsible because they are in competition with one other, or by public authorities which, it is admitted, have the right to disregard their commitments? In a

---

[4]  According to Nataf (1997a).

competitive system, each producer is trying to do better than the others and it can therefore be expected that all of them will produce sound currencies, that is, currencies which are as stable as possible and which have an area of circulation as large as possible.

Certainly, to avoid resorting to monetary competition, there can also be an attempt to impose limits on the discretionary power of monetary authorities, that is, to impose what may be called a 'monetary constitution' or a 'monetary rule' (in the words of Milton Friedman). This monetary constitution essentially compels the monetary authorities not to exceed a certain growth rate of either the monetary base or the money supply. Depending on whether real growth is more or less high, the result is a more or less high inflation rate. Milton Friedman advocated maintaining the rate of monetary growth decided a priori regardless of circumstances, which avoids a cyclical evolution and which allows reliable information to be given to individuals. The adoption of such a rule eliminates the implementation of an active monetary policy which would aim at adjusting monetary growth to the phases of economic activity. This active monetary policy is in fact itself at the origin of monetary and economic cycles because of the many time-lags which exist: time-lags between the occurrence of economic phenomena and the corresponding awareness of them, between awareness and decision-making, and between a decision and its effects. To the extent precisely that the business cycles nowadays are due to the instability of monetary policy, it is better to have a stable monetary policy (with a rate of monetary growth as low as possible), regardless of circumstances.

The 'monetary rule' of Milton Friedman has in fact been reinterpreted and, instead of deciding upon a monetary growth target, a number of central banks have adopted the inflation rate as the goal of monetary policy. Thus the European Central Bank is required not to exceed a rate of inflation of 2 per cent in the eurozone, but now it is even alleged that it needs to achieve a target of a 2 per cent inflation rate, a lower rate being considered – wrongly – as a rate of deflation, and deflation being generally regarded as harmful, wrongly also, as we know. But, taking into account the time-lags mentioned above, the inflation target is difficult to meet and may in fact lead to monetary instability, and this is why the strict 'Friedmanian' monetary rule is preferable.

In all these cases, however, there is a risk that monetary authorities do not respect the limits that are imposed upon them, on the pretext, for example, of exceptional events. This risk is all the greater in that there is no sanction when the 'monetary constitution' is not respected. It is different in a system where currencies are produced by producers in competition, because they know that they might go bankrupt if they produce a poor-quality currency, that is, a currency rejected by the users of money. A public producer, on the contrary, enjoys a captive clientele thanks to the fact, for instance, that there are legal tender laws or the legal obligation to pay taxes with the national currency. That is why, in order to avoid a high inflation rate and monetary instability, it would be preferable to adopt a system of monetary competition between private currencies.

Finally, let us recall that it is quite often considered that it is possible to limit money creation by making central banks independent. This certainly means that they are independent of political power, which is desirable. In fact there are countless cases of situations, in the modern world, in which governments have used money creation by their central banks to finance public deficits, which are sometimes considerable. The independence of central banks is intended in principle to cut this relationship between public deficits and money creation. But it is not sufficient. In fact, first of all, independence can be used to do good or bad things and this is why it is above all necessary to set limits on the discretionary power of monetary authorities. It is also likely that a central banker, even if he is formally independent from the political power, can be influenced by political pressure or by the state of public opinion, so that he can be induced to implement an expansionary monetary policy.

# 23. Monetary integration in Europe[1]

The only relevant question concerning European monetary integration and the euro is the following one. If a change of monetary system is to be decided, it has to be justified by the adoption of a better one; but what are the criteria that may be used to evaluate the quality of a monetary system? The answer is very simple: a good monetary system is a system which makes it possible to produce a 'good' currency, in the same way as a good transportation system is a system which provides good transportation services. Now, how can we evaluate the quality of a currency? Simply by referring to the role of money.

## 23.1  OPTIMAL MONETARY SYSTEMS AND MONETARY AREAS

As we know, money is a 'generalized purchasing power', that is, it constitutes a good the characteristic of which is to be (more or less) tradable at any time, against anything and with anyone. The better it plays this role the better a currency is; the better a monetary system is, the more it makes it possible for a currency to play this role. The tradability of money is higher, the larger its circulation area and the better it maintains its purchasing power over time (namely, it is less 'inflationary'). Let us consider both these characteristics of money in turn.

First, a currency is more useful, and therefore more desirable, the larger is its circulation area. In fact, since a currency is held as a tradable purchasing power, it is more useful to its holder, the more easily he can exchange it against a greater number of goods with a greater number of persons. Moreover, exchanging one currency against another implies transaction costs and risk costs. Thus, undoubtedly, enlarging the circulation area of a currency brings gains to those who hold it. From this point of view the supporters of the euro were not wrong whenever they argued, before the creation of the euro, that adopting the euro would bring gains to

---

[1]  More about monetary integration can be found in my book, Salin (2015), already mentioned.

Europeans. However, most people rarely make exchanges with residents of other countries and, in any case, this is not the most important problem.

Let us assume that increasing the circulation area of a currency does bring marginal gains. These gains are necessarily decreasing: the usefulness of a currency dramatically increases whenever there is a shift from one to two money-users, but the gain is equal to zero whenever there is a shift from $n-1$ money-users to $n$ money-users, specifically if $n$ is very great (for instance, all the inhabitants of the world). Now the practical problem consists in knowing what is the dimension of the area beyond which the marginal gain obtained from increasing the circulation area is perceived as negligible. From this point of view, we cannot know in advance the optimal dimension of the monetary area.

At this point, it may be useful to recall that, beginning in the 1960s, there has been a very interesting literature on optimal monetary areas, inspired by the path-breaking work of Robert Mundell (1961). This approach is still quite often used as a clue in any discussion about monetary unification in Europe or elsewhere. The very idea of an optimal monetary zone is interesting, but the literature from this period (and following ones) has been inspired by Keynesian-type concepts. An optimal monetary area is defined as the area inside which economic adjustment is optimal, adjustment being evaluated through the usual concepts concerning the impact of fiscal and monetary policies on employment, inflation and the balance of payments. The real scope of this literature thus depends on the validity of the underlying theory. Without developing a detailed analysis of the role of fiscal and monetary policies, it may just be recalled what has already been stressed, namely that it is an illusion to believe that monetary policy can cure unemployment problems. But I stress in particular the following statements.

Firstly, there is an obvious relation between monetary policy and inflation. But the relations between monetary policy and real variables (for instance, employment) are only short- or medium-run ones and may go one way or another. In the long run, monetary policy and real variables are mainly independent from one other. However, steady inflation decreases the efficiency of the productive sector – since individuals have less real cash balances – and a changing rate of inflation introduces more uncertainty, with further negative effects on economic activity. Therefore, if any, an expansionary monetary policy can only have negative effects on production and employment, at least in the long run.

Secondly, employment depends on variables which have no possible relation with the public deficit (or surplus), which means that it is completely illusory to believe that any government may use its public budget as an instrument of economic policy to stimulate economic activity and employment. To be sure, tax policy influences incentives, but the traditional literature on optimum monetary areas does not consider this aspect of fiscal policy.

Thirdly, as we have seen previously, there is never any problem of balance of payments, so that the balance of payments cannot constitute a target for economic policy. In fact, this is quite obvious whenever flexible rates prevail. But it also ought to be obvious under a fixed rate system. In fact the only valid understanding of this system implies that there is a rule of the game which consists in adjusting monetary policy to the balance of payments. Thus, if ever there is a 'balance of payments deficit', it does not mean that this deficit has to be cured, it does not mean that there is some 'balance of payments problem', but it does mean that monetary policy has to become less expansionary, that is, there is a 'monetary policy problem'. Under a fixed rate system, an independent monetary policy cannot in fact exist; which, by the way, means that there cannot be any inflation target.[2]

To summarize, the traditional approach of optimal monetary areas, along the lines developed by Robert Mundell, defines an 'optimal policy mix', with two instruments – monetary policy and fiscal policy – and three targets – employment, inflation and balance of payments. Instead of that, we are left with purely one-to-one relations: on the one hand, a relation between monetary policy and inflation (under flexible rates) or balance of payments (under fixed rates); on the other hand, a relation between tax policy (and not fiscal policy) and economic activity. This means that an 'optimal currency area' cannot be defined as an area of optimal macroeconomic adjustment. In a very small monetary zone, as well as in a very large one, it is possible to use monetary policy in order to avoid inflation (or to maintain the fixed rate system) and it is also possible to determine the best tax policy. The only remaining monetary problem consists in determining to what extent it is desirable to enlarge a monetary zone (that is, a zone of fixed exchange rates). This cannot be solved without referring to the roles of money.

However, there may also be a deeper reason not to accept the traditional theory of optimal currency areas. In fact this traditional approach attributes a collective meaning to the word 'optimum', although the concept of 'optimum' cannot have any meaning, except at the individual

---

2   More precisely – as stressed in Chapter 21 – in a fixed rate system with *n* participants, one of them can independently decide its monetary policy and the *n–1* others cannot have any independent monetary policy; or, all of them have to decide a common monetary policy for the whole zone and each of them has to adjust its own monetary policy to the common one (which, by the way, is more or less impossible, as was experienced under the former European monetary system).

level. And this is the very reason why I am proposing a different approach of the optimal monetary zone, based on the individual perception of gains and costs brought about by the use of various currencies. It is only by acting that an individual can express what is optimal for him, and it is the interaction between all individuals which induces everyone to steadily change their actions in order to reach what they consider as optimal. Therefore, a policy-maker or an economist cannot legitimately decide from outside that some situation is optimal or not. It has to be revealed by acting people.

As regards currency areas, this simply means that one ought not to decide a priori that Europe – or any other part of the world – is an optimal currency area, which would imply for instance that it would be optimal to have only one single currency in Europe. In fact, we do not know whether it is optimal to have one single currency in Europe, and the only possibility to know this consists in experimenting, that is, introducing monetary competition, as was suggested by Friedrich Hayek as early as 1976.[3] From this point of view the minimal proposal would have consisted in allowing competition between existing national currencies. Thus, monetary competition and monetary integration would have prevailed in Europe for a long time if governments had simply decided to suppress exchange controls – which have never had any justification – legal tender laws and the obligation to pay taxes with the national currency. But real competition would obviously imply freedom to produce and to use any currency and not just national public currencies.

The idea might be supported according to which, even if the marginal gain obtained by money-users becomes negligible when the monetary zone reaches some (unknown) dimension, which might be smaller than that of Europe, nevertheless gains cannot become negative if the currency area is extended to the whole of Europe (or, why not, to the whole world). However, it is necessary to apply exactly the same theory when speaking of money and when speaking of any other good, namely competition theory, at least if one abandons the dominant approach – that of pure and perfect competition – and adopts the idea according to which competition just means freedom to enter a market, which implies in turn that it is a 'discovery procedure', as has been so frequently stressed by Friedrich Hayek. One of the greatest merits of competition comes from the fact it induces producers to differentiate one from the other in order to offer a better good than other producers. Contrary to what is implied by the traditional 'pure and perfect competition theory', real competition does not mean homogenization of

---

[3]   See Hayek (1976).

products but, on the contrary, diversification. This has important consequences as regards the process of monetary integration.

A constructivist approach may let people think that diversifying goods
would imply a waste of resources, so that it would be preferable to adopt
a 'rational' way of producing 'each' good by offering buyers one single
model, for instance the one which is considered by engineers or experts as
the best. In reality, diversifying goods can be considered as equivalent to
an investment: more precisely, an investment in innovation. As any investment, it implies bearing present costs in order to obtain future gains. Thus,
one may have dreamt in the past of a world with one single computer standard, since people have to bear costs from having to shift from one standard
to the other when several exist. However, Apple played a useful role in
stimulating technical improvements in the computing industry by choosing
another way than homogenizing standards. The same is true for monetary
unification. Constructivists dream of a European currency or, even, of a
single world currency. However, if monetary diversification was forbidden,
money-users would have to bear the risk of having a bad currency, without
any possibility for anyone to propose a better one. This risk does exist in
Europe. But, contrary to the dreams of constructivists, nothing could be
worse than a single world currency, particularly if the issuers of this currency were to benefit from a legal monopoly in the production of money.

If one accepts this approach of the monetary zone, it follows that there
is no reason to believe that there ought to be one single currency in Europe
(or the world). The monetary needs of people being probably very diversi-
fied, it may be the case that individuals (in Europe or in the world) would
desire currencies with different characteristics, adapted to their specific
needs, if a larger freedom of choice was to prevail. From this point of
view it is fallacious to wonder whether 'the' currency ought to circulate
over a more or less large area, as the proponents of the theory of optimum
monetary areas are doing. In fact, one of the main reason for not accept-
ing the euro approach comes from the fact it is nothing but an expression
of monetary nationalism. Its founders started from the idea according to
which there is necessarily a coincidence between the monetary zone and
the institutional zone. And since many want to build a European super-
nation-state, they consider that this state must have its own currency. This
approach is wrong, for both the reasons just presented, and because there
is no justification for the idea according to which money has to belong to
the state sphere. Even those who believe in the existence of so-called public
goods would meet a lot of difficulties in trying to apply the traditional
definition of public goods to money. Anyhow, for European nationalists
who believe that money is an expression of national sovereignty, building
a European nation implies creating a single European currency.

The dimension of its circulation area thus plays an important role in determining the quality of a currency. The other aspect concerns its ability to maintain its purchasing power, which means that a currency is the better, the less inflationary it is. The inventors of the euro believe that they have solved this problem just by claiming that the European Central Bank has a single target, namely maintaining the stability of the euro, and that it is independent. But these institutional guarantees are not sufficient for the euro to be a 'good currency', as I explain below.

In fact, there are many reasons to be sceptical. One main reason is related to the very design of the institutional system, as we will see later on. Let me just mention for the time being that defining a European inflation rate is necessarily arbitrary. Each potential money-holder may have a different definition of price stability from his own point of view, taking into account goods which are of particular interest to him, and this is an additional reason to think that diversifying currencies may be desirable.[4]

Not only for this reason, but also for another, more fundamental one, one ought to be sceptical about the target of monetary stability, in spite of the fact it is now widely accepted. It seems that adopting this target makes it possible to go back to the long-lasting period of price stability which had been made possible by the gold standard. But there is a fundamental difference between that gold standard and modern price stability policies. In fact, under a gold standard, money benefits from a definition and the producers of national currencies give an exchange guarantee at a fixed price between their own currency and gold: whenever there is an over- or underissue of money, it is necessarily signalled by losses or accumulations of gold, so that monetary stability is only the result, non-explicitly decided in advance, of the working of the monetary rule. Modern monetary policies claim that price stability is their target. They are more or less reliable, but they do not give any price guarantee, which means that the quality of a currency is not the outcome of any promise, given by money producers, to exchange without limits their own currency against gold or any other good or set of goods. Instead of giving a concrete guarantee, they just deliver a vague intention. It is to be regretted that the opportunity has not been taken of the creation of a new monetary system in Europe to give back a definition to money.

In short, it has never been known whether Europeans need one single currency or several, or whether Europe ought to belong to a larger monetary area, which means it is not known whether Europe (composed of a

---

[4]  For instance, a trader in raw materials may desire a currency the definition of which makes it possible to maintain the purchasing power of this currency in terms of raw materials.

more or less vast set of countries) constitutes an 'optimal monetary zone'. But there is no reason for one single European currency to exist, in other words for any coincidence between the zone in which a currency is circulating and the frontiers of one or several countries. Also, Europeans – and others – certainly need currencies which they view as able to maintain a certain purchasing power or, at least, currencies the definition of which is clear, durable and backed by exchange guarantees at fixed prices between them and one or several goods. This does mean that the very idea according to which Europe needs a single currency has no justification.

If there was free banking – which excludes the existence of central banks and monetary authorities – and if there were several producers in a European (or world) private monetary cartel, one could theorize that free entry or the potential defection of one member, proposing a better currency, would discipline the cartel. A single currency in one given area, but with several (private) producers, would make it possible to exploit potential economies of scale but, meanwhile, would make 'free-riding' and free entry possible, so that competition would not be suppressed. Potential flexibility of exchange rates would thus contribute to an international monetary order.

To the contrary, the creation of a European Central Bank may constitute the worst solution to the European monetary problem, since the creation of a – necessarily public – monopoly prevents potential competition in money creation. If ever the European Central Bank, producing a single currency, proposes a 'bad' currency, that is, an inflationary currency, Europeans may have no option to use a better currency. History repeats itself, and it has taught us that, whenever a government is supplying a bad currency, it obliges citizens to use it through exchange controls or legal tender laws. From this point of view, the existence of a single European currency is a risk for Europeans, as they cannot be absolutely certain that European monetary authorities will not abuse their power and will not impose an overproduction of money. In other words, the only cause of monetary disorders can be found not in the existence of flexible exchange rates (that is, competition), but in the existence of national monopolies in money production. The aim of European monetary integration has been the creation of a European monopoly in the production of money: by reducing competition, it creates a risk of monetary instability.

A European monetary order does not imply a single currency or fixed rates, if the optimal size of a monetary area is not Europe. But it certainly implies freedom of choice for money-holders, as well as potential and actual differentiation of activities inside the existing banking systems, and processes for adjustment to changing conditions. Needless to say, free competition is the best solution, since competition induces producers to improve their products. In the case of money, competition induces money producers to limit or to avoid inflation and monetary instability. However, even if perfect free banking seems to be unrealistic for the time being, partial moves towards more freedom in some activities is desirable and, at least, competition between the 'supra-national currency' – the euro – and the national currencies still existing in Europe may limit the propensity of money producers to inflate.

Thus, the plea in favour of a single currency in Europe could be justified by considering one characteristic of money – the dimension of the monetary zone – while forgetting the other, most important one: its purchasing power. However, the practical problem is that we do not know to what extent economies of scale and externalities do exist in the production of money and in various financial activities, so we cannot decide a priori what ought to be the optimal dimension of a monetary zone. Thus, there was no reason to believe that it was optimal to have fixed rates within the European Union area, or even a single currency. If, instead of creating the euro, there had been free competition between the existing European monetary systems, the possible existence of economies of scale would have been revealed by the working of the market: one currency or a couple of currencies would gradually have replaced all others. In that sense the only path towards a real process of European monetary integration would have been that of free banking and flexible rates between competing currencies. This remains true insofar as all European countries do not belong to the eurozone, so that competition could potentially exist if it was decided that all Europeans could use the currencies they prefer. The free choice of people would make it possible to determine which currencies are the best from the point of view of those who use them, as regards both the dimension of the monetary zone and the capacity to maintain the purchasing power of money. It also means that monetary integration could have prevailed in Europe for many years before the creation of the euro, if it had been decided that exchange controls and legal tender laws were abolished.

Fixed rates between currencies issued by national and public cartels of banks correspond to the creation of a public cartel of cartels and the disappearing of competition. The existence of such cartels can be explained, similarly to that of any other public organization, by the working of the political market. Instability in such cartels is the necessary consequence of the politicization of decisions. The experience of the former European Monetary System (EMS) gives clear examples thereof. Exchange rates were supposed to be fixed between European currencies, but parity changes were accepted. The designers of the EMS had been clever enough to define their system as an 'adjustable' system (although a system ought to have been based on intangible rules), which meant that the system was supposed to work well when exchange rates remained fixed, and it was supposed to work well when they changed.

## 23.2   THE EURO

There is an astonishing contrast between the spontaneous character of the emergence of the gold standards – at least, those which emerged originally – and the impressive administrative machinery which was set into operation to introduce this constructivist currency[5] named the euro: thousands of reports, of expert or politician meetings and of seminars, surrounded the birth of the euro; whereas no one can attribute any precise date to the launching of any currency under some kind of gold standard, nor quote any meeting of heads of state to introduce such a currency. As stressed previously, these currencies from the past were the outcome of spontaneous processes. If the gold standard has worked well – at least before being managed by central banks – it is obviously because it was born spontaneously in order to meet concrete needs of money-users.

Contrary to this historical example, the euro is typical of the dominant ideas of our time. It is characterized by both state interventionism and nationalism. It is a technical construction and not the result of an institutional process. It relies on centralized legal procedures and not on a contractual basis which would allow the free interplay of personal responsibilities. The way the euro has been created is also symbolic of a characteristic feature of our time, namely that ideas and theories in the monetary field are quite often unrelated to the general economic theory, as if money was a specific good, the role of which could not be understood by referring to the general laws of human behaviour.

'No single market in Europe without a single currency, no single currency without a European Central Bank': this is the dominant approach concerning monetary integration. This approach is obviously accepted by all those who consider the ultimate target of European integration to be substituting a super-nation for existing nations. Given the fact that, nowadays, the monetary zone and the national zone usually coincide, it is quite naturally admitted that the European institutional zone and the European monetary zone should be made to coincide. The supporters of this approach think that the diversity of currencies would imply an obsta-

---

[5]   The term 'constructivist' has been particularly used by Friedrich Hayek in order to qualify systems or organizations which are built from scratch by using an a priori approach, instead of being the spontaneous outcome of the working of interacting processes between human beings.

cle to trade, so that it would not be compatible with the single market: transactions between European countries with different currencies are assumed to be more difficult than transactions inside one country, since it is necessary to shift from one currency to another when trade takes place across frontiers.

But there are, in any field of activity, two conflicting approaches of European integration. According to the first one – which may still be dominant – political unification and economic unification imply a process of harmonization of all sorts of regulations, taxes, economic and monetary policies.

According to the other approach, competition is necessary not only among individuals – and I have already applied this idea to the problem of currency choice – but also among governments. In fact, people learn from their differences, and both very useful information and efficient incentives are lost when all individuals are obliged to live in exactly the same environment in a broad zone such as the European one. Competition among individuals is useful because it gives the incentive to any one of them to do better than others. Similarly, competition among governments is useful because it gives the incentive to a government to do better than others. Thus, it may be expected that, under a system of competitive governments, legislation, tax systems, regulations, money production or economic policies would be better adjusted to the real needs of citizens.

Obviously the constructivist characteristic of the euro is derived from the first approach. But I consider it more justified to use the second approach in order to evaluate the ways and means of organizing monetary systems – analysed as monetary cartels – and to evaluate the possible working of the European monetary system based on the euro. We will then see why this system cannot prevent systemic risks and why other possible solutions would be more desirable in order to achieve a type of monetary integration better fitted to the real needs of individuals.

In any human system the problem consisting of determining the optimal combination of diversification and homogenization has to be solved.[6] There are many goods (shoes and books, for example) for which there is an extreme need for diversification. Homogenizing production for these goods would mainly bring a loss of satisfaction (the 'European or world single book'). But there are also fields in which there is a need for homogenization. Such is the case, for instance, for telecommunications (it cannot be imagined that each individual would have their own telephone system), transportation and, obviously, money, for reasons we have already met.

---

[6]    See my article, Salin (2001).

But the problem which has to be discussed now consists in determining how this optimal mix of diversification and homogenization can best be obtained.

Competition – that is, freedom to enter a market both for sellers and buyers – makes it possible for individual needs to be revealed. Let us then assume that an 'optimal' dimension of the monetary zone thus emerges from the mere working of the market. How ought such a zone to be organized? In reality, one of the great merits of competition comes precisely from the fact it induces producers not only to produce goods as close as possible to what consumers desire, but also to organize production in the most efficient way.

From this point of view also, the inventors of the euro have given the most oversimple answer: since, they assume, there is a need for a single currency in Europe, this single currency has to be produced by a single European Central Bank. This bank has been given all the usual characteristics of central banks in the twentieth century: it is a public firm and it benefits (within certain limits) from a monopoly for the production of money on all the territories of the member countries of the European monetary zone (the 'eurozone'). Thus, the European monetary system is endowed with exactly the same characteristics as nearly all the current monetary systems, which are public, national and hierarchical (with a first-rank bank and second-rank banks). As we know, none of these characteristics is necessary in order to produce money, and one may even say that a monetary system works better when they do not exist.

This monetary monopoly attributed to a central bank is full of risks for the future. In fact, history quite often repeats itself. Now, it is obvious that never in history has money been as badly managed as during the twentieth century, a period in which the monetary system based on a monopoly of the central bank was chosen all over the world. These banks have imposed bad currencies on the inhabitants of their respective zones, by protecting themselves from competition thanks to exchange controls and legal tender laws. It is true that the development of international trade and changed minds may make it more difficult for monetary authorities to impose such restrictions nowadays. However, the assumption cannot be dismissed that, under the pretext of protecting Europeans from so-called external instability, monetary authorities in Europe duplicate exactly the errors of the past. Since we have in Europe a super-state with a super-central bank, we have the risk of suffering all the usual disorders of state monopolies.

From this point of view the so-called independence of the European Central Bank is not sufficient to guarantee a satisfying implementation of monetary policy. What is meant by 'independence' is obviously independence from the political power. It is assumed that this is easily obtained by forbidding national governments or European Union institutions to give any instruction to the managers of the European system of central banks and of the European Central Bank. Moreover, the international character of this central bank may reinforce its independence. But being independent is not sufficient to induce it to decide upon and implement a good monetary policy, insofar as this means that the managers are institutionally irresponsible: they can make good or bad use of their independent position, without the threat of any sanctions. Now, if the members of the Board or the Council[7] are independent, they nevertheless necessarily hold personal prejudices, they have a specific monetary culture, they care about their own careers (for instance, in their own country) or they have to face pressures from public opinion and governments; for instance, if the opinion prevails in Europe at some point of time that monetary policy ought to be more expansionary in order to stimulate economic activity, the managers of the bank may well yield to such pressure to avoid being blamed, even if it would not be justified. From this point of view, a system such as that of New Zealand is to be preferred: there is a contract between the governor of the central bank and the public authorities regarding the rate of inflation, and the governor can be dismissed if the target is not reached. There is an agreed-upon target, which is known by everyone and which cannot be changed at will.

Unhappily, it is probably a modern tendency, in order to cope with excessive state intervention, to believe that the working of a system can be improved by committing it to the care of autonomous offices and 'regulating' institutions. Generally speaking, in order not to abuse their power and not to encroach upon the rights of others, individuals always need an external control system; which, precisely, independence cannot provide. There is however a well-known and efficient control system, namely competition. Instead of creating an independent institution, it would have been much preferable to impose the discipline of competition upon it.

The European monetary system is more or less duplicated from the American one. It is a sort of federal system in which national central banks – which survive – are dependent on the decisions taken by the European Central Bank. Such a system can be analysed as a cartel of national central banks. But the actual working of such a cartel definitely depends on the distribution of powers and the processes of decision. Now, it is difficult to forecast precisely how it may work at any time in the future; which, by the way, brings a major cause of uncertainty as regards monetary policy. It seems that the European system is an independent and

---

[7]   The European Central Bank is managed by an Executive Board, composed of six members, and the European system of central banks by a Governing Council composed of all the governors of national central banks.

centralized cartel. But, although it may seem strange at first glance, the complex interplay between the managers of the European Central Bank, those of the national central banks, public opinion and the concerned governments plays a role which is more important and more unforeseeable, in that the system was conceived as a centralized system. Even if the distribution of tasks between the European Central Bank and the national central banks changes over time, for the time being the real decision power is located in the European Central Bank and national central banks play a purely technical role. In fact, the targets and instruments of monetary policy are decided at the central level for the whole monetary union, and national central banks are in charge, for instance, of the practical working of open market operations in their own national area, according to the centrally decided general rules. Therefore, it cannot be disputed that the European monetary system is a centralized and hierarchical system: the ultimate decision power belongs to the European Central Bank which decides the monetary policy implemented by national central banks, which are themselves placed above commercial banks.

Now, it is wrong to believe that decisions concerning the production of money necessarily have to be taken by a single centre: 'a single currency' ought not to mean 'a single central bank'. On the contrary, as is clearly demonstrated by both theory and history, a decentralized system, based on numerous and independent decision centres, probably works better than a centralized one. Let us take the example of the gold standard; not the pseudo-gold standard which has been managed by central banks in the nineteenth and twentieth centuries, but the system which was working in the eighteenth century. In fact, under any gold standard, currencies (banknotes and deposits) benefit from a convertibility guarantee in gold at a fixed price. But, as stressed in Chapter 20, what is essential is knowing who is offering the guarantee: is it a responsible person – who will have to honour its liabilities – or an irresponsible person? Private bankers issuing currencies are certainly responsible, as they want to avoid the risk of failure. The governor of a public central bank is necessarily irresponsible, since his bank cannot fail and he does not bear the harmful consequences of his own decisions.

It is quite clear that, in the case of private money producers, such as those studied earlier, there may be a need for homogenization. But, whenever a need does exist and people are free to enter into contractual arrangements, it may be supposed that this need will be satisfied, at least if it can be in a profitable way. As regards the decentralized monetary systems we are considering, the coordination of the money production processes will certainly take place. Different ways can be imagined, but all of them will lead to the same result: namely, that the currencies issued by all the banks of the system will be seen by money-holders as perfectly substitutable to one other, so that they will indifferently hold one or another of them. This system can be described as a voluntary cartel of money producers.

Usually, it is considered that a cartel aims at creating a monopoly situation in order to extract additional resources from consumers. This is certainly true as regards public cartels which can use coercion in order to obtain and to maintain their monopoly positions, by preventing any freedom of entry into their own markets. But it is impossible for private cartels. In this case, on the contrary, the role of a cartel is precisely to better satisfy the needs of customers by offering them a homogenous good, which they desire.[8] This is exactly what happens in the monetary field. But monetary systems in our time – including the European monetary system – are compulsory public cartels which benefit from a monopolistic position and use it quite often to offer low-quality currencies.

The shift from the spontaneous systems of the past to the monetary systems of our time has introduced two major changes which have already been stressed in Chapter 20: first, there has been a shift from a decentralized system to a centralized system, from a voluntary and non-hierarchical cartel to a compulsory and hierarchical cartel; and second, central banks have been nationalized, which means that there has been a shift from a system based on contractual commitments to a world of discretionary decisions taken by a public monopoly.

The lesson which can be drawn from these considerations for Europe is clear: until recently, Europe did not suffer from the fact it did not have a central bank but, on the contrary, from the fact there were central banks. Obviously, reinforcing the centralization of the monetary system by creating a public supra-national central bank does not help to solve the 'European monetary problem'. Thus, the euro is the outcome of an approach which mixes monetary nationalism, politicization of money, substitution of pseudo-independence to an external control by competition, and the use of a compulsory and constructivist process, instead of a spontaneous one. All these elements are sources of potential dangers for monetary management.

Had the European monetary system been designed in a much more decentralized way, it could work more efficiently. In such a case, the European Central Bank (ECB) would issue European base money (according to rules appropriate to limit the production of euros) and each national central bank would have to maintain the convertibility at a fixed price between this base money and its own currency. It would simply mean that exchange rates between existing currencies would be rigorously fixed

---

[8]   See 'Cartels as Efficient Productive Structures', Chapter 3 of my book, Salin (2015).

(without any flexibility band or parity change). Each central bank would then be free to use the instruments of monetary policy which it deemed the most suitable to maintain the convertibility guarantee. Such a decentralized cartel would make it possible to preserve something important: the right to secede. Thus, if ever a national central bank was not satisfied by the European monetary management – which, for instance, it might consider as too expansionary – it could easily leave the system, just by abandoning the convertibility guarantee for its own currency in terms of euros and by again issuing a purely national currency which might benefit from better guarantees. The system which has been adopted in Europe for the time being is, on the contrary, centralized and discretionary, since monetary policy does not depend on precise and general rules, but is decided in the short run by the managers of the system. Therefore disagreements about European monetary policy are necessarily solved by some sort of political compromise which makes it impossible to guarantee a good quality euro. It would be better to have a system in which a base money is issued according to strict and credible rules which would guarantee its good quality, and in which national central banks would either have to accept this monetary strictness or leave the system.

Institutional uncertainties concerning the ECB are reinforced by the presently blurred design of targets and instruments. Choosing them is a classical problem in relation to which one could not expect anything original from European monetary authorities. Before the creation of the ECB, the European Monetary Institute considered five possible strategies in order to reach the ultimate target of monetary stability: an exchange rate target, an interest rate target, a gross national product (GNP) target, an intermediate monetary target and a direct inflation target. The first three were happily excluded, and it was recommended that the ECB should only consider two possible strategies: a monetary rule (intermediate monetary target) and an inflation rule. But the inflation target has been adopted as the only official target. As previously mentioned, it has been accepted that the target ought not to be a zero inflation rate, but rather a 2 per cent inflation rate, since people wrongly fear deflation and it is now quite usual to consider an inflation rate lower than 2 per cent as a situation of deflation. This is regrettable, since such a target means a loss of purchasing power of money cash balances equal to 2 per cent, which is significant (it means a negative real rate of interest of –2 per cent on money cash balances).

Meanwhile, more and more people are pleading for the ECB to design monetary policy not only with an inflation target, but also with an unemployment and a real growth target. We know that monetary policy is unable to reach such targets, but to the extent that people disagree with this statement, there is a risk for the future.

It may be regretted that so many uncertainties have been accepted, even though the target – substituting a single currency for existing national currencies – is debatable; even though other, more gradual, ways were possible, for instance reinforcing competition between existing currencies, restoring the gold standard in a more decentralized system, or issuing a parallel currency competing with existing ones. Insofar as not all the countries of the European Union are members of the eurozone, these latter options ought to be considered.

One obvious consequence of the euro is a higher synchronization of business cycles. This phenomenon will not stem from some process of contagion via intra-European trade, but from the existence of a single monetary policy and, therefore, of a single source of instability. The single currency does not suppress instability, but it does synchronize it.

It is obvious that the best solution to achieve European or world integration would simply consist in re-establishing freedom of choice in the currency markets. But those who consider themselves to be realistic and believe that such a solution would be illusory, because it would not be acceptable for public opinion (or, rather, for politicians), may accept other solutions, in-between the two extreme ones: monetary freedom or the euro. Thus, for the time being, the European Central Bank controls the whole monetary policy in the eurozone and national central banks are only operating institutions. But it would be preferable for the euro system to be more decentralized. As already stressed, this would be the case if, for instance, the European Central Bank issued base money in euros and if each national central bank was in charge of giving convertibility guarantees at a fixed price between this base money and the currency it issued.

Many other intermediary solutions can be imagined, with more or less banking freedom, more or less centralization. Thus, creating a European parallel currency which would compete with existing national currencies, without suppressing them – a solution which has already been suggested and which was supported by British authorities in the past – would have the advantage of reconciling the aims of the 'Europeans', who desire a European monetary symbol; of the nationalists, who do not want the disappearance of national currencies; and of free-market supporters, who would interpret it as a way towards more competition. Moreover, this parallel currency could benefit from a gold convertibility and it could even be imagined that European citizens would regain the freedom of producing and holding currencies with a gold guarantee.[9]

---

[9]   A very precise proposal along these lines has been made in Nataf (1997b).

# Conclusion: the future of monetary systems

As we have seen, monetary policy – if ever it exists – should have only one target: allowing the currency to be as good as possible, which means maintaining its purchasing power as much as possible. And as we have also seen, the ideal decision would consist in not producing additional nominal cash balances, which just means not implementing any monetary policy. It is obvious that such a change in the habits of thought and action would probably not be easily accepted. But it ought to be a reference point for consideration.

Now, even if one is convinced by such a target, some necessary steps have to be made to reach it or, at least, to come closer to it. From this point of view the independence of the central bank is not sufficient. But there are many ways to control it and to prevent monetary authorities from abusing their freedom of action. Traditionally, being obliged to maintain the convertibility of the currency in terms of an external asset – for instance, gold – is deemed to play this role. But history shows that public monetary authorities can easily discard such a constraint. Such is the real meaning of a devaluation. Things were completely different in the monetary systems of the eighteenth and nineteenth centuries, during which the gold convertibility guarantees were not given by a public authority, but by private banks. In such cases, a convertibility guarantee was a contractual engagement between a capitalist banker and his customers and, in such a private and therefore civilized world, a contract had to be respected. The incentive to decide an expansion of the quantity of money was thus efficiently constrained. This certainly means that the most important thing does not consist in knowing whether one should go back to a gold standard or not, but in defining an institutional context in which the convertibility guarantee is respected.

Therefore, it is necessary to go beyond a mere debate within the present institutional arrangements. There is, in fact, a surprising paradox in monetary theory: people debate about the best monetary policy, although the best solution would be not to have any monetary policy. This was the case in a pure gold standard (that is, without central banks). It would be the case in the future if ever public monetary monopolies were to disappear and competition was reintroduced in monetary activities. Are the new 'internet currencies' a route to such a new, non-inflationary world?

Going back to private and competing systems of production of money would be the most efficient solution to make it possible for individuals to hold a sound currency. There are, in fact, two possibilities in order to achieve a currency with stable or even increasing purchasing power. The first has already been mentioned, namely the existence of a convertibility guarantee in terms of some goods (gold, silver, a raw material or even a basket of assets), in a private competitive system; that is, a system in which the issuer of the currency is responsible and, therefore, motivated to maintain the guarantee. The other possibility consists in creating a fiat currency but offering a credible promise that the total amount of money to be created should not be greater than a given quantity. Such is the case with the bitcoin: people hold bitcoins inasmuch as they are confident that the system will be able not to allow any additional issue of bitcoins beyond the maximum amount which has been announced, according to a computing program. Therefore, if the demand for bitcoins increases, while the supply is stable, the purchasing power of this currency increases.

Now, let us imagine, as an extreme situation, very far from the one which we presently know, that private currencies have so efficiently competed with present monopolist and public currencies that these have disappeared. Would there be an inflation threat? Probably not, since this shift in the use of currencies would have been caused by the fact that, generally speaking, people do not like currencies with a decreasing purchasing power. As already stated, the good quality of these currencies would be maintained either because they benefit from credible convertibility guarantees or because people are convinced that the total amount of nominal cash balances cannot be increased in a discretionary way. In such a case, these various currencies would certainly have different rates of change in their purchasing power, but it can be assumed that, generally speaking, they would be deflationary rather than inflationary. Moreover, the definition of a rate of inflation (or deflation) might be different for each of these currencies, since they may be used for very different uses, so that the definition and measure of the same index of prices for all of them would be impossible.

As there would no more be local, national or regional monetary monopolies, the various areas of circulation of these currencies would be overlapping and the definition, for instance, of a national rate of inflation (or deflation) would be meaningless. But of most importance in this possible future new world would be that money creation – if any – would no longer imply a simultaneous creation of artificial credit. Therefore, interest rates would be determined by the supply and demand of voluntary savings.

And, as there is no reason for the demand and supply of savings to change in important and unpredictable ways, there would be no more instability of interest rates and, therefore, no more business cycles of monetary origin. Thus, it is not only the threat of inflation that would be suppressed, but also the threat of economic instability.

Such a monetary world is highly desirable. Unhappily, it is difficult to imagine that monetary authorities would easily agree to abandon their monopolies, unless there was great pressure of public opinion in favour of currency competition. We are far from such a situation, but one never knows what will happen and, in any case, I consider it my duty to analyse and to spread the ideas that I consider to be correct, and to be the only ones which are able to offer a considerable improvement in the monetary and economic environment of all people around the world.

# References

Frenkel, Jacob A. and Johnson, Harry O. (eds) (1976), *The Monetary Approach to the Balance of Payments*, London, UK: George Allen & Unwin and Toronto, Canada: University of Toronto Press.

Friedman, Milton (1968), 'The Role of Monetary Policy', *American Economic Review*, 58(1), pp. 1–17.

Hayek, Friedrich A. (1976), *Choice in Currency*, London: Institute of Economic Affairs.

Mises, Ludwig von (1949), *Human Action*, New Haven, CT: Yale University Press.

Mundell, Robert (1961), 'A Theory of Optimum Currency Areas', *American Economic Review*, 51(September), pp. 657–65; reprinted 1968 in R.A. Mundell, *International Economics*, New York: Macmillan.

Mundell, Robert (1971), *Monetary Theory: Inflation, Interest and Growth in the World Economy*, Pacific Palisades, CA: Goodyear.

Nataf, Philippe (1997a), 'Peut-on faire disparaître les cycles économiques? Le secret de la banque libre', Paris: Institut Euro 92, unpublished.

Nataf, Philippe (1997b), 'The Case for Abolishing Central Banks Altogether', *European Journal*, January, pp. 22–4.

Salin, Pascal (2001), 'World Regulations and Harmonization', *Independent Review*, 6(1), pp. 59–80.

Salin, Pascal (2009), 'La crise financière: causes, conséquences, solutions', Lausanne: Institut Constant de Rebecque.

Salin, Pascal (2014), *Money and Micro-economics*, London: Institute of Economic Affairs.

Salin, Pascal (2015), *Competition, Coordination and Diversity: From the Firm to Economic Integration*, Cheltenham, UK and Northampton, MA, USA: Edward Elgar Publishing.

White, Lawrence H. (1992), *Competition and Currency: Essays on Free Banking and Money*, New York: New York University Press.

# Index

Printed and bound by CPI Group (UK) Ltd, Croydon, CR0 4YY

23/04/2025

14660958-0004